ECONOMIC COMMISSION FOR EUROPE
Committee on Environmental Policy

ENVIRONMENTAL PERFORMANCE REVIEWS

REPUBLIC OF MOLDOVA

Second Review

UNITED NATIONS
New York and Geneva, 2005

Environmental Performance Reviews Series No.23

NOTE

Symbols of United Nations documents are composed of capital letters combined with figures. Mention of such a symbol indicates a reference to a United Nations document.

The designations employed and the presentation of the material in this publication do not imply the expression of any opinion whatsoever on the part of the Secretariat of the United Nations concerning the legal status of any country, territory, city or area, or of its authorities, or concerning the delimitation of its frontiers or boundaries. In particular, the boundaries shown on the maps de not imply official endorsement or acceptance by the United Nations.

CAUTION

This publication (ECE/CEP/130*) supersedes in its entirety an earlier version issued under the same title and symbol (ECE/CEP/130), published in April 2006. Errors in the first publication necessitated its recall.

ECE/CEP/130*

UNITED NATIONS PUBLICATION
Sales No. E.06.II.E.4
ISBN 92-1-116939-9
ISSN 1020-4563

Foreword

Environmental Performance Reviews (EPRs) for countries in transition were initiated by Environment Ministers at the second "Environment for Europe" Conference in Lucerne, Switzerland, in 1993. As a result, the UNECE Committee on Environmental Policy decided to make the EPRs a part of its regular programme.

Ten years later, at the fifth Ministerial Conference "Environment for Europe" (Kiev, 2003), the Ministers confirmed that the UNECE programme of EPRs had made it possible to assess the effectiveness of the efforts of countries with economies in transition to manage the environment The EPR programme also gave tailor-made recommendations to the Governments concerned on improving environmental management to reduce their pollution load, to better integrate environmental policies into sectoral policies and to strengthen cooperation with the international community. The ministers also reaffirmed their support for the EPR programme as an important instrument for countries with economies in transition, and they decided that the programme should continue to proceed with a second cycle of reviews. This second round, while taking stock of the progress made since the first review, puts particular emphasis on implementation, integration, financing and the socio-economic interface with the environment.

Through the Peer Review process, EPRs also promote dialogue among UNECE member countries and harmonization of environmental conditions and policies throughout the region. As a voluntary exercise, the EPR is undertaken only at the request of the country itself.

The studies are carried out by international teams of experts from the region working closely with national experts from the reviewed country. The teams also benefit from close cooperation with other organizations in the United Nations system, including the United Nations Development Programme, and the Organisation for Economic Co-operation and Development.

This is the second EPR of the Republic of Moldova published by UNECE. I hope that this Review will be useful to all countries in the region, to intergovernmental and non-governmental organizations alike and, especially, to the Republic of Moldova, its Government and its people.

Marek Belka
Executive Secretary
United Nations Economic Commission for Europe

Preface

The second Environmental Performance Review (EPR) of the Republic of Moldova began in November 2004 with the preparatory mission, during which the final structure of the report was discussed and established. Thereafter, the review team of international experts was constituted. It included experts from Belarus, Estonia and Lithuania with experts from the secretariats of the United Nations Economic Commission for Europe (UNECE) and the Organisation for Economic Cooperation and Development (OECD).

The review mission took place from 12 to 19 April 2005. A draft of the conclusions and recommendations as well the draft EPR report were submitted to the Republic of Moldova for comments in July 2005. In October 2005, the draft was submitted for consideration to the Ad Hoc Expert Group on Environmental Performance. During this meeting, the Expert Group discussed the report in detail with expert representatives of the Government of the Republic of Moldova, focusing in particular on the conclusions and recommendations made by the international experts.

The EPR report, with suggested amendments from the Expert Group, was then submitted for peer-review to the UNECE Committee on Environmental Policy on 10 October 2005. A high-level delegation from the Government of the Republic of Moldova participated in the peer review. The Committee adopted the recommendations as set out in this report.

The report takes stock of the progress made by the Republic of Moldova in the management of its environment since the country was first reviewed in 1998, in particular in the implementation of the recommendations of the first review. It also covers eight issues of importance to the Republic of Moldova, concerning policy-making, planning and implementation; the financing of environmental policies and projects; and the integration of environmental concerns in economic sectors and promotion of sustainable development. Among the issues receiving special attention during the review were compliance and enforcement mechanisms; economic instruments and environmental funds; and environmental management in agriculture and forestry and in industrial activities.

The UNECE Committee on Environmental Policy and the UNECE review team would like to thank both the Government of the Republic of Moldova and its experts who worked with the international experts and contributed with their knowledge and assistance. UNECE wishes the Government of the Republic of Moldova further success in carrying out the tasks before it to meet its environmental objectives and policy, including the implementation of the conclusions and recommendations in this second review.

UNECE would also like to express its deep appreciation to the Governments of Hungary, the Netherlands, Norway, Switzerland and the United Kingdom for their support to the Environmental Performance Review Programme, and to the United Nations Development Programme for their contribution to the work in the Republic of Moldova, the preparation of this report and its translation and publication into the national language.

LIST OF TEAM MEMBERS

Ms. Catherine MASSON	ECE secretariat	Team Leader
Mr. Antoine NUNES	ECE secretariat	Project Coordinator
Mr. Jyrki HIRVONEN	ECE secretariat	Introduction
Mr. Aare SIRENDI	Estonia	Chapter 1
Mr. Eugene MAZUR	OECD	Chapter 2
Mr. Mikhail KOKINE	ECE secretariat	Chapter 3
Ms. Natalya GOLOVKO	Belarus	Chapter 4
Mr. Jaromir CEKOTA	ECE secretariat	Chapter 5
Mr. Oleg DZIOUBINSKI	ECE secretariat	Chapter 6
Mr. Bo LIBERT	ECE secretariat	Chapter 7
Ms. Dalia STREIMIKIENE	Lithuania	Chapter 8

The mission for the project took place from 10 April to 20 April 2005. The peer review was held in Geneva on 10 October 2005. The UNECE Committee on Environmental Policy adopted the recommendations set out in this publication.

Information cut-off date: 10 October 2005

UNECE Information Unit   Phone: +41 (0)22 917 44 44
Palais des Nations   Fax: +41 (0)22 917 05 05
CH-1211 Geneva 10   E-mail: info.ece@unece.org
Switzerland   Website: http://www.unece.org

LIST OF NATIONAL CONTRIBUTORS

Constantin Mihailescu	Minister, Ministry of Ecology and Natural Resources
Violeta Ivanov	Head, Division of Environmental Policy and European Integration Ministry of Ecology and Natural Resources
Mihai Iftodi	Head, Division of Prevention of Environmental Pollution Ministry of Ecology and Natural Resources
Mihail Coca	Head, Division of Natural Resources and Biodiversity Ministry of Ecology and Natural Resources
Tatiana Plesco	Consultant, Division of Environmental Policy and European Integration Ministry of Ecology and Natural Resources
Valentina Caldarus	Deputy Head, Division of Natural Resources and Biodiversity Ministry of Ecology and Natural Resources
Valeriu Cazac	Head, State Hydrometeorological Service
Ghene Jalalite	Head, Agency for Geology "AGeoM"
Adam Begu	Head, National Institute of Ecology
Maria Nagornii	Consultant, Division of Environmental Policy and European Integration Ministry of Ecology and Natural Resources
Gavriil Gilca	Head, Department of Environmental Quality Monitoring State Hydrometeorological Service
Liudmila Marduhaeva	Consultant, Division of Prevention of Environmental Pollution Ministry of Ecology and Natural Resources
Stefan Stasiev	Consultant, Division of Prevention of Environmental Pollution Ministry of Ecology and Natural Resources
Inga Podoroghin	Main Specialist, Division of Environmental Policy and European Integration, Ministry of Ecology and Natural Resources
Nicu Vrednic	Consultant, Division of Environmental Policy and European Integration, Ministry of Ecology and Natural Resources
Mihai Mustea	Deputy Head, State Ecological Inspectorate
Elena Belousova	Consultant, Protection of Water Resources and Atmospheric Air Division, State Ecological Inspectorate
Mihai Nadchernicinii	Head, Division of Logistics and Environmental Security State Ecological Inspectorate
Valeriu Mosanu	National Institute of Ecology
Ion Panciuc	Head, Central Territorial Ecological Agency State Ecological Inspectorate
Radu Bajureanu	Deputy Head, Environmental Agency "Centru" Ministry of Ecology and Natural Resources
Ion Sava	Head, Orhei District Ecological Office, State Ecological Inspection
Anatolie Spivacenco	Vice Minister, Ministry of Agriculture and Food Industry
Iurie Senic	Consultant, Division of Agro chemistry, Ecology and Plant Protection, Ministry of Agriculture and Food Industry
Dumitru Haruta	Ministry of Agriculture and Food Industry
Dumitru Drumea	National Institute of Ecology
Vladimir Brega	National Institute of Ecology
Iacob Vlas	State Ecological Inspection
George Sarmaniuc	State Ecological Inspection
Marin Molosag	Vice Governor, National Bank of Moldova
Valeriu Binzaru	Director, Capital Investment Department, Ministry of Finances
Iaroslav Baclajanschi	Public Expenditure Management Analyst DFID technical assistance project, Ministry of Finances
Oleg Cara	Vice Director, National Bureau of Statistics
Elena Orlova	Head, General Division of Agriculture, Forestry and Environment, National Bureau of Statistics

Valeriu Cosarciuc	Chairman of the Committee on Agriculture, Parliament
Vladimir Crivciun	Department of Investments and Innovation, Ministry of Economy
Elena Subina	Department of Structural Changes, Ministry of Economy
Stela Melnik	Ministry of Economy
Nicolae Triboi	National Energy Regulatory Agency
D. Galupa	Forestry Research Institute
Serafim Andries	Research Institute of Pedology and Agrochemistry
Elean Pintilie	Service Standardization and Metrology
Svetlana Suvorkina	Ministry of Transport and Road Management
Petru Stratulat	Agency for Forestry "Moldsilva"
Dan Nour	Agency of Land Relations and Cadastre
Leonid Volosciuc	Institute for Plant Protection
Larisa Ghies	Head, Division of Regulation and harmonization of legislative and normative acts, Ministry of Industry and Infrastructure
Petru Groza	Deputy Head, Division of Regulation and harmonization of legislative and normative acts, Ministry of Industry and Infrastructure
Ilie Timofti	Head, Division of technical -scientific cooperation and transfer of technologies, Ministry of Industry and Infrastructure
Stela Ginju	State Pedagogical University "Ion Creanga"
Vlad Raileanu	Head, National Agency for Energy Conservation
Raisa Cecan	Chief engineer, Apa- Canal Chisinau
Ion Junea	Technical Director, Apa –Canal Chisinau
Mihail Pencov	State Water Concern "Apele Moldovei"
Constantin Ojog	ACSA
Ion Salaru	National Scientific and Practical Center of Preventive Medicine, Ministry of Health and Social Protection
Alexandru Sirbu	Agency for Regional Development
Ianina Spinei	Consultant, Transparency International Moldova
Alexandru Ursul	Director, Microproject Department, Moldova Social Investment Fund
Iurie Hurmuzachi	Agroinform
Vasile Mirzenco	National Farmers Federation
Marcela Vatamaniuc	Assistant manager, Biodiversity Office
Stela Drucioc	Head, Carbon Office
Alexandru Teleuta	Head, Biodiversity Office
Vasile Scorpan	Head, Climate Change Office
Andrei Isac	Director, Regional Environmental Center (REC) Moldova
Valentin Bobeica	Regional Environmental Center (REC) Moldova REC
Iuliana Cantaragiu	Finance Consultant, Regional Environmental Center (REC) Moldova
Ilya Trombitsky	NGO Eco – TIRAS
Valentin Ciubotaru	NGO, BIOS
Pavel Zamfir	NGO Eco-Lex
Alexei Andreev	NGO, BIOTICA
Vladimir Garaba	Head, Ecological Movement from Kishinev
Angela Lozan	
Sergiu Magdil	Agricultural Pollution Project
Svetlana Leu	Cleaner production and energy efficiency centre

LIST OF INTERNATIONAL CONTRIBUTORS

Francis Delaey	Head of Office, EBRD Resident Office, Chisinau
Margareta Petrusevschi	Programme Analyst, UNDP
Ludmila Radautan	Monitor, Tacis and the Balcans/Cards Monitoring Programme
Veaceslav Scobiola	Monitor, Tacis and the Balcans/Cards Monitoring Programme

TABLE OF CONTENTS

LIST OF FIGURES

LIST OF MAPS

LIST OF TABLES

LIST OF BOXES

ACRONYMS AND ABBREVIATIONS

ACSA	National Rural Extension Service
AMAC	Association Moldova Apa-Canal
ANRE	National Agency for Energy Regulation
BAT	Best Available Technique
BOD	Biological Oxygen Demand
BOP	Balance of Payments
CAS	Country Assistance Strategy
CBD	United Nations Convention on Biological Diversity
CC	Climate Change
CCI	Chamber of Commerce and Industry
CDM	Clean Development Mechanism
CFCs	Chlorofluorocarbons
CHP	Combined Heat and Power
CIS	Commonwealth of Independent States
CITES	Convention on International Trade in Endangered Species of Wild Fauna and Flora
CLRTAP	Convention on Long-range Transboundary Air Pollution
CMS	Convention on Conservation of Migratory Species of Wild Fauna
COD	Chemical Oxygen Demand
CP	Cleaner Production
CPEE	Cleaner Production and Energy Efficiency
CPI	Consumer Price Index
DEPEI	Division on Environmental Policy and European Integration
DDT	Dichlorodiphenyltrichloroethane
EAP TF	Task Force for the Implementation of the Environmental Action Programme for Central and Eastern Europe
EBRD	European Bank for Reconstruction and Development
EC	European Commission
EEA	European Environment Agency
EECCA	Eastern Europe, Caucasus and Central Asia
EGPRSP	Economic Growth and Poverty Reduction Strategy Paper
EIA	Environmental Impact Assessment
ELV	Emission limit values
EMAS	Eco-management and Audit Scheme
EMEP	Cooperative Programme for Monitoring and Evaluation of the Long-range Transmission of Air Pollutants in Europe
EMS	Environmental Management System
EPR	Environmental Performance Review
EU	European Union
FDI	Foreign direct investment
FSU	Former Soviet Union
FSP	Food Security Programme
G7	Canada, France, Germany, Italy, Japan, United Kingdom and United States of America
GDP	Gross domestic product
GEF	Global Environmental Facility
GHG	Greenhouse gases
GMO	Genetically modified organisms
HCB	Hexachlorobenzen
HCFC	Hydrochlorofluorocarbon
HDI	Human Development Index
HM	Heavy metals
HMS	State Hydrometeorology Service
HPP	Hydropower plant

IBRD	International Bank for Reconstruction and Development
ICPDR	International Commission for the protection of Danube River
IFI	International financing institution
IEMS	Integrated environmental monitoring system
IMF	International Monetary Fund
INECO	National Institute of Ecology
IPPC	Integrated pollution prevention and control
ISO	International Standardization Organization
IUCN	World Conservation Union
LA 21	Local Agenda 21
LEAP	Local Environmental Action Plan
LEF	Local Environmental Fund
MAC	Maximum allowable concentration
MDG	Millennium Developments Goal
MEA	Multilateral environmental agreement
MENR	Ministry of Ecology and Natural Resources
MoAFI	Ministry of Agriculture and Food Industry
MoE	Ministry of Economy
MOEYS	Ministry of Education, Youth and Sports
MoF	Ministry of Finances
MoFAEI	Ministry of Foreign Affairs and European Integration
MoHSP	Ministry of Health and Social Protection
MoJ	Ministry of Justice
MSIF	Moldova Social Investment Fund
MTEF	medium-term expenditure framework
MTPP	Moldovan Thermal Power Plant
NATO	North Atlantic Treaty Organisation
NCPM	National Scientific and Practical Centre of Preventive Medicine
NDA	National designated authority
NEAP	National Environmental Action Plan (Programme)
NEF	National Environment Fund
NEHAP	National Environment and Health Action Plan
NGOs	Non–governmental Organizations
ODS	Ozone-depleting substance
OECD	Organisation for Economic Co-operation and Development
OSCE	Organization for Security and Co-operation in Europe
PAH	Polyaromatic hydrocarbon
PCB	Polychlorinated biphenyl
PCPP	Polish Clean Production Programme
PEE	Public Environmental Expertise
POP	Persistent Organic Pollutant
PPI	Producer price index
PPP	Purchasing power parity
PRTR	Pollutant Release and Transfer Registers
REC	Regional Environmental Centre
RES	Renewable Energy Sources
SEA	Strategic environmental assessment
SEE	State Ecological Expertise
SEI	State Environmental Inspectorate
SME	Small and Medium Enterprises
SoE	State of Environment
SPM	Suspended particulate matter
Tacis	Technical Assistance to Commonwealth of Independent States
TEA	Territorial Ecological Agency
TPES	Total Primary Energy Supplies

UNCSD	United Nations Commission on Sustainable Development
UNCCD	United Nations Convention on Combating Desertification
UNDP	United Nations Development Programme
UNECE	United Nations Economic Commission for Europe
UNEP	United Nations Environment Programme
UNFCCC	United Nations Framework Convention on Climate Change
USAID	United States Agency for International Development
USD	US Dollars
VAT	Value-added tax
VOC	Volatile organic compound
WB	World Bank
WG	Working group
WHO	World Health Organisation
WHO-ROE	World Heath Organization Regional Office for Europe
WMO	World Meteorological Organization
WPI	Water Pollution Index
WSSD	World Summit on Sustainable Development
WWTP	Waste Water Treatment Plant

SIGNS AND MEASURES

..	not available
-	nil or negligible
.	decimal point
ha	hectare
kt	kiloton
g	gram
kg	kilogram
mg	milligram
mm	millimetre
cm^2	square centimetre
m^3	cubic metre
km	kilometre
km^2	square kilometre
toe	ton oil equivalent
l	litre
ml	millilitre
min	minute
s	second
m	metre
°C	degree Celsius
GJ	gigajoule
kW_{el}	kilowatt (electric)
KWh	kilowatt-hour
kW_{th}	kilowatt (thermal)
MW_{el}	megawatt (electric)
MW_{th}	megawatt (thermal)
MWh	megawatt-hour
GWh	gigawatt-hour
TWh	terawatt-hour
Bq	becquerel
Ci	curie
MSv	millisievert
Cap	capita
Eq	equivalent
H	hour
kv	kilovolt
MW	megawatt
Gcal	gigacalorie
Hz	Hertz
Mtce	Mega-ton of coal equivalent
ktce	Kilo-ton of coal equivalent

CURRENCY

Republic of Moldova
Monetary unit: Leu (plural Lei)

Year	Lei/ US$
1998	5.37
1999	10.52
2000	12.43
2001	12.87
2002	13.57
2003	13.94
2004	12.33

Source: IMF. International
Financial Statistics, April 2005.

EXECUTIVE SUMMARY

This second Environmental Performance Review (EPR) of the Republic of Moldova was carried out seven years after the first Review in 1998. It intends to measure the progress made by the country in managing its environment since then, and in addressing upcoming environmental challenges.

Overall context

The Republic of Moldova is emerging from a long economic recession...

The economic crisis bottomed out in 1999. Since then, the Republic of Moldova has shown signs of a slow economic recovery although in 2005 it still had the lowest GDP amongst European nations. Despite this crisis a significant restructuring of the economy and administration has taken place, and this has had repercussions on the management of the country's environment.

...from the privatization process...

Privatization is almost complete and currently the private sector accounts for 80 per cent of GDP. With the exception of the largest enterprises, nearly all agricultural land, 80 per cent of housing stock and all small and medium-sized enterprises are private. In the countryside, organization of rural life and of agricultural practices has been changed fundamentally by the privatization process. Land ownership is now spread among a multitude of small farmers and municipalities that have yet to gain experience in land management and environmental protection. Industry and energy sectors are in a dire economic situation and are not working to full capacity due to high depreciation on the value of capital, a degradation of fixed assets, and lack of investment. In such a context, environmental economic incentives and enterprise management systems are for the most part ineffective.

...from administrative restructuring...

Since 2001, the country has been divided into 32 local districts (rayons), two administrative units (Gagauz Yeri and Transnistria) and three urban municipalities (Chisinau, Balti and Bender). This restructuring reduced the financial autonomy of the municipalities and affected the environmental protection institutions. Some environmental competencies, previously at municipal level (e.g., solid waste management, drinking water supply and wastewater management) were recentralized into the territorial administrative structures of the ministry of environment.

...and wants now to adjust to EU practices.

Another important development that will affect environmental management is the Republic of Moldova's intention to integrate into the European Union (EU). With Romania's forthcoming accession to the EU, the country will become an EU neighbour, and as such is entitled to benefit from the EU Neighbourhood Policy. The joint EU-Moldova Action Plan (2005) contains environmental and sustainable development objectives and prepares the Republic of Moldova for the introduction of EU requirements.

POLICY-MAKING, PLANNING AND IMPLEMENTATION

Legal and policy-making framework

The policy framework has greatly improved...

The environment management system has acquired real strengths since the first review. The policy base was developed extensively by the introduction of a number of new environmental laws, strategies, programmes and plans. The establishment of the Ministry of Environment in 1998 improved the structure and standards of environmental institutions.

...but the legal basis is slow to develop and is still media specific.

After an active period of enacting legislation, not much has happened since 1999 although a number of recent policy concepts and action plans have called for new or adjusted environmental legislation. While the organizational principles for environmental management are rational, the excessively narrow scope of the legislation, which deals separately with every environmental media (air, water, soil, waste, etc.), is of concern. Each law tends to specify its own implementation regime, which makes it difficult to move forward to an integrated management approach. Measures need to be taken to ensure equivalence of practice across all media and to promote a holistic approach to environmental management.

...and has to evolve towards EU practices...

The 2005 EU-Moldova Action Plan envisages the adoption of additional legal acts for key environmental sectors, based on EU environmental *acquis*. To that end, emissions limit values should be revised and streamlined gradually, and technical and performance requirements considered at the project design stage. As a first step, main principles should be established and enterprises should be given time to implement these new measures. Also, there is very little common approach across sectors between environmental management and the management of other economic sectors. This common approach will need to be improved and developed further.

...with the help of a strengthened staff of professionals.

There is a need for sufficient, competent and professional staffing in the environment administration. Currently the level of staff is critically low and is too limited by far to cope with these new tasks or to acquire the knowledge and advanced competencies that are necessary for dealing with integrated and crosscutting issues. Therefore, to enable the country to fully implement adopted environmental policies and strategies and to further develop related legislation, it is necessary to strengthen institutions and improve administrative capacity. Staff training will also be necessary.

Compliance and enforcement mechanisms

Environmental permits are not integrated...

Environmental permits cover all environmental areas (air, water, waste, soil) separately. They regulate too many substances through permitting rules that are the same for all polluters, irrespective of their size and their environmental impact. This makes it difficult for the small number of inspectors to monitor and enforce permit compliance effectively. It also places a heavy administrative burden on environmental agencies and enterprises. An integrated permit limited to industrial installations with significant environmental effects would be more efficient.

...but the enforcement tools are more transparent.

The Republic of Moldova has made progress in terms of greater transparency in environmental assessment. However, more emphasis could be put on the use of environmental assessment instruments, i.e., Environmental Impact Assessment (EIA), State Ecological Expertise (SEE) and Public Ecological Expertise (PEE), especially for those projects with significant environmental impact. Industrial enterprises are not attaining a sufficient level of compliance with their environmental obligations, and their compliance should be monitored and promoted. In addition, inspectors are not using feedback from their inspection findings for the improvement of the overall enforcement process.

However, the overall system of sanctions is still inefficient.

The State Environment Inspectorate (SEI) possesses a variety of enforcement tools, but it cannot impose sanctions directly. Penalties and fines for administrative violations go through a court procedure (except for water-related violations), which takes a long time and results in negligible penalties for the violator. Courts are not competent enough to deal with environmental offences and the rate of fines is too low to have any deterrent effect. The percentage of penalties paid is very low. All actions related to sanctions should be carried out with increased SEI transparency and accountability.

Information, public participation and education

Environmental monitoring has improved...

The observation network for surveying the quality of the environment has been enlarged, covering more territory, more media and new chemical components. However this is still not enough to meet national legislation requirements and international obligations. Monitoring does not fully cover groundwater pollution, diffuse pollution of surface waters or background pollution. There is no comprehensive nationwide monitoring programme and the integrated environmental monitoring system is not operational.

...but still covers too many pollutants.

With the exception of drinking water, lists of ambient quality parameters have not been revised since independence. Due to an excessively large number of regulated pollutants, unrealistic monitoring and enforcement requirements are imposed on public authorities. Yet, at the same time, some hazardous substances remain unregulated. A number of standards are below the threshold of analytical detection.

Environmental information has improved unevenly ...

Some institutions have increased the number of indicators in their environmental databases and have improved their management and reporting of environmental information. However, modern information technologies have not been introduced into all sectors and information is not easily accessible to decision-makers and the public.

...as has public participation in environmental decision-making.

The Ministry of Ecology and Natural Resources (MENR) uses plans and programmes to invite the public to participate in decision-making on policies. Nevertheless, the legal and regulatory framework needs to be elaborated further to implement more effectively the public participation requirements of the Aarhus Convention on Access to Information, Public Participation in Decision-making and Access to Justice in Environmental Matters (which the country ratified).

Environmental education is handled seriously.

This is the case, demonstrated by a comprehensive and well-thought-out system in pre-school, primary and secondary schools, and higher education. However there are no permanent environmental training courses for public officials and there is almost no environmental education for adults.

International agreements and commitments

The tremendous progress made in international cooperation...

The Republic of Moldova has actively participated in most global and regional environmental events. It has ratified most environmental agreements of regional and global importance and is implementing them by preparing national contributions and adjusting existing or drafting new national policies on various environmental subjects. It has also hosted a series of international meetings and conferences that have helped the country to raise its profile and attract international resources and assistance to help solve national environmental problems. It has continued to develop bilateral relations with neighbouring countries.

...has been hampered by weak implementation...

At the same time, implementation of the ratified agreements and commitments remains rather weak and poorly coordinated. International support is often donor-driven and does not always address the real needs of the country. The MENR lacks the capacity to inform potential donors of the country's needs and priorities for investments and environmental assistance. The country is not concentrating its efforts on these agreements even though they have the potential to benefit the country greatly: it is neither following ongoing projects nor streamlining its priorities.

MOBILIZING FINANCIAL RESOURCES FOR THE ENVIRONMENT

Economic instruments and environmental funds

Market-based instruments are more effective than before, although their role as an incentive is not strong.

The effectiveness of market-based instruments used in the country has improved considerably since the 1998 EPR. Excise tax on imported fuel and cars, introduced in 1996, and the new 2003 tax on environmentally harmful products form an essential part of environmental fund revenues. However, numerous tax exemptions diminish the solid revenue performance of these environmentally related taxes. The system of emission charges remains inefficient and plays a negligible role. The incentive to reduce emissions to which pollution charges apply could be enhanced considerably by raising charges and imposing them on just a few major sources with easily measurable emissions.

Better pricing is reflecting true costs...

While significant advances towards cost-reflective pricing has taken place in transport and energy sectors, the pricing of water services remains less satisfactory as it neither covers operating costs, nor capital-cost recovery. Further reforms in existing market-based instruments are needed for a more comprehensive and efficient reduction of pollution discharges and decoupling of environmental pressures from economic growth.

...and environmental funds are much stronger.

Both the financing and the functioning of environmental funds (national and local) have improved considerably since 1998. Since 2000, revenues have increased substantially. Nevertheless, the management of funds and their operational efficiency still fall short of internationally recognized good practice. Actual evaluation of the effectiveness and impact of fund-financed projects is rarely done. The increasing carryover amounts in national and local fund budgets mean that existing resources are not fully utilized. The introduction of output-oriented budgeting could improve the effectiveness of spending of available financial resources and their allocation to priority environmental projects.

Expenditure on environmental protection

Revenue has increased and environmental expenditure has developed in parallel...

However, both revenue and expenditure remain low in absolute and per capita terms, as well as in terms of share of GDP. With a very limited contribution of financial resources from abroad (less than ten per cent), State funding still predominates and environmental funds have become the main source of funding since 2000. Eighty per cent of environmental expenditure is spent on operating expenses; the rest is spent on investments.

...but environmental priorities for financing are not being clearly targeted...

At the same time, the country has developed many new policy documents for environmental improvement, but they often do not contain clear measurable targets and do not indicate the necessary financial resources to achieve their objectives. The Government tends to change its priorities and does not provide all necessary funding, which hampers implementation of these environmental programmes. The *Economic Growth and Poverty Reduction Strategy Paper* (2004-2006) is an exception and unique, as it lists environmental protection among the priority areas and sets clear corresponding funding requirements.

...and the precise amount of environmental expenditure is unknown.

Total expenditure for environmental protection is about 0.8 per cent of GDP. This may be underestimated because certain environmentally related expenditure is not included in the reporting. Sectoral ministries and other governmental agencies may have expenditure that includes environmental components but they do not account for it separately. Information on environmental expenditure by the private sector is scarce. Neither the National Bureau of Statistics, which collects and processes statistical reporting forms on environmental expenditure, nor the Ministry of Ecology and Natural Resources, attempt to identify all environmentally related expenditure.

INTEGRATION OF ENVIRONMENTAL CONCERNS INTO ECONOMIC SECTORS, AND PROMOTION OF SUSTAINABLE DEVELOPMENT

Environmental management in agriculture and forestry

Agriculture exerts a high amount of pressure on the environment, ...

With 20 per cent of the labour force and a 19.2 per cent GDP contribution, agricultural production is still a dominant economic activity, but it is not very profitable. One the one hand agriculture is very damaging to all environmental media: soil erosion is on the increase, soil fertility is decreasing, green protection belts have shrunk because of land privatization and consolidation, pasture is overgrazed, and the meagre forest coverage has not significantly increased. On the other hand, the economic crisis has had positive a side effect with a drastic reduction in the use of fertilizers, pesticides and irrigation water.

...although there have been serious attempts to improve agricultural practices.

In spite of tight financial resources, efforts are being made to minimize negative environmental effects: extension services have been developed to help new inexperienced farmers, diffuse pollution is being combated, and organic agriculture and good agricultural practices are being promoted. With the economic situation improving and with agriculture continuing to be an essential contributor to the economy – it is the basis of a profitable food-processing industry – farming practices are becoming more intensive again. In this context of tight profitability, it is not easy to introduce elaborate schemes for environmental protection.

Water quality, pasture and ecosystems are still strained.

Pasture that is now owned by municipalities is overgrazed; improving its management would bring economic as well as environmental gains. A law on soil and a regulation on pasture have been developed but are still waiting for official approval. Another serious problem is the quality of drinking water, as water uptakes are in general not protected. Ecosystems have been degraded and dismantled by intensive agricultural activities, and their continuity should be re-established. The country should improve protection of its biodiversity and work actively towards establishing a National Ecological Network.

Land privatization has brought major changes...

The distribution of small plots and livestock to initially inexperienced farmers has profoundly modified farming and agricultural practices. This new state of affairs exerts different environmental pressures from before. To introduce measures to combat land degradation successfully, and to improve land management, good information on the land is necessary together with the integrated effort of farmers, municipalities, scientific institutions, extension services, and competent authorities over all the territory. The country lacks a geographical information system, which would ease joint efforts on land management and protection. Scientific and educational capacity is well developed but should focus more on improving practices such as counteracting soil erosion, re-establishing integrated crop management, making forecasts for plant diseases and giving advice on the efficient use of pesticides and fertilizers.

Forest needs to be better protected.

The country is working to increase forest acreage, which currently covers only 11 per cent of land. This would improve land and soil protection, prevent diffuse pollution and protect biodiversity. Four out of the existing five strictly protected nature reserves (scientific reserves located in forest zones) are managed by the forestry sector, and not by authorities able to ensure their protection. There is a need for a better-balanced share of responsibilities between the authorities that manage forest resources and those who are entrusted with their protection; a concern still unresolved since the first review.

Environmental management in industrial activities

Data on industrial pollution are far from sufficient.

Industrial production increased by about 30 per cent from 1998 to 2003. The analysis of the little data available on environmental pollution in industry shows that water use, waste generation, greenhouse gases emission and atmospheric pollution are gradually reducing while economic activity is picking up (i.e., positive decoupling trends). Other information about the environmental impact of industry is very limited and does not allow for the setting of targets for emissions reduction or for the identification of priorities and measures to achieve these targets.

Sectoral environmental policies are not well implemented.

Since 1998 the country has elaborated various environmental strategies, action plans and programmes covering the most important environmental issues relevant to industrial activities. The liberalization of the energy sector and the setting of cost-reflective energy prices have had a positive impact on energy efficiency and have mitigated the environmental impact of the sector. The waste management strategy, cleaner production centres and cleaner production pilot projects for each of the main industrial sectors have produced successful results. However, implementation of environmental policies in industry needs to be improved regarding their priorities and targets, their monitoring and the weak coordination between responsible ministries. The lack of appropriate economic incentives and financing mechanisms has compromised expected improvements.

Environmental standards should be streamlined.

Environmental emissions standards inherited from the Soviet past are too numerous and are unrealistic. Air emission limit values for major pollutants should be introduced step-by-step, starting with large thermo power installations and extending gradually to other sources and pollutants. In addition, pollution charges have no incentive effect and are applied to too many emission standards. They should therefore be revised. Taxes should be increased and only main pollutants should be subject to charges. An approximation to the Integrated Pollution Prevention and Control (IPPC) Directive should be considered as the long-term target and its gradual implementation should be started soon.

INTRODUCTION

I.1   The physical context

The Republic of Moldova[1] is a landlocked country covering 33,800 sq km and located on the south-western part of the East European Plain. It is bordered to the north, east, and south by Ukraine (border length 939 km) and to the west by Romania (border length 450 km). The terrain of the country is primarily a hilly plain interspersed with deep river valleys. The average elevation is 147 m above sea level.

The country has four main geographic areas. The Northern Moldovan Plain, with broad flat valleys, has an elevation of between 250 to 300 metres. The Dniester Uplands are situated on the western bank of the Dniester River. The Codrii Hills, rising to a maximum elevation of about 429 m at Mount Balanesti, occupy the central portion of the country, while the semi-arid steppe of the Podolian Plateau is in the south. The hills at the central part of the country are densely forested, while cultivated crops have replaced the natural grass cover of the plains and steppes in the north and south. Grassy salt marshes are common in some river valleys.

Moldova has a continental climate mostly affected by the Black Sea. Summers are warm with an average daily temperature of +24 °Celsius in July, although the daily highs occasionally can reach +40 °C. Winters are mild with an average daily temperature between −5 and −3 °C in January. Precipitation is light and irregular and varies between regions. Droughts are common in the south of the country where the precipitation average is 350 mm per year, but at higher elevation areas the precipitation can exceed 600 mm per year.

Three-quarters of the country is covered with the fertile chernozem soil type, which is ideal for agriculture. Rich soil and a favourable climate support substantial and diverse agricultural production ranging from wheat, corn, barley, tobacco, sugar beets, soybeans, and sunflowers to extensive fruit orchards, vineyards, and walnut groves. Beef and dairy cattle are raised on a family farm scale, and beekeeping and silkworm breeding are widespread. The country does not have any

---

[1] Hereinafter "Republic of Moldova" and "Moldova" are used interchangeably. This document does not cover Transnistria.

major mineral deposits but natural resources include deposits of lignite, phosphorite and gypsum.

Moldova is part of the Black Sea watershed and has a large river system consisting of more than 3000 rivers and streams. The two largest rivers are the Dniester (Nistru in Moldovan), with a total length of 1,352 km and 657 km within the country, and the Prut with a total length of 976 km and 695 km within the country. The Dniester River flows through the eastern portion of the country to the south forming part of the country's border with Ukraine in the northeast, then cuts through Moldova's interior, meets the Ukrainian border again in the southeast and then empties into the Black Sea. The Prut River, a major tributary of the Danube River, delimits Moldova's entire western border with Romania.

I.2   The human context

The country's population figures vary considerably depending on whether or not the Transnistrian population is incorporated into the total. The United Nation Economic Commission for Europe (UNECE) figures give a total population of 3.613 million in 2003, excluding Transnistria since 1993. The average population density is 120 persons per sq km. The population is concentrated in the northern and central parts of the country and about 41 per cent of the inhabitants live in urban areas.

The capital and biggest city is Chisinau (pop. 779,900) located on the Bicu River in the central part of the country. Other important towns include Bender (pop. 141,500) located on the Dniester River, and Balti (pop. 149,000), in north central Moldova.

Demographic indicators have changed noticeably since 1990. The birth rate (per 1000) fell from 17.1 in 1991 to 11.3 in 1998. The trend continued with a fall to 10.1 in 2003 with the fertility rate halving from 2.3 in 1991, to 1.2 in 2003. The infant mortality rate (per 1000) has diminished greatly from 19.3 in 1991, to 17.2 in 1998 and to 14.3 in 2003, but unfortunately the mortality rate (per 1000) has increased from 10.5 in 1991 to 10.9 in 1998 and to 11.9 in 2003. Taking into account the

Fgure I.1: Land use, 2003

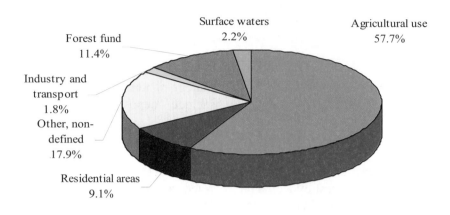

Source: Ministry of Ecology and Natural Resources. Republic of Moldova. State of the Environment Report 2004. Chisinau, 2004.

dismal economic situation, poverty, a drop in the living standards, and significant changes in other demographic indicators it is remarkable that there was almost no change in life expectancy during the 13-year period from 1991 to 2003 (See table I.1).

The country has three major ethnic population groups. Moldovans constitute about 65 per cent of the total population. The second largest group is Ukrainians, with about 14 per cent share of the population, followed by Russians, who constitute about 13 per cent. Russians and Ukrainians live almost entirely in major urban centres, where they constitute slightly more than half of the population. Other small ethnic groups include Gagauz and Bulgarians; these two groups reside primarily in the southernmost regions.

There has been a slight decline in the country's Human Development index (HDI) measured by the United Nations Development Programme (UNDP). In 1998 the country's HDI, was 0.7 (on the scale of 0.0 to 1.0) and Moldova was 102nd out of 174 countries reviewed, belonging to the group of countries with medium human development. Latest available figures in 2002 show that Moldova's HDI was 0.681 and that it was the 113th country out of 177.

I.3   The historical and political context

The Republic of Moldova declared its independence in August 1991, although it remained part of the USSR until the Soviet Union was formally dissolved in December 1991. A conflict flared up in Transnistria and despite several attempts over the years to settle the differences (in particular the 1997 political memorandum granting Transnistria a certain amount of autonomy) the

Transnistrian conflict has not been resolved. Several attempts were made with the involvement of various mediators (Organization for Security and Co-operation in Europe (OSCE), Russia, Ukraine) to reunite Moldova under a federal system, the most recent of them in 2004. This unresolved situation has important effects on international cooperation. Since Transnistrian authorities do not report on environment to the Moldovan Government this publication does not cover its territory.

The President elected in 1996 managed to institute some reforms (e.g. the land privatization programme), but his tenure was marked by a constant legislative struggle with the Parliament. Several times the Parliament considered votes of no confidence in the President's government. In 2000, Parliament passed a decree with the presidency to be decided by parliamentary vote. Later that year no candidate gained the majority of Parliamentary votes and when Parliament failed three times to elect a new president, the President dissolved it and called for new parliamentary elections.

Widespread popular dissatisfaction with the Government and the state of the economy led to a substantial majority of Communist deputies elected to the Parliament. The new President proceeded with his predecessor's plans to privatize several important state-owned industries. In the local elections in May and June 2003, Communists again won the largest share of votes, but lost in the country's highest-profile race, for mayor of Chisinau. The electorate's strong and consistent support for the Communist Party continued in the latest March 2005 parliamentary election when Communist Party Moldova won 46.1 per cent of the votes and 56 out of the 101 seats in Parliament.

Table I.1: Demography and health indices, 1991, 1996-2003

	1991	1996	1997	1998	1999	2000	2001	2002	2003
Birth rate (per 1000)	17.1	12.0	12.5	11.3	10.6	10.2	10.0	9.8	10.1
Fertility rate	2.3	1.6	1.7	1.5	1.4	1.3	1.3	1.2	1.2
Mortality rate (per 1000)	10.5	11.6	11.6	10.9	11.3	11.3	11.0	11.5	11.9
Infant mortality rate (per 1000)	19.3	20.7	19.6	17.9	18.5	18.4	16.4	14.8	14.3
Life expectancy at birth (years)	67.7	66.7	67.0	67.9	67.6	67.8	68.3	68.1	68.1
Female life expectancy at birth (years)	71.0	70.4	70.6	71.6	71.4	71.5	71.9	71.8	71.7
Male life expectancy at birth (years)	64.2	63.0	63.3	64.2	63.8	64.0	64.5	64.4	64.4
Population aged 0-14 years (%)	27.8	25.8	25.9	25.1	24.2	23.3	22.3	21.7	20.3
Population aged 65 years or over (%)	8.3	9.1	9.2	9.3	9.3	9.4	9.5	9.6	9.8

Sources: WHO. Health for All database. http://hfadb.who.dk/hfa/ or www.who.dk on 5.1.2006.

I.4   The institutions

The new constitution was approved by referendum and ratified by parliament on 28th of July 1994. Moldova is an independent and neutral republic, having Moldavian as the official language. The Constitution guarantees voting rights for all citizens aged 18 and older and provides for various other civil rights and freedoms.

The president is the head of state. Before the Constitutional amendments in 2000 the president was directly elected. Currently the president is elected by the Parliament to a four-year term and may serve no more than two consecutive terms. The president can dissolve the Parliament. The constitution provides that the president may be impeached for criminal or constitutional offences.

The president nominates the prime minister and, upon his or her recommendation, the cabinet. The prime minister and the cabinet must be approved by the Parliament. The current government, set up after the elections in March 2005, has 15 ministries (Table I.2).

A unicameral Parliament (*Parlamentul*) is the supreme legislative body. It has 101 deputies who are directly elected for four-year terms. The Parliament convenes for two ordinary sessions per year and may hold extraordinary sessions as well. In addition to enacting laws and performing other basic legislative functions, the Parliament can declare a state of emergency, martial law, and a war.

The judicial system includes three higher courts: the Supreme Court of Justice, the country's highest court; the Court of Appeals; and the Constitutional Court, the highest authority on constitutional matters whose decisions are not subject to appeal.

Tribunals and courts of law adjudicate at the local level. The president appoints judges to the Supreme Court of Justice and the Court of Appeal after the Higher Magistrates' Council makes its recommendations.

The Higher Magistrates' Council, composed of 11 magistrates and serving for a period of five years, acts to ensure the appointment, transfer, and promotion of judges. Council is composed of the Minister of Justice, the President of the Supreme Court of Justice, the President of the Court of Appeal, the President of the Court of Business Audit and the Prosecutor General, with three additional members selected by the Supreme Court of Justice and a further additional three selected by Parliament from amongst accredited university professors.

Table I.2: Ministries

Ministry of Agriculture and Food Industry
Ministry of Culture and Tourism
Ministry of Defence
Ministry of Ecology and Natural Resources
Ministry of Economy and Trade
Ministry of Education, Youth and Sports
Ministry of Finance
Ministry of Foreign Affairs and European Integration
Ministry of Health and Social Protection
Ministry of Industry and Infrastructure
Ministry of Information and Development
Ministry of Internal Affairs
Ministry of Justice
Ministry of Reintegration
Ministry of Transport and Road Administration

Source: Ministry of Ecology and Natural Resources, 2005.

Since 2001, the country has been divided into 32 local districts (or *rayons*), two Territorial Administrative Units (Gagauz Yeri and Transnistria), and three urban municipalities (Chisinau, Balti, and Bender). The municipalities are administered separately from the districts. All local jurisdictions are governed by locally elected councils. After being nominated by the local councils the prefects and mayors of districts and municipalities are appointed by the president.

I.5   The economic context

After gaining its independence Moldova was hit by one of the deepest and most prolonged recessions among the transition economies. In 1991 it belonged to group of middle-income countries but it is now the poorest nation in Europe with its GDP per capita below the average of the Commonwealth of Independent States (CIS) and the Central European Countries. Structurally its economy resembles more the Central Asian republics, than those of the other states on the western edge of the former Soviet Union.

GDP

The secession of the industrialized Transnistria left Moldova with an undiversified economic base almost totally dependant on agricultural and food production. In 1998, agriculture and forestry accounted for 25.8 per cent and industry, 16.7 per cent of GDP. The share of agriculture dropped to 19.3 per cent of GDP in 2003 and industry's share increased to 17.8 per cent. However, agriculture still governs GDP because the small industrial sector is dominated by food processing. According to the 2003 Statistical Yearbook, industry accounts for only 12 per cent of the labour force, while agriculture's labour force share is 43 per cent.

The economy was already contracting before 1991 but the break up with the Soviet Union speeded up the process. GDP fell almost continuously from 1989 to 1998, when it bottomed out at 55.9 per cent of its 1989 level. The only exception was the year 1997 when a slight 0.9 per cent increase over the previous year occurred due to the good weather causing an excellent agricultural output (see Table I.3).

Causes for this economic free-fall were many. First, Moldova was fully integrated into the USSR's economic system and its independence ended the central government subsidies and transfers. Second, the breakdown of the established Soviet Union-era trade links caused obstacles to the movements of goods and restrictions to accessing emerging markets. Third, the lack of its own energy resources and raw materials made the country's economy highly dependent on the rest of the former Soviet Union. This dependency caused import price shocks due to energy price increases in the Russian Federation.

And finally there were "internal" causes: the transition from a centrally planned economy to a market economy, the loss of the industries situated in the Transnistrian area, drought, and civil conflict. However, the robust GDP growth since 1999 seems to indicate that the economy is finally on a more solid footing, although it has to be remembered that according to the latest available 2003 figures GDP is still only at 73.4 per cent of the 1989 level. The substantial incoming flow of money from Moldovans working abroad has softened the effect of the economic downfall.

Figure I.2: GDP composition by sector in 1996, 1998 and 2003 (per cent of total GDP)

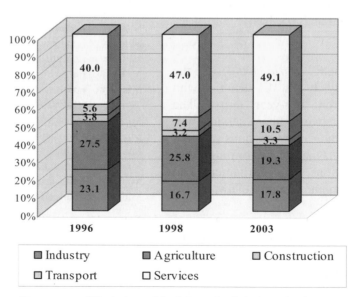

Source: Department of Statistics and Sociology. Statistical Yearbook 2004. Chisinau, 2004.

Inflation

Inflation rocketed to almost 1,200 per cent in 1993 but was brought down to 8 per cent in 1998. However, the devaluation of the Russian Rouble in the same year caused a sudden noticeable inflation increase to 39 per cent. Moldova made great progress bringing inflation under control to 5.2 per cent in 2002; but due mainly to a drought-driven rise in agricultural prices, inflation increased to 11.6 per cent in 2003 and continued to rise in 2004 reaching 12.4 per cent.

Trade deficit

Moldova's expenditure on imports far exceeds its export earnings causing a very serious trade deficit problem. The trade deficit topped 20 per cent of GDP in 2002 and rose to more than 30 per cent of GDP in 2003. This reflects Moldova's considerable energy import requirement and increasingly strong import demand. The growth in import demand is fuelled by the massive inflows of remittances, which are funnelled into household consumption. The export side is dependent on a very narrow range of export products, which complicates efforts to penetrate Western markets. Exports are dominated by agricultural goods and by the food and beverages sector. Food and beverages typically account for around 40 per cent of exports each year. The bulk of these exports have traditionally gone to markets in the CIS and Russian Federation in particular.

Privatization

Since independence most prices have been liberalized and subsidies on most basic consumer goods have been phased out. Nearly all agricultural land, about 80 per cent of all housing units and nearly 2,000 enterprises have been privatized. Moldova's small and medium-sized enterprises (SMEs) were privatized in the early post-independence years through a mass privatization programme based on vouchers. With a few exceptions, opposition has thwarted large-scale cash privatizations. The sale of key state owned enterprises in the wine and tobacco sectors was a particularly sensitive political issue between 1998 and 2001, and parliament only approved the required legislation to privatize these sectors in 2002. Currently the private sector is estimated to account for 80 per cent of GDP and its share of employment ranges from over 95 per cent in agriculture to around 55 per cent in services.

Energy sector privatization is a politically sensitive issue but also critical and important, given Moldova's energy intensive import mix and chronic problems with non-payment. In 2003 several smaller companies and two wineries were privatized, but the government was not able to privatize several larger state enterprises, notably Moldtelecom and two electricity distribution companies. Sporadic and ineffective enforcement of the law, combined with economic and political uncertainty, continues to discourage inflows of direct foreign investment.

Unemployment

The official registered unemployment is very low. Since 1992 it has never been higher than 2.1 per cent and the latest unemployment figure for 2003 is only 1.2 per cent. However, the official data does not capture the large number of unemployed, a number of which, according to the International Labour Organization (ILO) definition, averaged 7.9 per cent of the workforce in 2003. This was more than one percentage point higher than 2002, but down from the ten per cent recorded in the late 1990s. These figures do not take into account the 10-15 per cent of the workforce on unpaid leave or working only part time. In addition, a large portion of the active labour force (about 15 per cent) work abroad.

Financing

During 2002, Moldova rescheduled its loan payments to avoid potential default. In 2003 debt servicing claimed 32.5 per cent of the budget and in mid-2003 Moldova informed its bilateral creditors that it would no longer service its debts. Despite difficult negotiations, the International Monetary Fund (IMF) and World Bank had resumed lending to Moldova in July 2002, but then suspended it again in July 2003. Hoping to secure a new IMF programme, Parliament approved the government's *Economic Growth and Poverty Reduction Strategy Paper* (EGPRSP) in December 2004. The government needs to accept the fiscal adjustment and wage restraint that IMF deems necessary; otherwise relations with the multilateral creditors are very likely to remain strained. However, World Bank is resuming the financing of projects in Moldova through its Country Assistance Strategy (CAS), which sets out the lending and non-lending support to the country for the period 2005-2008.

Transfers and workers' remittances

The inflow of transfers and especially remittances from abroad are very important for keeping the Moldovan economy working. In 2001-03, total inflows of grants, assistance and humanitarian aid to Moldova were around US$ 150 million annually, equating to 8-10 per cent of GDP. However, the country's economic situation would be much worse if it did not receive the remittances from the Moldovans working abroad. These remittances have risen sharply in recent years as a result of mass emigration of the labour force.

In 2003, net inflows of foreign currency from Moldovans abroad equalled almost US$ 450 million (around 22 per cent of GDP). This is up from 15 per cent of GDP in 2002 and, according to unofficial estimates, probably underestimates the actual volume of remittances. Despite a deficit on trade in goods and services that was 31 per cent in 2003, the increasing worker remittances have helped to bring the current account deficit down from an annual 19.7 per cent of GDP in the late 1998 to 7.3 per cent in 2003. The combined income and transfers surplus covered more than 80 per cent of the merchandise trade deficit in 2003 and the remittances will certainly continue to be very important in offsetting the trade deficit in the future.

Moldova's heavy reliance on remittances is problematic and precarious. Firstly, the remittance money flowing into the country increases consumption to a greater extent than production and hence is driving up the imports and inflation. Secondly, if an important host country (like the Russian Federation or Italy - 54 per cent and 18 per cent of the migrants respectively) clamps down on Moldovan migrant labour, the remittance income might dry up very quickly and cause a short-term negative shock effect on the economy. In the long term it is also likely that the money sent home from abroad will diminish as many of the migrants settle down to a new life outside of Moldova.

I.6   The environment

Environment protection commitments

Moldova has actively taken part in international efforts to protect the environment. It signed the UN Rio Declaration on Environment and Development in 1992 and later, in 2002, participated in the Johannesburg World Summit on Sustainable Development and signed the document adopted in the meeting. In addition Moldova participated in the regional "Fifth Ministerial Conference - Environment for Europe" in Kiev in 2003. Since 1991 Moldova has developed an extensive environmental framework of laws, concepts, strategies, programmes and plans to cover all major environmental areas (see Annex III). According to the 2004 State of Environment (SoE) Report the most urgent current environmental problems are: protection of soil resources, improvement of the quality of drinking water, safe management of obsolete pesticides and toxic waste, biodiversity conservation, minimization of transboundary effects and diminution of the anthropogenic impact.

Soil degradation

Moldova's economy is dependent on agricultural production and 57.7 per cent of its land area is in agricultural use. The intensive exploitation of agricultural land and the use of ecologically harmful technologies have led to a significant reduction in productivity and a destructive impact on soil. The condition of the soil is crucial for agriculture and a basis for the development of a productive, export-oriented agriculture and food-processing industry. At present however the yield potential of agricultural soil is declining, which hinders the growth of the agro-industrial sector and affects the national economy as a whole.

The eroded land area covers 858,564 ha or 33.9 per cent of agricultural land and it is increasing annually by 0.9 per cent, causing a loss of 26 million tons of fertile soil. The annual estimated production loss and damage costs to the national economy from soil degradation are about 3.1 billion lei (US$ 251 million). Erosion also has social implications since it strongly affects the families who practise subsistence agriculture. These families belong to the poorest population group and therefore lack the financial resources to address this problem.

Soil degradation has multiple interlinked causes. The lack of information and know-how, especially the rural population's limited access to information on the efficient use of land, leads to the use of poor cultivation technologies and insufficient crop rotations. The diminished application of mineral or organic fertilizers has caused negative humus and nutrient balance of the soil. The use of mineral fertilizers fell from 191,000 tons in 1991 to 72,700 tons in 2003. Other factors like diminished pesticide use, salination of the land, deep ploughing and illegal cutting of protective forestry belts around agricultural land have contributed to erosion.

Water

The surface water quality varies. According to the Water Pollution Index (WPI) the main rivers Dniester and Prut are moderately polluted (category III-IV) while smaller rivers like Reut and Bicu are more polluted (category IV-VI), on a scale where I is the least and VI the most polluted. Dniester's water quality is important, since it is the main surface water body in the country, providing water for 82 per cent of the population of Chisinau and being the source of 56 per cent of the total abstracted water.

The majority of underground water does not meet the quality standards and requirements for potable water because of the excessive concentrations of chemical substances (fluorine, iron, hydrogen sulphide, chlorides, sulphates and excessive mineralization). According to the 2004 State of Environment, pollution in underground aquifers is widespread and the poorly managed underground water is subject to continuous deterioration. In rural areas, where most of the population draw their drinking water from the substandard underground sources and where only 17 per cent of families use central supply sources, bad water quality has a direct impact on the population's health, causing increased morbidity and generating additional health-related expenditures for the state budget and economy.

In the 1990s the water usage pattern changed significantly towards a drastic reduction in consumption. The groundwater abstraction was halved from the 277 million m^3 in 1991 to 132 million m^3 in 2001. The reduction of the use of water to agricultural irrigation was even more dramatic. Irrigation water consumption dropped from 898,000 m^3 in 1990 to 92,000 m^3 in 1998 and to 46,000 m^3 in 2002.

The wastewater discharged from residential or industrial areas is a major pollution contributor to surface waters as most of the wastewater treatment plants (WWTP) are not operational anymore. Out of the 580 WWTPs built before the early 1990s,

only 104 were still in use in 2003. The total capacity of these plants is 614,000m^3/day but only 32 per cent of the capacity or 198,000 m^3/day is effectively used, most of the plants being out of order. As a result, the quantity of untreated or insufficiently treated wastewater has dramatically risen since 2000 (see Figure I.3). Another big polluting source is individual domestic discharges because 70 per cent of housing does not have a proper connection to the sewer system.

Air

The energy and heat generation sector is by far the biggest stationary air pollution source in Moldova. Currently Moldova has 2,289 registered stationary sources, mainly in the energy and heat generation sector but also in industry and services (including 529 petrol stations). During the past few years two factors have reduced stationary emissions; firstly the decrease in energy demand and secondly the large replacement of solid and liquid fuels by natural gas in combustion units. The emission total has decreased from 30,500 tons in 1998 to 16,000 tons in 2003. During the same time period sulphur dioxide emissions dropped to 20 per cent of the initial emissions, nitrogen oxide to 63 per cent and carbon monoxide to less than 56 per cent.

In 2003 road transport accounted for 85.5 per cent of total mobile emissions. Road transport emissions depend on a number of factors such as the technical condition of cars, quality of the gasoline used and the state of the roads. In 2003 there were 281,000 cars in the country. Half of the car fleet is more than ten years old and the number of new cars is relatively small. The enforcement of the use of unleaded petrol and desulphurised diesel has contributed to the reduction of emissions and caused the imports of unleaded petrol in a few years (1999-2003) to increase from 70 per cent to 99 per cent of total imports. The financial resources allocated for road maintenance and traffic security are very low and the state of the roads is not going to be improved in the near future. During 2003, the State Ecological Inspectorate, together with the road police, inspected exhaust gas emissions of 14,740 cars. 7.3 per cent of gasoline cars and 12.6 per cent of diesel cars did not comply with the emission standards and regulations.

Table I.3: Selected economic indicators, 1995-2003

	1995	1996	1997	1998	1999	2000	2001	2002	2003
GDP (1989=100)	60.2	58.2	58.7	55.9	58.9	64.2	67.4	70.3	73.4
GDP (% change over previous year)	-4.1	-3.4	0.9	-4.9	5.4	9.0	5.0	4.3	4.5
GDP in current prices (million lei)	6,480	7,798	8,917	9,122	12,322	16,020	19,052	22,556	27,297
GDP in current prices (million US$)	1,441	1,694	1,928	1,699	1,172	1,288	1,481	1,662	1,980
GDP per capita (US$)	399	471	538	465	321	354	408	459	548
GDP per capita (US$ PPP per capita)	2,223	2,138	2,217	2,059	2,020	2,112	2,300	..	..
Industrial output (1989=100)	47	44	44	37	33	35	40	44	50
Agricultural output (% change over previous year)	3	-13	12	-12	-8	-3	6	..	..
Gross output of agriculture (1989=100)	46	40	45	40	36	35	37	..	..
CPI (% change over the preceding year, annual average)	30	24	12	8	39	31	10	5	12
PPI (% change over the preceding year, annual average)	53.7	32.2	20.0	9.7	44.0	28.5	12.3	4.7	7.8
Registered unemployment (% of labour force, end of period)	1	2	2	2	2	2	2	2	1
Balance of trade in goods and non-factor services (million US$)	-70	-260	-348	-388	-137	-294	-313	-378	-622
Current account balance (million US$)	-95	-192	-275	-335	-68	-116	-68	-52	-142
" (as % of GDP)	-7	-11	-14	-20	-6	-9	-5	-3	-7
Net FDI inflows (million US$)	66	23	78	76	38	136	146	116	58
Net FDI flows (as % of GDP)	4.6	1.4	4.1	4.5	3.2	10.6	9.9	7.0	2.9
Cumulative FDI (million US$)	134.0	157.1	235.4	311.7	349.5	485.5	631.6	747.7	806.1
Foreign exchange reserves (million US$)	257	312	366	144	186	222	229	269	302
" (as months of imports)	3.81	3.46	3.55	1.67	3.64	3.47	3.12	3.11	2.54
Net external debt (million US$)	597	761	921	1,308	1,308	1,348	1,313	1,393	1,649
Exports of goods (million US$)	739	823	890	644	474	477	567	660	806
Imports of goods (million US$)	809	1,083	1,238	1,032	611	770	880	1,038	1,429
Ratio of net debt to exports (%)	80.8	92.5	103.5	203.3	275.9	282.6	231.6	211.1	204.5
Ratio of net debt to GDP (%)	41.5	45.0	47.8	77.0	111.7	104.6	88.7	83.8	83.2
Exchange rates: annual averages (lei/ US$)	4.497	4.604	4.624	5.370	10.517	12.433	12.867	13.570	13.946
Population (1000) UNECE (excluding Transnistria)	3,611	3,599	3,587	3,650	3,647	3,640	3,631	3,623	3,613
Population (1000) WHO HFADB on 18.3.2005 (inc. Transnistria)	4,339	4,325	4,310	4,297	4,285	4,271	4,254	4,236	4,267

Sources : UNECE Common statistical database 2005, National Statistics 2004, and WHO Health for All Database 2005.

Table I.4: Estimated air emissions, 1995-2003

Table I.4 a: Stationary sources

thousand tons

	1995	1996	1997	1998	1999	2000	2001	2002	2003
Total	40.6	36.7	33.7	30.5	20.4	15.2	14.5	17.0	16.0
of which:									
Sulfur dioxide SO_2	19.0	16.9	14.5	12.0	8.0	3.9	2.5	2.3	2.5
Nitrogen oxide NOx	4.3	3.9	4.0	4.0	2.8	5.6	3.0	3.0	2.5
Carbon monoxide CO	8.0	7.7	7.7	8.1	4.9	4.5	3.9	5.7	4.5

Source: Ministry of Ecology and Natural Resources. State of the Environment Report 2003. Chisinau, 2004.

Table I.4 b: Mobile sources

thousand tons

	1995	1996	1997	1998	1999	2000	2001	2002	2003
Total	238.2	100.5	215.6	174.4	110.0	118.8	122.9	130.9	..
of which:									
Volatile Organic Compounds VOC	41.6	16.5	39.2	29.6	19.2	20.7	22.2	12.9	..
Nitrogen dioxide NO_2	19.8	7.0	25.6	13.4	9.1	9.9	10.7	15.1	..
Carbon monoxide CO	160.8	72.7	144.4	121.7	74.4	80.7	85.8	87.2	..

Source: Department of Statistics and Sociology. Statistical Yearbook 2004. Chisinau, 2004.

Total air emissions almost halved from 1995 to 2002 decreasing from 278.8 to 147.9 thousand tons a year. However there are differences between the development of the stationary and mobile source emissions. There was a downward trend in stationary emissions up to 2001 and then a slight rise, while mobile source emissions bottomed out in 1999 but have increased since then. The composition of total emissions is also changing. The share of mobile source emissions has always been large but during 1995-2002 it became even more dominant. During the same period, the stationary source emission share diminished from 17 per cent in 1995 to 13 per cent in 2002.

Waste

The collection and disposal of household and industrial waste is a problem but Moldova has made some progress with it in past years. The overall amount of waste has been decreasing since 1997 when the total existing waste stock was 9 million tons. At the end of 2003 the stock of waste was 3.7 million tons. The generation of waste in 2003 decreased and waste reuse increased compared to 2002.

The annual average waste generated per person is 340 kg although in Chisinau it is slightly higher (400 kg/capita). Moldova has about 1,700 landfills, of which only 670 are legal. In 2003 landfills covered about 1,300 ha and about half of the area belonged to legal landfills. Most of the rural settlements or small towns have no legal dumpsites

and consequently, a significant part of domestic households and industrial waste is dumped illegally on unequipped areas such as roadsides, riverbanks, and ravines.

The decrease in industrial waste can be attributed to reduced economic activity. Toxic waste has diminished dramatically from 350 tons in 2002 to only 112 tons in 2003. Stocks of obsolete pesticides are a special threat. There are 1,712 tons out-of-use and 865 tons of prohibited toxic pesticides, deposited in 340 warehouses, of which 80 per cent are not suitable for storage. Another problem is the 23,920 tons of contaminated oils used in the power sector, part of it containing polychlorinated biphenyls (PCB). The problem is aggravated by the lack of waste sorting and processing plants, lack of financial resources at the national and local level, and the use of unsuitable storage for these substances.

Biodiversity

Moldova has not succeeded in increasing its protected areas that in 2005 still cover the same 1.96 per cent of the territory as in 1998. The country has five scientific reserves that were created for strict nature protection. Two of the areas are allocated for the preservation of the forest ecosystem, two to preservation of floodplain willow and poplar forests and the fifth is dedicated to the aquatic ecosystem of the Dniester River. The total area of these five reserves is 19,378 ha. In addition to these strictly protected areas, Moldova has 130

Figure I.3: Trends in economic growth, energy consumption, air and water pollution

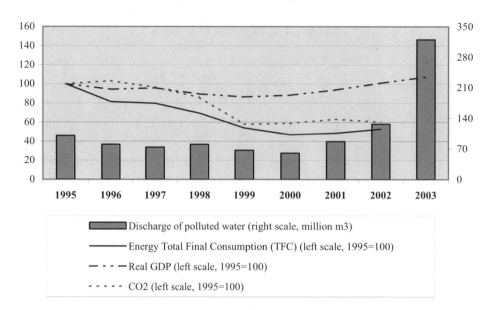

Source: Department of Statistics and Sociology, Ministry of Ecology and Natural Resources, International Energy Agency, IEA database, April 2005.

Note: Indices are based on the following data: GDP at previous year's prices, discharge of insufficiently purified water in million m3, emission of CO2 into atmosphere (stationary sources and transport) in thousand tons, and total final consumption of ene

Figure I.4: Energy intensity comparison TFC/GDP (PPP)

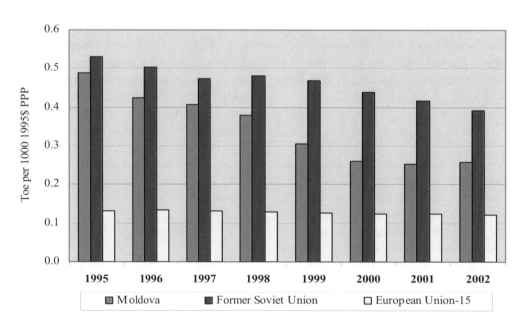

Source: International Energy Agency, IEA database April 2005.

Notes : TFC = Total Final Consumption of Energy

PPP = Purchasing power parity

natural monuments, 63 managed nature reserves and 41 protected landscapes.

The protected area is much smaller than in most European countries. For example the share of total protected land area is 3.3 per cent in Ukraine, 6.4 per cent in Belarus, 8.9 per cent in Hungary, 18 per cent in the UK and 25 per cent in Austria. The relatively small share of the total territory and fragmented character of these areas, added to the low level of protection regime in some areas, might not provide effective conservation of biological diversity.

According to the Land Cadastre, the forestry fund covered 403,400 ha (11.9 per cent of country's territory), and this included 362,700 ha of forest (forestation level of 10.7 per cent). The current share of afforested area is considered insufficient for an effective environmental balance and a factor contributing to the high level of soil erosion, landslides, degradation of water resources, and intensified droughts. Over the last decade authorized and unauthorized cuts have reduced the forests, but other issues such as excessive grazing, low level of ecological knowledge on forests, and lack of efficient local management and administrative controls, have also been features to a diminishing share of the forested land.

I.7 Decoupling

Achieving the strategic environmental objectives and reducing pollution pressures can be possible over the long-term only if environmental pressures are decoupled from GDP growth. The available data imply that progress since 1998 has been uneven. Most emissions declined rapidly during the 1998-99 recession but started to rise in subsequent years. Air pollution has increased since 1999, due to the rapidly growing road transport emissions (emissions from stationary sources fell until 2000, fluctuating until 2003), and the total final energy consumption has had an upward trend from 2000 onwards.

The volume of untreated and insufficiently treated wastewater grew much more rapidly than GDP, air pollution and energy consumption in recent years (Figure I.3); this worrisome trend reflects a rapid deterioration of sewage treatment facilities caused by underinvestment. The energy intensity measured by total final consumption (in physical units) per unit of GDP (at 1995 purchasing power parities) declined until 2000, remaining practically constant thereafter (Figure I.4). It still mostly reflects the effect of the collapse of economic activities. Although this measure of energy intensity remained well below the average of the former Soviet Union countries, it continued to significantly exceed the EU-15 average.

The broad trends illustrated by Figures I.3 and I.4 imply that environmental policy has achieved only partial decoupling of environmental pressures from economic growth and needs to better integrate environmental concerns into economic decisions.

Map I.1: Map of the Republic of Moldova

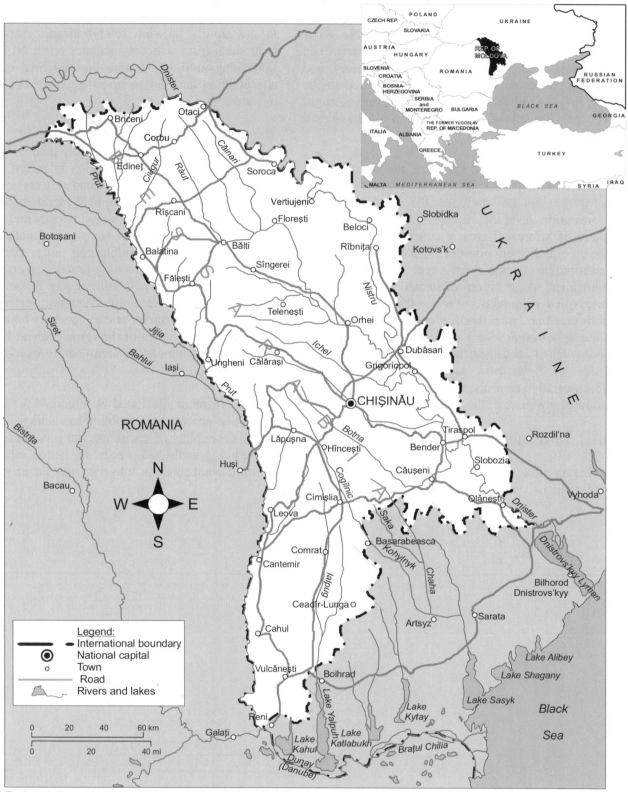

PART I: POLICY MAKING, PLANNING AND IMPLEMENTATION

Chapter 1

LEGAL AND POLICY-MAKING FRAMEWORK [1]

1.1 The institutional framework

Management Structures

In 2001 the Parliament of the Republic of Moldova established 32 regional *rayons* (districts) with social and economic, but no direct environmental, competencies. These regional *rayons* work in parallel to the four regional environmental agencies and have staff in each administrative district. Local self-government is exercised by 1442 municipalities with elected local councils and their own budgets.

The 1998 *Law on Local Public Administration* enlarged the functions of local authorities on natural-resources management and environmental protection. Environmental departments were created in local councils to deal with these issues. As a result, the delimitation of functions between these local authorities and the regional environmental agencies is sometimes unclear. The local administrations tried to assume the functions of environmental control, i.e., to duplicate the activity of territorial branches of the Ministry of Ecology and Natural resources. The main tasks of environmental departments created within the local governments were to prioritize local environmental matters, to develop local environmental action plans and to raise the environmental awareness of the public. The provision of environmental services such as municipal solid waste management, drinking water supply and wastewater collection and treatment were the responsibilities of the municipalities but due to the re-centralisation started in 2001 these functions are now moving away from the municipalities to the regional and local structures of Ministries. In some local councils the environmental departments continue to be active, although the financial autonomy of local administrations has been reduced by the 2001 amendments to the Law.

The framework within which the public authorities operate is set out in the 1995 Law on State Service. Ministries draw up and implement policies either directly or through their executive authorities. They operate at regional or local level in different configurations, using technical, research and any other necessary skills from their specialized organizations.

In 1998, the Department for Environmental Protection was upgraded to the Ministry of Environment, which was restructured in 1999 as the Ministry of Environment and Territorial Management. In 2001 it was reorganized as the Ministry of Environment, Construction and Territorial Development. In 2004 construction and territorial development issues were separated from the Ministry, which became the Ministry of Ecology and Natural Resources (MENR).

In October 2005, the MENR has been reduced to 25 staff and is responsible for most of the elements constituting the corpus of environmental laws. It has one executive authority, the State Ecological Inspectorate (SEI) that helps in implementing environmental policies and laws. The structure of the MENR is given in figure 1. Its internal structure is as follows:

- The Division of Environmental Policy and European Integration has the task of developing and implementing the State policy on environmental protection. It also has the task of coordinating the improvement of national environmental legislation and for the approximation of its content to European Union (EU) legislation.

- The Division on Natural Resources and Biodiversity develops and promotes State policy on conservation and sustainable use of natural resources. It develops the legislation on forest protection, hunting, fishing and land resources and implements programmes and plans on protection and conservation of natural heritage. It coordinates the activities connected with biological diversity conservation and

---

[1] The present chapter reviews progress since the 1998 UNECE Environmental Performance Review of Moldova

protected areas management, and also develops related legislation.

- The Division for Environmental Pollution Prevention deals with the issues of pollution prevention and waste management, and also with the implementation of State ecological expertise plans, programmes, schemes and strategies. It develops related legislation.

- The Division of Accounting and Foreign Relations deals with staff management, law service, accounting and international agreements.

There are other specialized institutions, such as the State Environmental Inspection and its Central Ecological Laboratory, the Agency for Geology "AGeoM", the State Hydrometeorological Service, the National Institute of Ecology and the Environmental Information Centre, working in air, water, monitoring, information and other areas. These institutions are ancillary to the MENR, providing a supportive role in research and information gathering and dissemination. These institutions have no executive responsibilities.

These specialized institutions may be national or regional, depending on their specific tasks. In certain fields, State companies exercise important management functions. In environment, these include the State Water Concern "Apele Moldovei", which is under the Ministry of Agriculture and Food Industry, and, ancillary to the Government, the Agency for Forestry "Moldsilva" that deals with forest management and identifies the areas, type and amount of cutting in coordination with the State Ecological Inspectorate.

The State Hydrometeorological Service has 415 staff and a meteorological observation centre. Consequently air and water monitoring responsibilities are key functions. The biggest problem for their effective operation is a lack of the required technical base. Most of the air pollution measurement stations work on non-continuous sampling systems. This gives information on pollution levels three times per day.

The Agency for Geology "AGeoM" provides control for the safeguarding of groundwater from pollution and exhaustion and keeps the State balance of mineral stocks. They participate in the issuing of permits for water abstraction.

The Environmental Information Centre, created in 2000, is responsible for the gathering and updating of environmental information and for making it publicly available.

The National Institute of Ecology, created in 1990, is in charge of carrying out scientific research on ecology in coordination with the Academy of Sciences. Their tasks also include consultancy on environmental impact assessment (EIA) and the elaboration of national reports on the State of the Environment. Furthermore they carry out expert evaluation of foreign or new technologies from an environmental point of view on the basis of their own experience without using data from the European Integrated Pollution Prevention and Control (IPPC) Bureau.

The Central Ecological Laboratory carries out the sampling and analysis of water, soil and other environmental samples. The technical base for their effective functioning is quite limited. Quality control and quality assurance systems are not implemented at the level of internationally recognized principles. There is a need to establish a national reference laboratory for environment quality measurements, which should be accredited by an international accreditation body.

The last three organizations cover functions that are overlapping and need to be co-ordinated with each other. In many EU countries, these functions are carried out by one single institution, such as an environmental agency.

In general, management and implementation structures are simple, with each policy - permitting, compliance procedures, monitoring and reporting - managed by distinct institutions for each sector. The strength of the institutional system is that the tasks of permitting and assuring compliance with permitting conditions (through inspection) are performed in two separate departments. Since both departments are within the SEI the information can be freely exchanged; and having two departments avoids the possibility of conflict of interest. Thus the principal responsibilities for the implementation of environmental protection requirements are shared between:

- The relevant division of the Ministry dealing with policy formulation and planning;

- The specialized divisions responsible for the preparation of legislation;

- The SEI, which is responsible for permitting;

- The relevant territorial environmental agencies (TEAs) responsible for inspection and control of the environmental performance of installations, which can appeal to the national inspectorate competencies;

- The operator (if required by authorities) for emission monitoring, and the relevant MENR institution for ambient monitoring; and

- The Environmental Information Centre and the National Institute of Ecology for reporting.

The General Division for Environmental Strategies and Policies coordinates the National Environmental Fund (NEF), set up in 1993. The NEF management is carried out by a steering committee that includes representatives from the MENR, Parliament, the Governmental Apparatus and environmental NGOs. The Minister of Ecology and Natural Resources is the president of NEF. See chapter 5 on Economic Instruments and Environmental Funds.

Interministerial co-operation mechanisms

Environmental information from other government bodies is not readily available to the MENR even though it is required by law and, in some cases, is stipulated in the formal agreements between institutions, such as the existing agreement between the MENR and the Ministry of Health and Social Protection. Therefore, the MENR relies on the information gathered by its inspectors. The other ministries lack specialists and/or departments to deal with environmental issues. In some ministries the Environment Unit has been dissolved, such as the Ministry of Economy and Trade.

A number of industrial enterprises are ISO 9000 certified. ISO 14001 has not yet been implemented. A number of programmes for cleaner production are under implementation, financed predominantly by international sources.

The frequent reorganization of national, regional and district structures since 1998, has certainly been a source of confusion and has complicated the horizontal cooperation of authorities enforcing environmental legislation. The changes in geographical coverage and the consequent transfers of files, changes in staff and leadership, and changes in priorities do not facilitate the development of interministerial cooperation mechanisms.

By decision of the President of the Republic of Moldova, the National Council on Sustainable Development and Poverty Reduction was established in 2004 in order to coordinate activities related to strategic planning on socio-economic policy, oriented towards sustainable development and improvement of the population's quality of life. This Council, if operational, would be an excellent framework for intersectoral and interministerial cooperation.

Staffing

Due to low salaries in the public sector, the recruitment of good quality staff is difficult and keeping new staff members even more so. Good coverage of crosscutting issues necessitates a fair distribution of skills and competencies across the environmental management structures, and therefore consequent training and retraining needs. At present there is no experience of integrated approaches to environmental management and the differing level in staff skills does not allow for an even quality of permit preparation. Moreover, training cannot be limited merely to environmental management; it also needs the involvement of industry and of local governments, including professionals such as operators for water supply and treatment facilities or landfills.

1.2 The policy framework

Concepts and strategies

The foundations for the environmental policy were set up by the 1993 *Law on Environmental Protection*, the 1995 *Concept of Environmental Protection*, the 1995 *National Strategic Environmental Protection Action Programme*, the 1996 *National Environmental Action Plan* and the 2001 *National Action Plan for Environmental Health*. At the same time a number of sector-specific strategy documents have been elaborated, including a series of provisions relating to environmental protection.

In the period 1995 to 2000, the "Environment for Europe" process drew particular attention to countries in the Eastern Europe, Caucasus and Central Asia (EECCA) region and to South-East European countries. The Republic of Moldova has participated actively in this process, being represented at the highest level in international environmental activities. It has also signed and ratified a number of international agreements. Their implementation has become a constituent part of environmental activities at national and regional levels. See chapter 4 on International Agreements.

A series of legal instruments, programmes and strategies have been adopted relating to other sectors of Moldovan economy. A series of changes has occurred in Moldovan society and in the structure of the national economy during the last years. The need to implement a unified policy on environmental protection and the use of natural resources, which integrates environmental requirements into the national economic reform along with the political desire for integration into the EU, has resulted in the revision of the existing environmental policy and the development of a new policy concept.

The 2001 *Concept of Environmental Policy* replaced the action plans and concepts that have been in force since the middle of the 1990s. It covers the adjustment of the ecological policy's major objectives to take account of the social and economic changes in the country, and incorporate

regional and global programmes and trends in order to prevent further deterioration of the environment. Its main objectives for environmental policy are:

- To prevent and mitigate the negative impact of economic activities upon the environment, natural resources and public health in the context of sustainable national development; and

- To ensure a safe environment for the country.

According to the Concept, the current environmental policy priorities are capacity building and cross-sectoral collaboration, including the use of "economy through ecology" and "cost-benefit" principles, regulation of environmental impacts, pollution prevention and rehabilitation of the environment. The Concept covers the issues of financing environmental activities, and public

Figure 1.1: Organizational structure of the Ministry of Ecology and Natural Resources

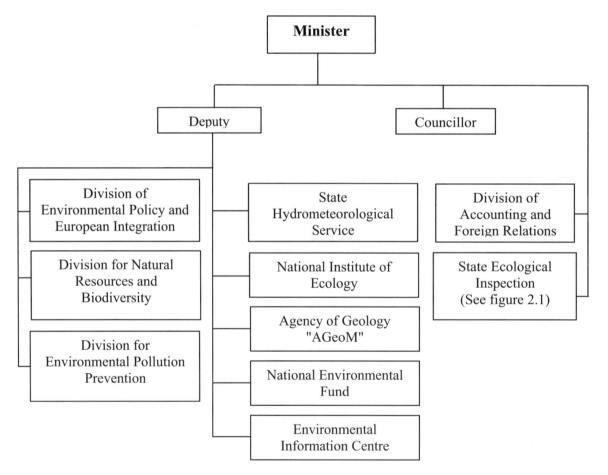

Source: Ministry of Ecology and Natural Resources, 2005

participation in the decision-making process in the context of environmental protection and rational use of natural resources. It calls for an extension in Environmental Information Centre activities and the creation of environmental information centres at local level. International collaboration activities in environment are driven by the development of a concept for international relations on environment and the political desire for European integration, with emphasis on approximation, strategies and programmes.

EU-Moldova Action Plan for Neighbourhood Policy

In September 2003 the country presented a *Concept for the Integration of the Republic of Moldova* into the European Union. In the Concept it welcomed the European Neighbourhood Policy and expressed its wish to be included in the Stabilisation and Association Process of the Western Balkan countries. In March 2004 the country recognized the importance of the Neighbourhood Policy for internal reform and considered it as a way to move closer to the EU. A joint EU-Moldova Action Plan was prepared for 2005-2008 and signed in February 2005. According to the Action Plan the country is invited to enter into intensified political, security, economic and cultural relations with the EU.

The EU acknowledges Moldova's European aspirations and Moldova's wish to integrate with the EU. The Action Plan covers the issues of sustainable development and asks for steps to be taken to better integrate environmental considerations into other policy sectors, particularly industry, energy, transport, regional development and agriculture. It also asks for steps to be taken towards strengthening environmental administrative structures and establishing procedures regarding access to environmental information and public participation. It covers issues of the implementation of the Aarhus Convention on Access to Information, Public Participation in Decision-making and Access to Justice in Environmental Matters, EIA and environmental education. The need for the adoption of additional legal acts for key environmental sectors is also specified. The possible participation in European Environment Agency activities is mentioned.

Economic Growth and Poverty Reduction Strategy Paper

In its chapter on Environmental Protection and Sustainable Use of Natural Resources, the 2004 Strategy highlights the necessity for the integration of sustainable development principles in all socio-economic activity spheres. Concrete action plans were developed for short-term goals to be achieved by 2006. Related objectives and actions were specified together with their estimated costs and an identification of financial sources.

Other Strategies, Plans and Programmes

A large number of other strategies, plans and programmes related to the environment, listed in Annex III, have been elaborated since 1998. Two of the most important are:

- The 2001 *National Strategy and Action Plan for Protection of Biodiversity* covers issues on the management of natural protected areas, their expansion and the structural and functional rehabilitation of the degraded ecosystems. Informing and educating the population on environmental protection and keeping them involved in decision-making about the protection and rational use of biological diversity, are other key issues of this Strategy. The implementation of the related Action Plan will cost an estimated US$ 18.7 million. The possible sources of financing include the State budget, subventions from different institutions and organizations, and contributions from national and local environmental funds; and

- The 2003 *Concept of National Water* Resource *Policy for 2003-2010* covers the purposes and tasks of water policy including the rational use and protection of water resources, water quality improvement, meeting population and national economy needs, and protecting the aquatic ecosystem.

In order to increase the population's access to good quality drinking water, the 2000 *Programme of Water Supply and Sanitation for Localities until 2006* was developed in 2002 and is under implementation. It is financed from State and local budgets, the NEF and credits and grants from international financial institutions and foreign countries.

1.3   The legal framework

Law development process

The Constitution of the Republic of Moldova refers several times to the environment and to the principle of sustainable development. It requires this and all other policies to be managed through laws. The laws must stipulate the regulations that should be elaborated to make these laws operational, and set a timetable for their adoption. Legal requirements are uniform for the entire country except Transnistria

Laws and their subsidiary ordinances tend to be prescriptive and make detailed provisions for the organization and implementation of the matter being regulated, setting out control practices or giving the location of offices established to implement them. Environmental laws and their subsidiary ordinances are similarly single-media in character. Voluntary approaches for environmental compliance are not integrated into legal requirements.

To a certain extend, the regulatory process is well implemented. On one hand, permitting and inspecting authorities give their opinion on legal acts drafts. But, on the other hand, feedback on policy setting from the legislative process and the permitting and inspection authorities has not been very effective. At present many policies and strategies are not implemented through the legislative framework as a lot of corresponding legal acts are still missing. The very large number of policy concepts and action plans on environmental protection has not systematically led to the development of new legislation. The basic legal acts from the 1990s are still in force with minor amendments.

The MENR drafts the legal acts and submits them to its four regional agencies for comments and then to the Ministry of Justice who considers them from a legal point of view. The latter may return them to the MENR for review. Once approved the draft is forwarded by the Government to the Parliament, where it goes through a parliamentary committee (on public administration, ecology and territorial development) stage and two readings before being presented to the President for signature. Laws bear signatures either of the President of the Republic or of the Chairman of the Parliament. The President can send the Act adopted by the Parliament back for revision. The environmental laws, approved by the Parliament, may contain provisions about the

time when they come into force. A law normally comes into force on the date of its publication in the Official Journal of Legal Acts. The period between adoption and publication can be quite long – an average of three months.

The Government issues implementing regulations for environmental laws when the implementation is the concern of more than one ministry. These regulations make detailed provisions for implementation. Balancing regulatory and non-regulatory instruments for implementation does not seem to be a priority for the country, which considers such an approach ineffective. Instead, the priority is put on the strengthening of the regulatory instruments with the establishment of sanctions to punish violation cases.

Environmental Protection

The basic legislation that covers environmental protection is given in Annex III. Most of these laws were elaborated between 1995 and 1999.

The fairly detailed nature of several of the environmental laws has a positive impact on the effective functioning of the regulatory cycle. Other laws can be rather declarative and require the development of detailed secondary legislation acts. However, the requirements specified in these laws are often not met and they lack implementation mechanisms.

The prescriptive and strictly single-media character of environmental laws generates a lack of interaction and cooperation between sectors, and an absence of a holistic view of environmental problems and their solutions. This is another factor that is likely to increase difficulties in the implementation of integrated pollution prevention and control because of the lack of experience in multi-sectoral practice. This single-media nature of environmental laws, and even more of their implementation procedures, raises particular concerns.

For instance, the 1993 *Law on Environmental Protection* requires that "economic agents" apply for and regularly renew their environmental and natural resource use permits. In addition, economic agents are required to use energy and water efficiently, to avoid polluting the soil, to minimize waste generation and the use of toxic substances and to reduce their air emissions. Sectoral laws require the "economic agents" to apply for a set of environmental permits, including one for discharges into the air, water and soil and one for waste. Further requirements relating to permits are established in different pieces of legislation dealing with air and water protection and others.

Maximum permissible limits of pollution are established via complex calculations based on ambient air and water quality standards, which are set down using GOST standards dating from the Soviet period. There is, by far, not enough capacity to check the excessive number (more than 1,000) of pollutants listed in the environmental quality standards, and the measuring equipment is not efficient enough to detect the low set cut-off values. The combined approach (where both environmental quality and emission limit values are followed when establishing permit conditions) as used in the EU has not been introduced. The provisions that relate to informing the public of permit applications and decisions on issuing permits are not expressed clearly enough and it is apparently not current practice to inform the public.

Ecological Expertise

The 1996 *Law on Ecological Expertise and Environmental Impact Assessment* gives citizens the right to request information on new economic developments/projects and on the results of the evaluation of their design documentation. The Constitution gives every citizen the right to take actions to the courts but there are no examples of people who have exercised this legal right yet. The main reasons for this may be that people do not often realize that the right for a clean environment is one of their fundamental constitutional rights and that the public has limited access to timely and intelligible environmental information. However, citizen actions are starting to take place, and citizens are starting to make use of environmental NGOs to initiate the actions.

Air protection

The 1997 *Law on Atmospheric Air Protection* states that a permit is required for facilities emitting substances into the air. Emission standards and the way they are calculated are based on dispersion calculations. The aim is to guarantee that ambient air quality standards are not exceeded. Air quality standards are still those of the Soviet times and have not been approximated to EU standards. There are no emission standards for certain industries (e.g., large combustion plants) and all standards are calculated on a case-by-case basis. The principle of best available techniques is not applied in the

country and the existing legislation does not give any grounds for it.

The emission limits for Volatile Organic Compound (VOC) emitting installations are also based on dispersion calculations. This means there is no evidence as to whether limit values set in EU legislation (the two VOC Directives) are followed because facilities in the country are still allowed to build higher stacks and ventilation systems as a way to meet the ambient air quality standards.

The *Law on Atmospheric Air Protection* also regulates emissions of mobile sources but again, the limit values used are those established for old Soviet cars and the number of components regulated is very limited - carbon monoxide, hydrocarbons for gasoline engines, and smoke density (relative indicator for PM content in exhaust gases) for diesel engines.

Water protection

The basic legal act of water legislation is the 1993 *Water Code*, which gives grounds for similar concerns as those described above on air quality management. The authorized discharge levels are based on ambient standards. The methodology for calculating discharge limits from ambient standards is based on the principle of dilution calculation and dates from former Soviet Union times. The main criterion for the calculation of emission limit values is that pollutants discharged into the watercourse should not exceed the maximum permissible concentrations in the receiving waters of designated use (fishery management limit values are being used by default). The ambient water quality standards are extremely stringent as they are based upon the concept of zero risk. As a result they are unrealistically strict which leads to a general acceptance that it is not possible to meet the legal requirements. Also, sometimes natural components in groundwater (e.g., sulphides) may have a higher concentration than the authorized limit value in the receiving water body, so it is impossible to follow the requirements. There is a need for a realistic linkage between ambient standards and discharge standards with both preferably being established directly by legislation.

Waste and hazardous substances

There is no legal obligation in the country for companies working with certain quantities of dangerous substances to develop accident prevention and safety management plans. The principles of EU legislation on the control of major-accident hazards involving dangerous substances are not yet included in the national law. The provisions that require installations to develop a policy for major accident prevention as well as safety management systems, including preparation of external emergency plans and a safety report, are missing. A series of pieces of legislation cover the issue of waste management. The most important of them are listed in Annex III.

The 1993 *Law on Environmental Protection* imposes general obligations on so-called economic agents, requiring them to introduce technologies that minimize waste generation, to keep a register of generated wastes and to process recyclable waste on site or in specialized enterprises. The current definition and categorization of waste is still based on classifications adopted under the Soviet system. International waste categorization has not been introduced so far.

The *Law on Environmental Protection* also provides for the establishment of taxes for the storage and treatment of industrial and domestic waste, and technical standards for transport, surface storage, incineration and landfill of the non-recyclable components of waste. The 1998 *Law on Payments on Environmental Pollution* implements these principles in detail.

The 1997 *Law on Industrial and Domestic Waste* requires the Government to develop a National Waste Management Plan. Under the Law on Environmental Protection local Governments are obliged to develop local Environmental Protection Plans that, where they have been developed, may include plans for local waste management. No waste management plans have yet been developed at *rayon* level in addition to the National Waste Management Plan.

The *Law on Environmental Protection* covers three main waste classes: solid and non-hazardous waste, toxic (hazardous) waste and nuclear waste. So far a list of wastes falling within these categories is still missing. There is no definition of hazardous waste corresponding to EU legislation in the country.

The *Law on Environmental Protection* forbids all imports and transits of nuclear waste on the territory of the Republic of Moldova.

One of the EU waste legislation's principles states that waste management is preferably dealt with at regional level. Such a proximity principle has not yet been incorporated into Moldavian legislation and such practices do not exist yet either. No existing legal act regulates environmental permitting of waste incinerators or lays down any emission limit values. Incinerators, if they are developed as is planned, would be regulated like any other pollution source, through dispersion calculations.

The country's legislation on landfill needs some major upgrading in order to set up a framework for the introduction of fees for waste disposal that reflect the real costs for landfill waste in an environmentally sound way.

Existing waste legislation does not cover specific requirements for waste oil, titanium dioxide waste, polychlorinated biphenyl (PCBs), sewage sludge, batteries and packaging. Some of these substances may be classified as toxic and are then part of a special regime, its main stipulation being reporting requirements for producers of the waste.

The legislation on classification, labelling and packaging of dangerous substances and preparations is not yet developed to an extent comparable to EU legislation. There is no formal requirement for the testing and notification of dangerous substances and preparations. There are neither authorities responsible for supervising the labelling and for setting the labelling requirement itself nor technical structures needed to manage the flow of information concerning placing of new chemicals on the market.

Others

The country is at the very start of introducing the concept of environmental management to industrial companies. There is no legislative support to promote the introduction of environmental management systems. There are no existing environmental management and audit schemes that industries can subscribe to for environmental management in enterprises. However, companies are not showing any interest in implementing such schemes. Economic resources are tight and there is not much incentive to improve their environmental performance. There have been companies that have set up a system in accordance with ISO 14000 requirements but they were not accredited by any national body. There is a tendency to approach such issues as environmental management in enterprises by developing obligatory standards rather than by setting up a voluntary scheme and programme to promote the idea and involve companies. The situation is similar with eco-labelling, a concept that is just beginning to be introduced.

The issue of genetically modified organisms has not yet been practically dealt with. The regulation for licensing for applied research on genetics and microbiology was adopted in 1998. This regulation contains some general provisions relating to genetically modified micro-organisms and genetically modified organisms but does not cover the full set of EU legislation in this field.

Nature protection

The most important pieces of national legislation covering the field of nature protection, biodiversity and forest management are given in Annex III.

The 1998 *Law on the Fund of Natural Areas protected by the State* and the *Law on Environmental Protection* designate the MENR as the authority responsible for regulating nature protection. The responsibility for the management of nature and forest areas has been delegated to the Agency for Forestry "Moldsilva". Local authorities also have the responsibility for nature protection, mainly for the management of natural monuments. The Law on Protected Areas gives a legal base for the designation of State-owned protected areas. It includes a list of protected areas and a list of protected species and requires the MENR to develop the related secondary legislation. Only one regulation, which designates wetland areas as scientific reserves, has been developed so far. The *Law on the Ecological Expertise and Environmental Impact Assessment* includes the obligation that the impact of new projects on protected areas must be taken into account.

As regards habitats, the national legislation is not yet in compliance with the EU habitat protection requirements. Habitats have not been identified as such and the resources and mechanisms for the management of habitats are so far quite limited. The 2001 *National Strategy and Action Plan for Protection of Biodiversity* provides the framework for a structured biodiversity and habitat protection policy and identifies steps to approximate the legislation to EU requirements.

Two main laws cover the conservation of wild birds, the 1995 *Law on Fauna* and the *Law on the Fund of Natural Areas protected by the State*. The latter includes a list of protected birds, including all the birds listed in the Bonn Convention on the Conservation of Migratory Species of Wild

Animals. Trade in species of wild flora and fauna is regulated in the *Law on Fauna* and the 2003 *Regulation on Creation, Registration, Addition, Storage (Custody), Export and Import of Collections of Plants and Animals from Wild Flora and Fauna*. The legislation that should cover the Convention on International Trade in Endangered Species of Wild Fauna and Flora (CITES) requirements is still missing.

Noise

The country has laid down maximum permissible ambient noise levels in the "Hygienic rules for admissible levels of noise on the territory of settlements" dated 1984. This document sets different noise levels, depending on the sensitivity of areas, and its implementation is the responsibility of the Ministry of Health and Social Protection.

There is no Moldovan legislation or standards for noise emission from construction plants and equipment. However the local authorities have the responsibility to address problems with construction noise. The country has not yet moved from an ambient-based noise regime to an emission standards-based regime. Standardized test methods, test facilities as well as a system for spot checks have not been introduced for the measurement of noise emissions from construction plants and equipment.

1.4   Conclusions and recommendations

The Republic of Moldova's environmental management system has real strengths, especially the well-developed strategic base and the dedication of its current staff. The issues that have been raised above do not put these into question and do not necessarily foresee the need for any significant structural change. However, the number of staff is already at the lowest critical level. Some institutional strengthening and raising of administrative capacity is necessary to ensure that the country can continue to move towards the effective practical implementation of its environmental policies and strategies.

Although the organizational principles for environmental management are rational, there is one area of significant concern, which is the excessively single-media orientation of the legislation. The problem is perhaps not that there is one law for air and separate legal acts for water and waste, for example, but rather that each of these laws tends to specify its own implementation regime, which introduces differences in practice that in turn makes an integrated approach to management difficult or even impossible. Measures need to be taken to reduce the gap, firstly by ensuring the equivalence of practice across all media. Subsequently, legislative adjustments would promote a holistic approach to management. There is a need to introduce advanced regulation mechanisms on environmental protection by establishing emission limit values in legal acts directly and combining this approach with an environment quality-based approach.

In a similar manner as ensuring that all cross-media problems are addressed, more attention should also be paid to strengthening the cross-sectoral approaches between environmental management and the management of other economic sectors.

The elaboration of a legislation based on EU environmental *acquis* would help the country to fulfil its wish to move towards EU practices. This does not mean that everything should be done at once, and that strict limit values or Best Available Techniques (BAT) requirements should be immediately implemented, but rather that principles should be established and the regulated community should get some time and transitional periods to implement the new measures.

Every change in practice, whether introducing new requirements or improving existing practice, calls for development of new competencies in the environmental authorities and their bodies through training and retraining. Training therefore should be a key component of any improvement strategy.

Recommendation 1.1:
Following the 2005 EU-Moldova Action Plan, the Government should acknowledge environmental

protection of natural resources as a national priority. For this purpose, it should strengthen the capacity of the environmental authorities and their bodies at national, territorial and local level, so that they are able to perform their functions and adequately respond to environmental priorities expressed in the policy papers. To facilitate the convergence to the EU environmental legislation, a new legal EU harmonization department should be established

Recommendation 1.2:
The Government should strengthen the Ministry of Ecology and Natural Resources to ensure that it fulfils main functions such as implementing international environmental commitments and collecting, managing and disseminating environmental information including the annual State of the Environment report and other reports.

Recommendation 1.3:
The Ministry of Ecology and Natural Resources should use new approaches in the development of environmental legislation, including convergence with key pieces and approaches to EU framework legislation, and identify ways of overcoming the gaps between strictly single-media oriented environmental laws. It should develop guidance documentation, best practice notes or other information on appropriate working methods.
See also Recommendation 2.1.

Recommendation 1.4:
The Government should ensure the effective functioning of the National Council of Sustainable Development and Poverty Reduction by including the Ministry of Ecology and Natural Resources as a member of this Council in order to improve integration of environmental considerations into other policy sectors, mainly agriculture, energy, industry, regional development and transport.

Chapter 2

COMPLIANCE AND ENFORCEMENT MECHANISMS[1]

2.1   Introduction

The principal instruments for compliance assurance are environmental assessment, permitting, compliance monitoring, enforcement, and compliance promotion. Ideally, they should be linked with each other in order to allow feedback and correction to improve the effectiveness of compliance assurance efforts. To make this process function properly, strategic planning and performance assessment capabilities of the environmental enforcement authority are key factors. The following analysis is largely based on sometimes incomplete or contradictory information received from the Moldovan enforcement authority itself.

2.2   Environmental Enforcement Authority: Responsibilities, Organization and Capacity

According to the 1993 *Law on Environmental Protection*, in the Republic of Moldova the State Environmental Inspectorate (SEI) is the environmental enforcement agency responsible for the compliance with the country's legislation in the field of environmental protection and use of natural resources. SEI is an autonomous subdivision of the Ministry of Ecology and Natural Resources (MENR) with the status of a legal entity. The Inspectorate is headed by a Chief Inspector who reports directly to the Minister.

The SEI's jurisdiction includes the protection of air, water and soil, and ensuring the rational use of mineral and biological resources. According to the "Statute of the State Ecological Inspectorate," the principal responsibilities of SEI and its territorial units include:

- State Environmental Expertise (SEE) of new and changing economic development projects;

- Regulation of environmental impacts by issuing permits for air emissions, water use, wastewater discharges, waste disposal, and logging;

- Monitoring of compliance with environmental requirements; and

- Imposition of administrative sanctions for violation of environmental legislation, including termination or suspension of any economic activity undertaken in violation of environmental requirements, claims for compensation for damage caused by environmental violations, and fines.

The SEI has a central office with divisions covering major environmental protection sectors and management functions (see Figure 2.1) and four zonal (territorial) ecological agencies[2] (TEAs): the Central TEA in Chisinau, the Northern one in Balti, the Southern one in Cahul, and a TEA for the Autonomous Territory of Gagauzi in Comrat whose organizational structure roughly follows that of the central office. The SEI central office regulates large industrial installations and supervises TEAs that carry out environmental assessment, permitting, monitoring and inspection activities with the help of their *rayons* (district units) (e.g., there are 16 such units in the Central TEA, the largest of the four). The district units work closely with local public authorities that no longer (since 2001) have their own environmental officials. The division of responsibilities between these, effectively, three levels of environmental enforcement agencies is not always clear, and inspectors themselves complain about the loss of cost efficiency in comparison with the previous system that comprised the central office and 12 TEAs.

In addition, there are six border environmental control posts (down from 60 in 1998) that collect (in cooperation with the customs authorities) charges on imported fuel and environmentally harmful products and control vehicle emissions. The Fishery Service (formerly, the Inspectorate for Fish Protection) is also an institutional part of SEI. It is responsible for monitoring fish populations and

---

[1] The present chapter reviews progress since the 1998 UNECE Environmental Performance Review of Moldova

[2] Before the administrative reform of 2001, there were 12 TEAs, one in each administrative unit (judet). The administrative reform replaced the judets with 32 rayons.

controlling fishery activities in the Dniester River and Prut River basins.

In 2004, the SEI had a total of 411 staff compared to 521 in 1998. The main reason for this cutback was the administrative reform that drastically reduced the number of TEAs. The personnel cuts have also affected the central SEI office. There are currently 264 inspectors (this term includes both permitting and enforcement officials) distributed among the major SEI units as shown in Table 2.1. District units usually have three inspectors with responsibilities for air and water pollution; mineral resource use; soil pollution and waste; and flora and fauna protection. There is currently approximately one inspector per 70 regulated installations, almost double the same indicator in 1998 (36). Further staff cuts are expected in the near future, particularly in the central office.

The SEI is funded from the state budget only at 60%, which is barely enough to cover staff salaries. Additional financial resources for the central SEI office come from charges collected by the environmental border control posts, while TEAs heavily depend on fees for paid services to industrial operators for sampling and analysis by state environmental laboratories, assistance with environmental assessment and permit applications, and environmental audits. In 2004, the revenues from paid services amounted to almost 2.3 million lei (US$ 184,000). While the use of state laboratories for industrial self-monitoring purposes can be acceptable if procedures are established to ensure impartial sample analysis, direct consulting and auditing services to the regulated community create an obvious conflict of interest and should be eliminated.The inspectors are guided in their activities by the Statute and instructions of the SEI, as well as compendiums of environmental legislation. While operational manuals for inspectors have been produced in the past (in 1999 and 2002 with the support of United Nations Development Programme (UNDP) and the World Bank, respectively), they are not utilized. There currently is no special training programme for inspectors.

It is important, at a minimum, to maintain the existing staff numbers at the SEI and work to systematically improve the staff's qualifications through regular training and recruiting new experts. Better operational guidance, including improved directions for data management and internal and external communication, is needed to increase the efficiency and transparency of the Inspectorate's work. New equipment is also badly needed but should be purchased based on sound priorities set in an SEI strategy.

Table 2.1: State Ecological Inspectorate (SEI) staff in 2004

State Ecological Inspectorate Unit	Number of inspectors	Total staff
Total	264	411
Central SEI Office	48	90
TEA Center (including district units)	78	114
TEA North (including district units)	50	80
TEA South (including district units)	21	36
TEA Gagauz Yeri	8	10
Fishery Service	19	31
Border environmental control posts	40	50

Source: State Ecological Inspectorate, March 2005.

2.3   Environmental Assessment

The 1996 *Law on Ecological Expertise and Environmental Impact Assessment* (with the latest amendments in 2003) lays down the framework for environmental assessment. The country is also party (since 1993) to the Espoo Convention on Environmental Impact Assessment in a Transboundary Context (entered into force in 1997) which requires it to notify neighbouring countries of all major projects under consideration that are likely to have a significant transboundary environmental impact.

The State Environmental Expertise is a mandatory procedure for all development projects with a potential environmental impact, regardless of their size, as well as for new programmes, strategies, and policies with environmental implications. (The latter corresponds to the notion of strategic environmental assessment, see below in this section.) SEE of development projects is performed by the SEI central office or by TEAs[3], depending on the project's potential environmental impact, in coordination with the Ministry of Health and Social Protection, and the Ministry of Economy and Trade, the Agency for Regional Development, and the Service of Standardization and Metrology. A survey of public opinion is required for construction projects within a sanitary zone around residential areas. Since 1999, the project proponent pays a fee for SEE, with most of the revenues going to the state budget and a small part to the SEI to cover part of its administrative costs.

---

[3] The projects for installations to be connected to the existing water infrastructure are usually considered by the TEAs.

Table 2.2: State Ecological Inspection

Central Administration

1	Ecological expertise and authorization Direction
2	Ecological logistics and security Direction [a]
3	Fauna and flora inspection Direction
4	Financial and accounting Section
5	Soil, subsoil, waste and chemicals inspection Section
6	Air and water resources inspection Section
7	Information systems Section
8	Judiciary Section
9	Personnel section
10	Control and bookkeeping National Ecological Fund Service

Note: [a] The Ecological logistics and security Direction monitors the activity of the Specialized Ecological Service

Territorial subdivisions

1 Ecological Agency [b]

Ecological Investigation Center [c]
District Ecological Section
Control and audit of natural resources Section
Ecological expertise, authorisation and information Section
Ecological inventorizing and testing Section [d]
Judiciary Section (Service)
Personnel section (Service)
Economical- ecological, financial and accounting Section
Logistics and technical personnel Service

Notes:
[b] The Ecological Agency is a juridical person
[c] The Ecological Investigation Center is a section within Ecological Agency
[d] The Ecological inventorizing and testing Section monitors the activity of ecological mobile posts

2 Fish resources Service [e]

Protection, ichtyological expertise and reglementation Section
Financial and accounting Section
Administrative, information, monitoring and permitting Section
Control and reproduction District Service

Note: [e] The Fish resources Service is a juridical person

3 Specialized Ecological Service [f]

Specialized Ecological Service Briceni
Specialized Ecological Service Cahul
Specialized Ecological Service Hincesti
Specialized Ecological Service Ocnita
Specialized Ecological Service Stefan Voda
Specialized Ecological Service Ungheni

Note: [f] The Specialized Ecological Service is performed as a Section and is not a juridical person

Source: State Ecological Inspectorate, 2005.

Note: All four subdivisions "North", "Central", "South" and "Gagauzia" have same structure.

In addition, the Law requires the preparation of an Environmental Impact Assessment (EIA) for new projects and programmes with significant potential environmental impact. The types of activities subject to an EIA are listed in an annex to the Law and cover main industrial sectors (with defined production capacity thresholds), large farms, large water supply and wastewater treatment plants, waste management installations, irrigation infrastructure and military bases. An *environmental impact statement* needs to be prepared by the project proponent at his/her own expense and submitted to the relevant environmental authority, the local authority, and other stakeholder government agencies. The local authority must then inform the public of the availability for a 30-day period of the EIA documentation for review and comment (with a possibility of a public hearing).

Public participation in environmental assessment is also ensured through the so-called "public environmental expertise" (PEE) which is a right for citizens and Non-governmental Organizations (NGOs) to access, discuss and comment on the EIA and other relevant project design documents, as well as develop "conclusions" of advisory status that may be published independently and used as an input to SEE. There are very few PEEs performed at the central level (once per year, on average) and slightly more at the territorial level, and their quality is considered poor by the SEI. (See Chapter 3 on Information, public participation and education).

In accordance with an established regulatory procedure, the SEE considers (within 45 to 90 days) the project design documents[4], the environmental impact statement (when an EIA is required), PEE conclusions, and comments from government stakeholders and the public. A regulatory "conclusion" (decision) is issued approving or rejecting the project. This decision can be appealed in court. An SEE conclusion on a project serves as a basis for issuing environmental permits. 393 project-level SEEs were performed by the SEI in 2004 (52% more than in 1998), of which 168 SEEs were done by the central office. The past SEE documents are practically never used again by the SEI in its permitting and inspection activities.

The first EPR of the Republic of Moldova recommended the increase of public participation in environmental assessment. This has not been fully implemented. Despite the promulgation in 2000 of the Regulation on Public Participation in Elaboration and Adoption of Environmental Decisions, the SEI is not proactive in seeking public comments as part of SEE and usually disregards PEE conclusions, while project proponents do not share their documentation with the public, using commercial confidentiality concern as an excuse.

The country signed the Protocol on Strategic Environmental Assessment (SEA) to the Espoo Convention at the Fifth Ministerial Conference "Environment for Europe" in 2003. UNDP is developing a manual on the implementation of this instrument, which is expected to be completed in late 2005. It will cover the SEA scope, responsibilities, procedure, and methodology. In the meantime, the MENR's Division for Environmental Pollution Prevention conducts assessments of government programmes and strategies that may have an environmental impact, following a methodology that does not comply with international practices and standards for strategic environmental assessments. However, such assessments are not systematic and are usually reduced to verification of the presence of a section on environmental impact in a given programmatic document. Recent examples of the strategies reviewed include a programme on the development of renewable energy sources and the nationwide scheme of oil storage and gasoline station locations.

2.4   Environmental Permitting

The SEI currently issues permits for "specialized water use" (water abstraction and wastewater discharges into water bodies)[5], air pollution, and logging[6]. Water permits for installations with wastewater discharges over 400 m³/day or with groundwater abstraction over 1 million m³/year are issued by the central SEI, while the respective departments of TEAs regulate installations with smaller effluent volumes. A similar situation exists for air emission permits. In 2004, 1,604

---

[4] SEE is conducted after the project site has already been selected (with a written SEI agreement) and a construction permit issued. The developer is required (under the Aarhus Convention ratified by Moldova and the 1996 Law on Principles of Urbanism and Territorial Planning) to notify local residents one month before the site selection, but this almost never happens in practice.

[5] The installations subject to wastewater discharge permits are typically Apa Canal water and wastewater utilities, since all industrial installations are connected (with or without pre-treatment) to public sewerage systems and, therefore, do not need a permit for their effluents. The quality of industrial wastewater discharged into the sewer is regulated by the receiving Apa Canal utilities.

[6] See Chapter 7 for a description of environmental regulations in the forestry sector.

environmental permits were issued, including 842 for air emissions, 116 for water use/pollution, and 646 for logging.

Although the 1997 *Law on Industrial and Domestic Waste* stipulates the issuance of permits for waste storage and disposal, the SEI does not issue any in practice, creating a regulatory vacuum in waste management. Non-toxic industrial waste is disposed of in landfills (where it is mixed with municipal solid waste) with a written consent, which is not a permit, from the local Center for Preventive Medicine (a branch of the Ministry of Health and Social Protection) and the district unit of TEA. Toxic waste is stored on-site without permits, but operators are required to report its quantities and pay pollution charges for it based on three categories of toxicity. Operators of landfills, waste incinerators and waste transportation vehicles get licenses for these activities from the Centers for Preventive Medicine.

There are currently no standard application forms for any environmental permit. The preparation of permit applications is either done by the enterprise itself or contracted out to a research institute or a private firm. However, SEI staff also provides free and paid consultations to permit applicants, which creates a potential conflict of interests at the Inspectorate. The functions of permitting and assuring compliance with permit conditions are performed by different departments within the SEI at both the central and regional level, but this division does not exist in the district units of TEAs, where there is very few staff.

For new or refurbished installations, the permits are issued following a positive SEE decision. The issuance of permits for water use/pollution requires endorsements from the State Water Concern "Apele Moldovei" (for surface water abstraction), the Agency for Geology "AGeoM", (for groundwater abstraction), and the local Centre for Preventive Medicine. Air emission permits do not require any stakeholder consultations. Local authorities and representatives of the public are not formally involved in the permitting procedure.

The principal part of any air emission or wastewater discharge permit is a list of emission limit values (ELVs) proposed by the applicant and approved by the SEI. For large air pollution sources permitted at the central level and for all wastewater dischargers into water bodies, these ELVs are calculated so as not to exceed the maximum allowable concentrations (MAC) of respective

pollutants in the receiving environmental medium. With respect to air emissions, for those installations that are unable to comply with such ELVs, "temporary agreed limits" are established, usually at the level of actual emissions, and a programme of environmental improvements is agreed. For smaller air pollution sources receiving their permits from the TEA, ELVs are set based on the emission inventory (conducted once every five years or when there are changes in the production process) or current compliance monitoring results, whichever value is lower.

There are no permit conditions on self-monitoring, emergency preparedness and response, resource use efficiency, or post-closure decommissioning. A revision of the permit conditions before the specified renewal date may be initiated by the permitting authority based on the changed regulatory requirements or by the operator planning significant changes to the production process.

Permits are issued free of charge (since 2004) and are valid for three years for air emissions (if there are temporary emission limits, for only one year) and for two years for wastewater discharges. There are no statutory time limits for issuing environmental permits, and usually the permitting authority spends very little time considering their content.

Not all polluters are required to have an environmental permit actually have one. Even among installations with significant environmental impact, which are regulated by the central SEI office, much less than half (according to some staff members' estimates, only 10-15%) of appropriate "specialized water use" permits have been issued. The installations that do not have a required permit are simply fined if they get inspected. The situation is significantly better with permitting of air pollution sources. While there is no national environmental permit register, permit information is maintained in a paper format by TEAs (a transition to electronic files is planned).

In summary, the environmental permitting system is loosely implemented, does not consider the overall environmental impact of an installation and emphasizes medium-specific, end-of-pipe technological solutions rather than pollution prevention. ELVs calculated to meet environmental quality standards in the receiving media (that are often unrealistic), do not factor in economic consequences of compliance and sometimes are technically unfeasible. Environmental permitting requirements and procedures are not proportionate to the polluting impact of installations: there is very little differentiation between small and large sources. A high administrative burden on the permitting authorities' limited staff is caused by a large number of installations, large and small, renewing their permits very frequently.

There is widespread agreement among SEI staff on the need to introduce integrated permitting for large industry within the framework of convergence with the European Union (EU) environmental legislation, in particular with the Integrated Pollution Prevention and Control (IPPC) Directive (96/61/EC). There have been several attempts in recent years to study and plan a transition to integrated permitting, e.g., in 2000-2001, a project funded by the European Commission on the country's prospective approximation to the EU legislation produced a draft strategy and recommendations and, also in 2001-2002, another EU-funded project on environmental approximation in the western NIS. Inspired by these two donor projects, a group of Ministry of Environment officials and local experts developed in 2001 a draft law on integrated environmental permitting ("On Regulation of Economic and Social Activities with an Environmental Impact"). However, the draft was not put in the context of other necessary legislative changes to enable the new system; it faced significant opposition from various key stakeholders, and as a result, was not approved by the Government.

To meet the objectives set in the 2005 *EU-Moldova Action Plan* , the country's efforts toward gradual convergence with the approach of the EU IPPC Directive should be resumed and *"should constitute a long-term target for pollution prevention and control"*, as recommended in the first EPR of 1998. A gradual transition (up to 10 years) is necessary in order to mitigate the cost impact on the existing industry.

At the same time as an integrated permitting system is developed to regulate large industry, appropriate permitting regimes would need to be introduced for regulating installations not covered by integrated permitting, including sector-specific general binding rules and simple registration for installations with insignificant environmental impact. Concurrently, the system of environmental quality standards would also need to be reformed to reflect realistic and affordable environmental objectives (see Recommendation 3.1).

2.5   Compliance Monitoring and Reporting

Enterprises must report annually on their air emissions, wastewater discharges and waste generation. However, very few of them are able to undertake actual measurements on their own. Currently, only two combined heat and power plants in Chisinau have the capacity to independently conduct instrumental self-monitoring. Others contract state environmental laboratories to take and analyze control samples but mostly estimate the regulated parameters based on the input and technology process data.

Currently, the reporting of air emissions includes volumes (in tons per year) aggregated across all emitted sources for each parameter, while wastewater discharges have to be reported separately for each source. The annual reports are sent to TEA and the local statistics office (for wastewater discharges they are also sent to "Apele Moldovei"). In case of accident, the installation must notify TEA immediately, but the emergency pollution release information is not reported separately but is incorporated into the annual report. Environmental reporting data is accessible by the general public upon request.

Table 2.3: State Environmental Laboratory activities, 2004

Laboratory	Number of technical staff				Number of samples analyzed		
	Air	Water	Soil	Total	Air	Water	Soil
Chisinau	5	4	4	13	5,057	409	605
Balti	3	3	2	8	553	418	706
Cahul	..	3	1	4	..	132	196
Ungheni	1	1	..	2	105	64	..
Otaci	..	2	..	2	..	246	..

Source : State Ecological Inspectorate, 2005.

The sampling and analysis for emission controls are undertaken through a network of laboratories: the central one in Chisinau and smaller ones in Balti, Cahul, Otaci, and Ungheni (the Causeni laboratory was recently closed down due to the lack of funding). Only the Chisinau and Balti laboratories

Overall, despite the good qualification level of their limited staff, SEI laboratories are presently poorly suited to support the Inspectorate's enforcement activity. Although the SEI laboratories' staff is paid from the State budget, no financial means are provided for sampling, chemicals, maintenance and upgrade of instrumentation. As a result, analytical equipment in all the laboratories is extremely obsolete, and sampling activities are reduced to a minimum. Most SEI laboratories can directly monitor only a limited number of ingredients from the range of parameters specified in the permits, and their capacity is enough to cover just 15-20% of industrial installations. None of the laboratories is equipped for adequate analyses of organic micro-pollutants in water, air and soil samples, except the central laboratory which can make measurements of pesticides and PCBs. Only the central laboratory in Chisinau is equipped with instrumentation allowing the analysis of heavy metals. The smaller laboratories continue to use analytical methods originally introduced in the Soviet Union. Despite the fact that in 2001 all five SEI laboratories went successfully through the accreditation procedure, quality assurance and control issues are not always reliable. As a result, laboratory analysis data presented by the SEI as evidence in court are often contested by defendants.

Inspections can be planned or unscheduled. According to a government decree of April 2003, *only one planned inspection per year* is allowed and it has to be sanctioned by the TEA Director (there is also a list of installations that should not be inspected at all based on some commercial confidentiality and security considerations). This measure was prompted by the desire to protect businesses from excessive interventions from regulatory agencies, but in practice it has significantly complicated the Inspectorate's access to regulated installations. Unscheduled inspections can be conducted based on reports of accidents or complaints.

The priority for inspections is given to larger installations, while small enterprises rarely get inspected at all. In 2004, about 2,851 installations were inspected for air emissions and 3,283 for water use and pollution. The SEI was unable to

can conduct pollution analyses for all three environmental media (see Table 2.3). The laboratories conduct both planned sampling and analysis on behalf of the Inspectorate and contract-based sampling on request from enterprises.

provide an exact number of installations inspected nationwide since the reporting is done by each specialized inspector separately. It is also unclear what share of these inspections was unscheduled. In the Orhei District, about 500 installations are inspected annually, with about one-third of the inspections being unscheduled.

An obligatory element of a regular inspection is checking whether the installation has a valid environmental permit and whether it complies with the permit conditions. The inspector checks the necessary documentation as well as the technological process and output data. If necessary, the inspector can also conduct sampling and analysis of air emissions or wastewater, although adequate equipment for that is often lacking. If the inspector reveals (through sampling or calculations) that ELVs have been exceeded, follow-up inspections may be conducted over a certain period of time. Inspection reports are filed in the paper and sometimes electronic formats and kept in TEAs for 5 years.

Inspections are conducted by TEA inspectors (from the main and district offices) specialized in different environmental components, with the occasional participation of inspectors from the central SEI office. In complex situations (large installations with significant environmental impact), inspections are undertaken together by the TEAs, specialists from the central SEI office, a local Center for Preventive Medicine and sometimes experts from research or design institutes. Although in the past most inspections used to be conducted separately by an environmental medium, the recent restrictions on their number have made integrated inspections (where one inspector checks compliance across the media) much more common. Information from individual inspection reports is recorded by all the TEAs but is not reported to the central SEI office (instead, it is aggregated into numerical indicators that are included into monthly TEA reports, see Section 2.7).

The efficiency of inspectors' work depends to a great extent on the information exchange within the Inspectorate as well as with other governmental agencies, the regulated community and the general public. Unfortunately, despite the recommendations of the recent World Bank's "Environmental Compliance and Enforcement Capacity Building Project" on establishing an effective and user-friendly information system on compliance assurance activities, nothing has been done in this regard. The SEI receives a lot of information on polluters through regular environmental and statistical reporting but manages it poorly. This information is hardly used by the MENR in its decision-making.

2.6   Enforcement Tools

The SEI possesses extensive enforcement powers and has at its disposal a variety of enforcement tools, including:

- directions for corrective actions;

- non-compliance fines;

- initiation of damage compensation suits; and

- suspension of the operation of the installation.

The decision concerning the type of sanctions to be applied depends on the character and scale of the environmental violation. If an environmental violation has been revealed during an inspection, this usually does not imply the immediate application of sanctions. If the offence is insignificant and is easily remedied, the inspector just writes an inspection report with directions for corrective actions and explains to the management of the installation the terms of personal liability for failing to implement them.

In cases of more significant violations, an administrative protocol (notice of violation) is issued, indicating the nature of the violation and respective penalties, which is then filed with a court that applies those penalties. If the installation exceeds ELVs stipulated in the permit or an accidental pollution release occurs, the operator has to pay a calculated speculative amount for the environmental damage that is based on the degree to which the ELV has been exceeded. If an environmental violation continues to cause significant environmental damage, SEI inspectors have a right to suspend the operation of the installation until the violation is corrected. There is no practice of criminal prosecution for environmental violations.

The most frequently used enforcement tools are notices of violation with associated fines (in 2004, 11,513 protocols were issued) while the least frequent are the orders for cessation of operations (86 cases in 1998, 149 in 2004). Fines for violations of water regulations are imposed directly by the SEI, according to the 2001 amendments to the *Code of Administrative Violations*. However, fines for all other types of environmental violations must be imposed by a court, based on the Inspectorate's notice of violation. Environmental damages can also only be imposed by a court.

The need for court action to impose administrative penalties hampers effective enforcement. The court procedure takes a long time and usually results in a minimum penalty for the violator. In 2004, out of 9,710 protocols on environmental violations brought to courts decisions were made only on 6,188 (64%). From these, in 4,639 cases the violators were given a fine (on average, just 50 lei or US$ 4 per violation), 1,289 violators were issued a warning, 224 cases were dismissed, and 36 returned to the Inspectorate to rectify their poor preparation. The tolerance of the courts toward environmental offenders is partly due to the lack of legal experts at the SEI and, therefore, poor preparation of the cases brought by the Inspectorate. The judges are not experienced in environmental issues and often pose unacceptable burdens of proof on environmental inspectors. A further hindrance is the lack of specific procedures in courts to deal with environmental offences.

As a result, the percentage of penalties actually paid is very low: 49% for fines and 24% for damage compensation in 2004 (in 1998, just 3% of damages were collected). When damage compensation payments are imposed by the court, it is often a challenge to make the enterprise pay, and delinquent enterprises are referred by the SEI to the prosecutor's office in order to enforce the payment (63 such cases in 2004).

Overall, the two types of penalties currently used most often by the Inspectorate (fines and damage compensation) are both too small and poorly administered that they do not have any deterrent effect on the violators.

2.7   Compliance Assistance and Promotion

The SEI does not have any special compliance assistance programme for industry, although occasional assistance is provided. Getting information about new environmental regulatory requirements is considered to be an obligation of industry itself. One of the sources of such information is publications issued by the SEI and the MENR (e.g., compilations of environmental laws and regulations, instructions on the environmental expert evaluation, and guidance on environmental inspections). In the past, SEI management has considered holding regular informational seminars for industry but did not have enough resources to do it. The SEI considers its main compliance promotion activity to be the paid consultations to operators, provided mostly during site visits (over 6,000 such assistance actions were recorded in 2004).

The SEI has an information department that plays the role of an interface between the Inspectorate and the general public. It answers up to 90% of complaints addressed to the MENR. National and local mass media (newspapers, TV and radio) as well as information bulletins issued by MENR and NGO publications are also used by the SEI to disseminate information about its work and promote environmental compliance (e.g., by singling out most egregious violators). The SEI also publishes and disseminates its annual report.

The SEI cooperates with environmental NGOs. Joint activities include not only organizing actions for planting trees, cleaning up the green areas, river banks, but also formal and informal public consultations on new developments that raise public concern (e.g., gasoline stations, hazardous waste incinerators). Together with other MENR departments and Regional Environmental Center, the SEI has developed and published an Ecological Guide for Local Authorities, which describes best practices of community environmental management. TEA district units are engaged in

environmental education (e.g., in Orhei the local unit is planning to create an environmental education center), especially since local authorities lost their environmental functions.

It is necessary to further advance compliance promotion efforts by a) organizing seminars and training programmes for enterprise managers to discuss environmental requirements and problems with, and opportunities for, compliance, b) promoting the adoption of environmental management systems in industry, and c) continuing to work with NGOs to build public support for compliance assurance activities.

2.8 Strategic Planning and Performance Assessment

SEI priorities are established on the basis of the evaluation of the Inspectorate's activity during the previous reporting period. The SEI elaborates an annual programme of activities, which is subject to approval by the MENR. On the basis of this annual programme, quarterly and monthly work plans are developed, focusing on specific environmental media or regulated industries where serious environmental problems have been revealed. The TEAs follow the same procedure. Activity plans at the district level are coordinated with district councils. In addition, the central SEI office includes in its annual plans the provision of methodological support to TEAs and the supervision of implementation of local environmental programmes. However, there is no SEI strategy that sets particular priorities for compliance assurance.

Table 2.4: Selected key State Ecological Inspectorate activity indicators for 1998 and 2004 *)

Indicators	1998	2004
Number of inspections **)	15,567	18,577
Number of violators	7,245	10,843
Number of notices of violation issued	7,245	11,513
Fines imposed, lei	33,977	319,280
Fines collected, lei	14,860	155,606
Value of damage compensation suits filed, lei	2,029,741	1,083,083
Value of damage compensation collected, lei	62,430	262,714
Number of installations temporarily closed	86	149
Number of public complaints considered	1,080	1,419

Source: State Ecological Inspectorate annual Activity Reports for 1998 and 2004.
Notes :

*) The monetary values are given in Moldovan lei without adjustment for inflation. The annual average value of the lei against the U.S. dollar in 1998 was 5.37 lei = 1 USD, and in 2004 12.33 lei = 1 USD.

**) The number of inspections should not be confused with the number of installations inspected as there is a lot of double counting: with several specialized inspectors visiting an installation, each submits his own inspection report.

In fact, the SEI does not have systematic information about its regulated community. There is no national database of regulated installations, and the detailed inventory of all polluters by district, completed in 2003, is mainly in a cumbersome paper format and is therefore difficult to use. In some districts (e.g., in Orhei), databases of local installations are maintained in an electronic format.

The territorial agencies regularly report to the SEI central office. This normally includes brief weekly and monthly reports and comprehensive quarterly, bi-annual and annual reports, as well as immediate notification of incidents of significant environmental impact within their jurisdiction.

Fifty-two activity indicators are used to assess the Inspectorate's performance. Data for these indicators are compiled by TEAs, reported regularly to the central office, and kept in the SEI's Statistical Database. Information on some of these indicators is presented in Table 2.4. Other indicators measure activity, e.g., number of environmental permits issued and SEEs conducted, different kinds of documents prepared, or volume of pollution charges collected.

Such activity indicators do not provide a good sense of the effectiveness of enforcement efforts as it is impossible to discern actual compliance rates. It is also unclear how these indicators are used to evaluate and correct the SEI's short-term enforcement plans. The emphasis on activity indicators gives inspectors no incentive to engage in compliance promotion.

At least formally, environmental quality data are not used as an indicator of the Inspectorate's performance. They are, however, extensively covered in the TEA annual reports. This creates a good basis for their future use in the SEI's performance assessment.

2.9   Conclusions and recommendations

Environmental permitting is still based on single-media regulation that makes compliance difficult, places a heavy administrative burden on environmental agencies and the regulated community, and hampers public participation. The large number of regulated substances and uniform permitting rules for all polluters, irrespective of their size and impact, makes it difficult to monitor and enforce compliance with permits effectively. These kinds of difficulties could be solved with the

adoption of an integrated permitting system that would be implemented in stages, and would be limited to industrial installations with significant negative effects on human beings or the environment. Initial steps in introducing BAT-based integrated permitting could be taken already in the short term (up to three years), including:

- Agreeing on the scope of the future integrated permitting system (in terms of industrial sectors and production capacity thresholds, if appropriate) and adopting an overall strategy for the transition and implementation plan;

- Drafting a new law on environmental permitting and amendments to the existing legislation to enable the reform, as well as developing implementing regulations;

- Making institutional changes to reflect the needs of the new system; and

- Launching pilot permitting projects for industry and training for permitting officials.

The current compliance monitoring system generally corresponds to the recommended EU Minimum Criteria for Environmental Inspection (2001/331/EC). However, its functioning is undermined by the low number of SEI laboratory and inspection staff.

Regarding environmental assessment, the Republic of Moldova has made progress in terms of greater transparency. However, more emphasis could be put on the use of environmental assessment instruments, i.e. the EIA, SEE and PEE, in particular for those projects with significant environmental impact. For example, proposed production techniques for new projects should already be assessed against best available techniques (BAT) at the design stage. EIA and SEE recommendations on mitigation of environmental impacts should be used as decision-making tools when setting conditions in environmental permits, and should help to define the corresponding long-term environmental management implications. Public participation in EIAs and SEEs should be further improved by providing full public access to documents and inviting their comments. It is essential that the environmental management mechanism is used to its full potential.

Sanctions against environmental violators are not efficient enough yet. They should push towards a better and more effective enforcement. The SEI should obtain the right to impose directly, without going through a court procedure, all fines for administrative violations (as it is presently the case only for water-related violations). The rates of the fines should be increased to enhance their deterrent effect. Costs for restoring damage to the environment should also be estimated and compensation mechanisms ruled by law. All this should be done in conjunction with increased SEI transparency and accountability. At the same time, an operator should have the right to appeal the sanction in court.

Therefore, the following recommendations are addressed to the Republic of Moldova:

Recommendation 2.1:
The Ministry of Ecology and Natural Resources should in the short term:

- *Draft legislation and necessary by-laws to introduce an integrated permitting system for installations having significant impact on the environment, following the approach of the EU IPPC Directive as a benchmark;*

- *Ensure that self-monitoring requirements for enterprises are included in the permits; and*

- *Institute a simplified permitting scheme for other installations.*
(See Recommendation 1.3)

Recommendation 2.2:
Building on actual partial compliance with the EU Minimum Criteria for Environmental Inspection, the Ministry of Ecology and Natural Resources should:

- *Improve the operational and human resources management of the State Ecological Inspectorate, including staff training, and upgrade its technical capabilities;*

- *Streamline the instruments used to achieve compliance and enforcement. A first step would be to identify particular groups of the regulated*

community and their impact on ambient environment conditions. Further priorities should then be set among the most problematic geographic areas and the most polluting installations, and enforcement tools selected that will effect the most appropriate enforcement response; and

- *Improve the existing set of indicators, which currently falls short of measuring both environmental improvements (e.g., pollution reduction amounts) and enforcement results (e.g., compliance rates and timeliness of compliance actions), so that the effectiveness of enforcement can be assessed more accurately.*

Recommendation 2.3:
The Ministry of Ecology and Natural Resources should improve the use of the three existing environmental assessment instruments (SEE, EIA and PEE) by linking them closer to the principles to EU EIA Directive and to other compliance assurance mechanisms and increasing public involvement in environmental assessment decisions.

Recommendation 2.4:
The Government should propose and submit for legislative approval important changes in the application of sanctions against environmental violators by:

- *Allowing administrative imposition of fines;*

- *Increasing the level of fines and indexing them to inflation;*

- *Making managers responsible for infringements; and*

- *Introducing environmental damage assessment based on actual remediation costs.*

Chapter 3

INFORMATION, PUBLIC PARTICIPATION AND EDUCATION

3.1 Introduction

The 1998 review of the Republic of Moldova recommended the country strengthen its environmental policy framework by, among others, the following measures:

- Streamlining the monitoring system between the different partners and gradually implementing a comprehensive nationwide monitoring programme;

- Expanding the existing inventory, monitoring and reporting systems for air pollution with regard to the most important air pollutants, and installing additional air monitoring stations on the borders with Ukraine and northern Romania to control transboundary air pollution;

- Revising procedures of public involvement in ecological expert evaluation and the evaluation of impact on the environment to make these procedures operational; and

- Building capacities of bodies involved in environmental issues at the national level, local governments and the environmental NGO community.

This chapter describes and evaluates the performance of the Republic of Moldova in implementing recommendations in the 1998 review in the areas of environmental monitoring, information management, public participation and education as well as legal requirements and policy objectives that the country has set in these areas thereafter.

3.2 Environmental monitoring

In the Republic of Moldova today, there are various types of environmental monitoring. They cover ambient environmental quality, state of natural resources like soils, forests and wildlife, and pollution emissions and discharges. Monitoring of pollution (compliance monitoring) is covered in chapter 2. The Ministry of Ecology and Natural Resources (MENR) plays a key role in environmental observations and data collection. Its six networks of environmental quality monitoring stations are presented in map 3.1. The main features of environmental monitoring in the country, including the role of individual governmental bodies and institutions, are presented hereunder.

Air quality monitoring

The State Hydrometeorology Service (HMS) through its Division of Environmental Quality Monitoring operates 17 ambient air monitoring stations in five main cities: Chisinau (6), Balti (2), Tiraspol (3), Ribnita (2), and Bender (4). In 2004, the HMS reactivated, after a decade of non-operation, its only transboundary air-monitoring station *Leova* at the border with Romania.

HMS stations measure a limited number of meteorological and chemical parameters (SO_2, NO_x, dust, CO, B(a)P and Pb) in urban air. Several chemical parameters required by national standards (Cu, Cr, Ni, V and Co) are not measured, and neither are air concentrations of NH_3, VOC (except B(a)P), O_3, PM_{10}, Hg and POPs. Since 2004, measurements have been made of aerosols, some POPs and some heavy metals (Cd, Hg and Pb) in precipitation at one station in Chisinau and at the Leova station.

The HMS has no automated stations and samples are taken manually three times a day for gas and dust concentrations in the air, and monthly for B(a)P and heavy metals concentrations in the air and for aerosols in precipitation.

The National Institute of Ecology had one air monitoring station in Hincesti that ceased to operate in 2000. The Ministry of Health and Social Protection (MoHSP) has 12 permanent air monitoring sites in urban areas. Maximum concentrations of six parameters (total suspended matter, O_3, NO_2, SO_2, CO and Pb) in air are measured monthly in residential areas and indoors.

Map 3.1: Networks of environmental quality monitoring in the Republic of Moldova

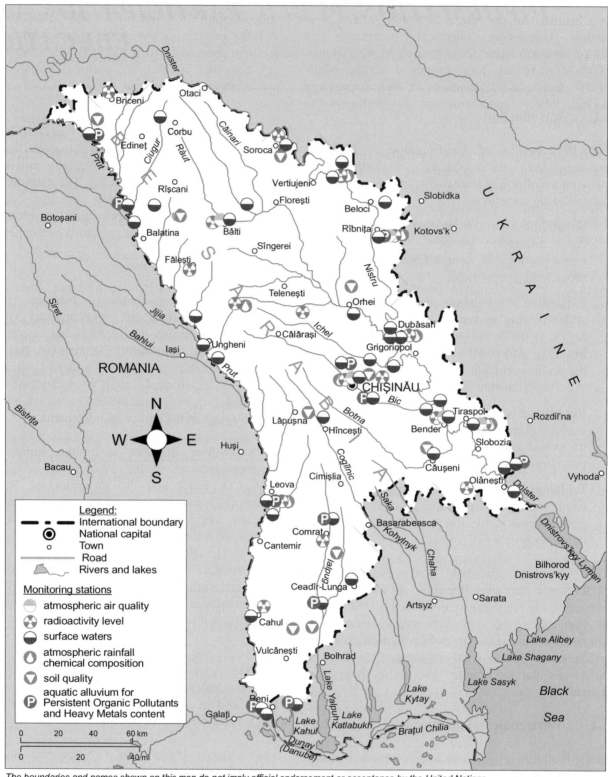

The boundaries and names shown on this map do not imply official endorsement or acceptance by the United Nations.

Source: Division of Environmental Quality Monitoring, State Hydrometeorology Service, 2004.

The current ambient air-monitoring network has remained unchanged since 1998, despite its inadequacy. To meet the requirements of national regulations (one monitoring station per 100,000 of urban residents) there should be two more stations in Chisinau and one more in Cahul. There is no station monitoring chemical parameters in background air. None of the stations in the Republic of Moldova (except four automated stations of the MoH) meets national standards for measurements of average daily concentrations of pollutants in ambient air.

To fully participate in the Cooperative Programme for Monitoring and Evaluation of the Long-range Transmission of Air Pollutants in Europe (EMEP) under the Convention on Long-range Transboundary Air Pollution, the Republic of Moldova has to automate the Leova station and install two further automated transboundary stations. The HMS is looking for € 445,000 to upgrade the Leova station and to install a second station in the village of Calinesti (Balti district, the boundary region of the Prut River) to monitor northwest air flows and a third one in the city of Dubăsari (on the left bank of the Dniester River, on the border with Ukraine) to monitor northeast and southeast air flows.

Water quality monitoring

Since 1998, the HMS has increased its observation network for surface water quality by four points on four different rivers and by five points on water reservoirs. Overall, it consists today of 49 observation points located on 16 of the largest rivers, six major water reservoirs and one estuary. The observation points are located near large urban areas. Diffuse pollution of surface waters is not monitored in the Republic of Moldova.

Samples are taken monthly to measure up to 42 hydro-chemical parameters and up to six hydro-biological parameters depending on the observation point. In 2004, the HMS started monitoring heavy metals and POPs (organo-chlorinated pesticides, including DDT and HCH) in sediments in the Prut and Bîc Rivers and all water reservoirs. In 2005, it took samples for PCB at five water-monitoring posts near electric energy installations.

The HMS implements a joint sampling programme with the Iasi Environmental Protection Agency (Romania) on the Prut River. Four automated monitoring stations were installed on Prut (2) and Dniester (2) Rivers in 2004, thanks to a NATO-funded project. The stations had been providing real-time data on pH, temperature, water level, conductivity, turbidity and dissolved oxygen until they ceased to operate because of inconsistencies between the stations' equipment and local telecommunication networks. The HMS expects that the project-implementing agency will fix the problem soon and that it might be also possible to upgrade the stations to monitor pollution by chemicals and oil products.

According to an assessment made jointly by Danish and Moldovan experts under the Denmark-funded project in 2002, to comply with monitoring requirements of the EU Framework Water Directive, the Republic of Moldova should create an additional eight river and 18 lake observation posts. To strengthen its water-quality observation network including transboundary water monitoring, the HMS prepared proposals for unspecified donor financing (some € 290,000) to install four supplementary automated monitoring stations as follows: two stations on the Răut River upstream and downstream of Balti city, one station on the Bîc River downstream of Chisinau city and one station on the Prut River at the confluence with Danube River. The HMS considers it necessary to also start observations at Telenesti on the Ciulucul Mic River, at Cupcini on the Ciuhur River, as well as at Floresti and Ghidesti at the Răut River, where important point-pollution sources are located. By contrast, the HMS has only some vague ideas about potential sites for background water observation points. There seems to be no discussions held on how, where and when to start monitoring of diffuse pollution of surface waters.

The groundwater-monitoring network of the Agency for Geology of Moldova "AGeoM", consists of 186 acting observation boreholes located on 33 fields. Since 1998 the total number of observation boreholes has decreased by 36. Groundwater analysis is made on 20 physico-chemical parameters and five heavy metals (instead of 13 required by standards). The frequency of water samples varies from one to ten per month depending on the borehole observation purpose. In large water intakes samples for hydro-chemical parameters are taken twice a year and once every 2 to 3 years for heavy metals. The network needs to be expanded as it does not cover, for instance, aquifers under filtration fields belonging to sugar refineries in Drochia, Hiroveti, Ocnita, Dondusenj, Alexandreni and Singerei and aquifers affected by sewage from 35 big cattle-breeding farms. These pollution sources pose a significant threat to human health today.

Territorial centres of preventive medicine of the MoHSP monitor the drinking water quality of 3,550 underground wells in rural areas and 11 surface water bodies. 12 production laboratories monitor drinking water quality at water purification plants. There is no monitoring of biological parameters of surface water sources of drinking water supply in the country, however. Waters for bathing are monitored in urban areas only (at seven posts at the Dniester River and eight posts at the Prut River). In rural areas bathing waters are not monitored, as responsible public authorities have not been designated.

Soil monitoring

The HMS monitoring network for soil quality covers 3,455 ha over ten districts: in the North (Briceni, Glodeni and Soroca); in the Center (Orhei, Hincesti, Anenii-Noi and Causeni); and in the South (Taraclia, Cahul and Gagauz Yeri). Samples are taken twice a year at 52 plots. In 2004, the HMS started soil sampling for POPs (DDT and its metabolites) in the vicinity of six abandoned pesticide storehouses in different regions of the country. In 2005, it took samples for PCB at ten plots near electric energy installations.

The State Ecological Inspectorate (SEI) takes soil samples (including for some pesticides) on and in the vicinity of sites of industrial and other polluters. Institutions of the MoHSP monitor soil quality in recreational areas, human settlements as well as in areas around drinking water intakes. The Agrochemical Service of the Ministry of Agriculture and Food Industry (MoAFI) monitors soil quality including some pesticide residues on agricultural lands. The Institute of Geography of the Academy of Sciences published in 2004 a map of degraded lands in the Republic of Moldova. The State Water Concern "Apele Moldovei" monitors irrigated land.

Biodiversity including forest monitoring

The national network of forest monitoring, managed by the Forest Agency "Modsilva", comprises 700 control plots covering the entire country forest area. The network density is 2x2 km or 1 plot per 400 ha. There is another network comprising 12 control plots, with a density 16x16 km or 1 plot per 25,600 ha. Data from this network are collected, validated and processed according to the Guidelines of the International Cooperative Programme Forest under the Convention on Long-range Transboundary Air Pollution.

The forest monitoring provides data on forest ecosystems viability, productivity and protection. It serves "Modsilva" by developing proposals on the extent of forest cuts versus the status of forests, forecasting the yield and quality of wood, evaluating the forests regeneration capacity and choosing appropriate measures for improving forest health.

Several institutes of the Academy of Sciences (e.g., Institutes of Zoology, Botany and Genetics), the State University of Moldova and the Agrarian State University study the country's wildlife at species level. Information on the status of selected species is usually published once every three years. The Red Book of the Republic of Moldova (second edition, 2001) includes 14 species of mammals, 39 species of birds, eight species of reptiles, one species of amphibians and 37 species of insects. The publications of "Animal World of Moldova" and "Plant World of Moldova" series started in 2003.

The information published in the Republic of Moldova makes estimates of conservation status difficult and the information reported is somewhat unreliable. Some of the species currently reported as threatened may prove to be more common, while many other species will be added to the list as the knowledge base grows.

Local people are permitted to collect plants on larger tracts of nature reserves. Unfortunately, there are no data about the types or quantity of plants collected or the impact this has on the reserve. Without such monitoring, collectors might completely eliminate species from the reserves.

Analytical laboratories

The HMS has its network of certified analytical laboratories located in the main cities such as Balti, Cahul, Chisinau, Dubasari and Tiraspol. The MoHSP operates 35 territorial analytical laboratories and a central laboratory at the National Scientific and Practical Centre of Preventive Medicine (NCPM).

Since 1998, the SEI, which is in charge of compliance monitoring and pollution control, has closed down one (in Causeni region) of its then six certified laboratories (one central and five regional). During the same period the total number of employees decreased from 59 to 33 while the total number of air, water and soil samples taken and analyses made increased from 7,764 to 8,491 and from 22,012 to 25,265, respectively.

The evaluation of SEI laboratory capacities undertaken in 2002 in the framework of the World Bank Environmental Compliance and Enforcement Capacity Building Project revealed that the equipment in SEI laboratories was obsolete. For instance, none of these laboratories are equipped for organic micro-pollutants analysis in water, air and soil samples. Only the SEI central laboratory in Chisinau makes analysis of heavy metals. In the framework of the project a gas chromatograph was supplied to the SEI central laboratory in Chisinau for measurements of pesticides and PCBs. "AGeoM" laboratories, on the contrary, remain poorly equipped.

There are no joint inter-calibration or training exercises organized in the country. Since the laboratories do not participate in the national and international inter-laboratory comparisons, the quality assurance and quality control issues are of concern.

Ambient quality standards

The Republic of Moldova continues to apply former USSR ambient environmental standards. The lists of ambient quality parameters have not been revised using or harmonized with international standards since Moldova received independence, except the drinking water quality parameters that are under revision in accordance with WHO requirements.

The system of standards is comprehensive and ambitious, covering more than 1,000 pollutants and mandating very low concentrations of pollutants. Overall, an excessively large number of regulated pollutants impose unrealistic monitoring and enforcement requirements on public authorities. Some of the Moldovan standards are below the threshold of detection, so it is impossible to know whether they are being achieved or not. Due to budget limitations, there is no routine monitoring of some pollution parameters that should be measured according to monitoring standards.

At the same time, existing standards do not take into account substances occurring naturally in the environment, which are characterized by seasonal variations (e.g., chlorides and sulphates in water

bodies). Some substances are unregulated (for example, phosphorus, which may lead to eutrophication, and carcinogenic substances in water). No water quality parameters are defined for recreation purposes and maintenance of aquatic ecosystems.

Existing ambient quality standards need to be amended and built on to provide a system that can work for all stakeholders. This change is also necessary in order to comply with the policy of the Moldovan Government to harmonize its standards with EU legislation. A new system of ambient quality standards should focus on hazardous substances, taking into account both international guidelines and specifics of the environment.

3.3   Information management and reporting

Information systems

In the Republic of Moldova, there is no national environmental information system as such. Individual ministries and departments develop their own decentralized databases of relevance to the environment following their own technical protocols and procedures. Progress is made largely thanks to external support.

For instance, under its project implemented in 2001-2003 on "Assistance to Moldova in the Implementation of the Aarhus Convention", Denmark provided the MENR and its institutions with hardware (a server and 22 workstations), software, expert advice and training to develop and install environmental databases, "Mediul Moldovei" at the HMS and "Controlul Ecologic" at the SEI. The purpose was to improve the Ministry's information system by establishing a network of interconnected personal computers equipped with a database application designed to deal with the data on the state of the environment (water, air and soil) and data associated with the environmental legislation enforcement. Both databases are not functioning after the completion of the project in 2003.

Coordination and data exchange

Coordination and data exchange between monitoring institutions remain sporadic and are frequently the result of the individual initiative of technical experts. Despite several inter-ministerial arrangements (e.g., the agreement on cooperation between the former Ministry of the Environment, Construction and Territorial Development and the former Ministry of Health, signed in 2000) currently there are few operational channels of information exchange. This generates duplication of efforts and information gaps, and does not allow environmental information to be fully used in decision-making.

The Republic of Moldova made some efforts to integrate environmental data and information stored at different institutions. In December 1998, the former Ministry of the Environment adopted a regulation on a so-called integrated environmental monitoring system (IEMS). According to this regulation, which focused on actual data exchange rather than on monitoring, 15 ministries, departments and the National Academy of Sciences were expected to designate responsible institutions to participate in the exchange of data on a broad set of indicators relating to social and economic development, waste, air, water, soils, mineral resources, flora, fauna and environmental policy instruments. The designated institutions were supposed to supply information to an environmental monitoring centre to be established at the former Ministry of the Environment. The centre was expected to coordinate actions of suppliers of environmental information, process the data, operate national databases and to submit complete, generalized and specific information on environmental conditions to decision makers and the general public. The Ministry together with the former Department of Statistics had to establish formats and time schedules for data transmission. These formats and time schedules have not been developed yet.

Under its project on "Assistance to Moldova in the Implementation of the Aarhus Convention", Denmark assisted the Republic of Moldova, inter alia, to prepare an inventory of monitoring data and institutions performing analysis and sampling of such data, followed by proposals for setting-up an IEMS. Denmark financed the staff of the IEMS Centre that was physically located at the HMS. It also provided the Centre with a server, personal computers, software and an Internet connection to assist it in the development of the IEMS.

The country does not seem to have followed up proposals elaborated under the above-mentioned project. No discussion was undertaken with high-level officials in the Ministries and Departments to which specific monitoring recommendations were addressed. The authority of the 1998 IEMS Ministerial Regulation happened to be insufficient to make the IEMS operational. Overall IEMS is not

functioning and the environmental data exchange remains greatly handicapped. As no functional links were established with the HMS and other key monitoring institutions in the country, the IEMS Centre practically ceased to exist after the completion of the project and the discontinuation of the Danish financial support late 2003.

No more time should be spared to reinvigorate the IEMS Centre. Human and technical resources from the IEMS Centre that are presently at the disposal of the HMS should be effectively used for the purpose. The HMS Division of Environmental Quality Monitoring might constitute a core for a strengthened Centre that could serve as a working vehicle to facilitate inter-departmental cooperation on environmental data collection and management in the country.

There is a successful example of inter-departmental cooperation on data exchange to build on. With the support of France, the MENR, in cooperation with the MoHSP, "AGeoM" and "Apele Moldovei", has recently created a water data centre. The centre operates a decentralized but harmonized database that contains data on:

- Water-monitoring stations (39);

- Water flow and physical and chemical parameters (some 30) relating to 1993-2000;

- Ten rainfall monitoring stations covering data for 1993-2003;

- Water consumption and pollution by 2,689 economic agents in 1996-2003;

- Groundwater quality and quantity covering 1,660 wells;

- Results of the inventory of lakes and water reservoirs and wastewater treatment stations undertaken by the SEI in early 2000s; and

- Water accounts established for 1994, 1998 and 2000.

The Republic of Moldova made efforts to strengthen coordination under some sectoral monitoring frameworks. The 2000 governmental regulation on monitoring environmental pollution with radioactive, toxic and bacteriological substances established institutional arrangements for data exchange in case of emergencies. Another regulation, that was adopted two years later, aimed at improving environmental health monitoring in the country. The latter regulation helped the MoHSP to make some progress in improving data collection and reporting.

Environmental statistics

The National Bureau of Statistics has recently expanded its collection of statistical data on the environment. In particular, it has introduced statistical reporting on emissions into the air of polycyclic aromatic hydrocarbons (PAH), heavy metals and POPs. Overall statistical data is collected today from economic agents and relevant public entities in 17 subject areas. It publishes aggregate data in its statistical yearbook and transmits a detailed environmental data compendium to the MENR.

Environmental reporting

The monitoring and data collection results are, to a various extent, reported to decision-making bodies and made available to the general public and the international community. For instance, the HMS publishes:

- A daily bulletin on ambient air quality that is submitted to the public authorities and is uploaded on the HMS web site (http://www.meteo.md);

- A monthly bulletin on air, water and soil quality and the background radiation circulated among the public authorities and transmitted to the Ecological Movement of Moldova, an NGO that is publishing the monitoring data in its widely-spread quarterly bulletin;

- Annual reports on air quality, water quality and soil quality; and

- Annual State Water Cadastre (jointly with "Apele Moldovei" and "AGeoM").

The NCPM of the MoHSP publishes a monthly bulletin and an annual report on sanitary and epidemic conditions in the country and posts them on the web site http://www.sanepid.md. The MoHSP and the MENR jointly published national environmental health reports for the European Ministerial Conferences on Health and Environment held in 1999 and 2004. Since 2006, the NCPM plans to publish such reports annually. It also envisages creating a database and publishing a bulletin on drinking water quality.

Some important types of data are not published at all or are not readily accessible:

- Forest monitoring data and inventories by "Moldsilva";

- Groundwater measurement data by "AGeoM"; and

- Emission monitoring data by the SEI. (Single paper copies of annual inspection results may be freely accessed at the State Ecological Inspectorate).

The National Institute of Ecology publishes annually the National Report on the state of the environment. The last (bilingual) one was published in 2004 in 1000 copies each and uploaded on Internet (http://www.cim.moldova.md). The report is largely descriptive, as it is not based on internationally agreed indicators. It is not used in policy or decision-making.

The country reports regularly to the United Nations Commission on Sustainable Development and to governing bodies of applicable multilateral environmental agreements (MEAs). In a particular case, it reported the complete emission data on heavy metals and POPs to the Executive Body on Long-range Transboundary Air Pollution in 2004. National communications, national strategies and other information relating to the country's participation in MEAs and international environmental programmes (or the information on how to access these documents) are, however, rarely circulated in the country or uploaded on official environmental web sites.

The Republic of Moldova is not taking advantage of all opportunities to build its monitoring and reporting capacities that are provided by the UNECE Working Group on Environmental Monitoring and Assessment. Its participation and contribution are sporadic.

3.4 Public participation

Role of civil society

The Republic of Moldova has a large network of environmental NGOs. The registration procedure is relatively simple and NGOs can register with the Ministry of Justice (MoJ), rayon authorities or primarias. There are no official statistics on NGOs but there are about 430 environmental NGOs in the country with some 100 operating in Chisinau only. A majority is involved in environmental education. Others deal (in order of priority) with public participation, biodiversity, environmental impact assessment (EIA) and compliance with environmental legislation.

Some 50 environmental NGOs are considered very active in the country as they have launched many environmental initiatives on national and local levels and they are actively implementing international projects. BIOS, Biotica, Eco Lex, ECOTIRAS, Environmental Movement of Moldova and INQUA Moldova are among these active NGOs.

NGOs suffer from lack of funds for their operation. They are not exempted of VAT and custom duties and do not benefit from any tax privileges. Only in cases of intergovernmental agreements on technical assistance may the Ministry of Finance (MoF) decide to waive some taxes.

International donors remain a major source of financing. Environmental NGOs receive support from the Environmental Fund. In 2004, for instance, the MENR provided grants to 22 NGOs amounting in a total of lei 230,000 (US$ 18,654). However, although the revenues of the Environment Fund have considerably increased since 1998, its expenditures for NGO support remain extremely low, less than one per cent of total expenditures.

Environmental NGOs are relatively well organized and since 2001 they have convened their forum annually. The forum held in 2003 resulted in a memorandum of cooperation signed by a number of NGOs with the then Ministry of Environment, Construction and Territorial Development. As a result, the Ministry regularly circulate environmental information among these NGOs and invite them to participate in various endeavours. A core of some 15 organizations cooperates with the Ministry on a permanent basis by participating in environmental projects.

The Regional Environmental Center (REC) of Moldova was created in 1998 to assist in resolving environmental problems in the country and promoting co-operation between NGOs, governmental bodies, local communities, the business sector and all other stakeholders. It has been assisting environmental NGOs in three main areas: providing small grants; capacity building; and information dissemination through a database, web site (http://www.rec.md), electronic bulletin, and information centre in Chisinau. REC operates an electronic database on environmental NGOs in the country and implements various donor-supported projects to support NGOs. It provided grants for some 250 small and transboundary projects, most of which promoted access to environmental information and public participation in

environmental decision-making. The projects helped to establish environmental information centres in several cities and towns. REC's two offices in Balti and Cahul are also playing the role of environmental information centres.

Awareness-raising

Environmental topics are regularly covered by mass media in the Republic of Moldova. Newspapers (e.g., "Natura", "Ave Natura", and "Vreau sa stiu") and magazines (e.g., "The Environment", "Alternatives" and "Gutta") are among the most active. At the National Radio, there is a regular "Ecoterra" broadcast on the air. The MENR regularly provides journalists with environmental information materials.

The MENR is actively promoting activities to raise environmental awareness in the country. It organizes press conferences and meetings of its staff with mass media. It publishes a journal "Mediul ambiant" (Environment) with six issues a year. It organizes various competitions for all categories of the population including a national competition for the "greenest" human settlement and an annual tree planting "Tree of Longevity" event. A new campaign "Water - Source of Life" has been recently launched to improve and maintain wells and springs. Resources from the the National Environmental Fund (NEF) are used for these activities.

Implementation of the Aarhus Convention

The Republic of Moldova ratified the Convention on Access to Information, Public Participation in Decision Making and Access to Justice on Environmental Matters (Aarhus Convention) in 1999. The MENR established a departmental working group with NGO representatives to promote the implementation of the Convention. The country is very active in the cooperation under the Meeting of Parties to the Aarhus Convention. See chapter 4 on international agreements and commitments.

Access to information

To facilitate public access to environmental information, the MENR compiled and posted on its web site a list of public authorities that collect and disseminate environmental information. It established also an Environmental Information Centre (http://www.cim.moldova.md/) open to the public in 2000. The Centre operates an environmental library, serves as a venue for roundtables, press conferences, briefings, and other informational events. It publishes a monthly electronic environmental information bulletin. The Centre has been recently downsized, however. The Ministry plans to promote the creation of local Aarhus centres to ensure public access to environmental information. A pilot centre has already been set up and is successfully operating in the district centre of Shtefan Vode.

The MENR provides financial support to the publication of collections of legislation, information bulletins and studies of individual environmental problems. In 1994 the Ministry set up a Consultative Council consisting of representatives from the academic sector, environmental NGOs and the trade unions. The main task was to give expert advice on scientific studies that would be published with the financial support from the Environmental Fund. The Council was short-lived and it is not operating today.

The 2000 *Law on Access to Information* and environmental laws provide a broad basis to ensure the right to access to information, including environmental information. These laws are generally consistent with the requirements of the Aarhus Convention, except the 1996 *Law on Principles of Urbanism and Territorial Planning*, which needs to be amended as it unjustifiably restricts access to town and physical planning documentation of public interest.

Apart from the MENR, ministries and departments have not designated information officers responsible for providing information to the public. Very often public authorities at rayon and local levels deny access to environmental information either because of lack of staff resources or of photocopying equipment. Furthermore, local authorities do not always have texts of environmental laws. In the Republic of Moldova, until recently, all legally binding documents have been available on the web site of the MoJ. Since summer 2005 it has become inaccessible thanks to the termination of external donor support. The MENR's web site provides access to key environmental legislation but only some 14 per cent of the country's population has access to Internet.

Public participation

The legislation of the Republic of Moldova contains general provisions to ensure public participation in environmental decision-making concerning laws,

regulations, standards, permitting, plans and programmes. However, procedures are not sufficiently detailed enough to make these provisions applicable in practice. Time frames are frequently not established for individual stages of public participation. For instance, although it requires the public to be consulted on town and physical planning schemes before approval, the 1996 *Law on Principles of Urbanism and Territorial Planning* does not provide for any time fames. The 1999 *Law on Green Areas in Urban and Rural Settlements* allows the Government, at its own discretion, to waive the environment protection requirements of this law. No obligation is established in the legislation to inform the public about the decision taken along with the reasons and considerations on which it is based, although the direct effect of the Convention itself could be said to entail such an obligation. The MENR is uploading draft legal acts and regulations for comments by the public on its web site, but it does not inform members of the public about how their comments have been taken into account in final texts.

In 2004 the MENR adopted the Instructions for the involvement of the public in the process of the development of and the decision-making on draft legal acts and regulations in the field of environmental protection and use of natural resources. The NGO community took an active part in the discussion of this regulation. Its entry into force is pending as it has not yet been registered by the MoJ.

The public is generally invited to participate in decision-making on policies, plans and programmes of relevance to the environment. The public has been involved in the development of the *National Concept of Environmental Policy*, the *National Programme of Water Supply and Sanitation for Localities* and the *Economic Growth and Poverty Reduction Strategy*. In 2004, the MENR involved the public in the discussions on master plans for siting of gasoline filling stations and motor-transport depots, for the protection of human settlements against flooding and for the protection of human settlements against earthquakes. A NGO representative, elected by NGOs themselves, sits on the Administrative Council of the Environmental Fund. The public is not represented, however, in the Inter-Ministerial Committee on Sustainable Development and Poverty Reduction or in the National Commission on Environmental Policy (the latter having been dormant since its creation in 2002).

There is some experience at local level with public participation in policy-making. For example, the authorities of the Stefan Voda rayon involved the public in the elaboration of the local environmental action plan. The REC Moldova, which is assisting in this activity, plans to transpose the experience gained onto other rayons.

The MENR initiated the preparation of a series of legal and regulatory documents to facilitate public participation in environmental decision-making. The 2000 *Government Regulation on Public Participation in the Elaboration and Adoption of Environmental Decisions* describes the ways in which the public may be informed of the intention to undertake projects involving an economic activity (e.g., by announcements in the press or on radio or television or by direct contact with NGOs). It describes how in practical terms the public should be provided with environmental information about the proposed activity and how the views of the public should be collected, taken into account and reflected in the decision-making. This regulation appears not to be being enforced in the country, as there is no evidence that project proponents and public authorities undertook the required action. Surprisingly, the Regulation is not included in the collection of EIA legislation that is published as manual for all ecological expertise officials in the Republic of Moldova.

The Laws on Ecological Expertise and EIA, and on Environmental Protection, as amended in 2003, provided details on the practical application of the right of citizens and NGOs to participate in the State ecological expertise and to organize a parallel public ecological expertise of projects that may have adverse environmental impact.

There is no experience known of public participation in the State Ecological Expertise of projects. The Environmental Movement of Moldova organizes public ecological expertise. It organized in 2004 ten such Expertises, of which their outcomes were unevenly appreciated.

The 2001 *Law on Biosafety*, the 2003 *governmental decree on the National Commission for Biosafety*, № 603 and the 2004 Regulation of the MENR *on Informing the Public and its Participation in Decision-making on Genetically Modified Organisms*, № 19 of 10 February promote public participation in permitting procedures relating to the release of genetically modified organisms into the environment.

Access to Justice

The legislation ensures the right to access to justice on environmental matters. For instance, representatives of the public have free access to administrative and judicial procedures to challenge acts and omissions by private persons and public authorities that contravene environmental law. There is no clear legal notion, however, of the protection of the right to a safe environment and therefore the courts frequently refuse to admit claims and consider cases on their merits. Judges often lack information on the environmental legislation and its practical application. The Centre for Improving the Qualifications of Officers of Justice organizes seminars on environmental law for judges, public prosecutors and barristers.

The public is still poorly informed about the opportunities for access to environmental justice. Citizens rarely apply to court in case of damage, because they are not convinced about the fairness of courts in general, and know that there are no judges specialized in environmental matters and doubt their capacity to assess the situation correctly. Access to justice is also low, in many cases, due to poverty, which does not allow paying court expenses. Cases of individual citizens or NGOs seeking a judicial review of the infringement on their environmental rights and upholding administrative decisions in courts are rare. Eco-Lex and Ecological Movement of Moldova, two NGOs, have some experience in this regard.

Further requirements

Overall, the legal and regulatory framework on public participation in decision-making and access to justice on environmental matters is still of an insufficient nature to implement the requirements of the Aarhus Convention more effectively. International donors (e.g., the European Commission, Denmark, Italy, and the Netherlands) actively supported the building capacity of the Republic of Moldova to implement the Aarhus Convention. Assistance was provided, for instance in drafting regulations and manuals, including handbooks, on the implementation of the Aarhus Convention for civil servants and for representatives of the public, and in organizing training workshops. Further support may be needed, especially at the local level, but it should be matched with a commitment of resources from inside the country.

The country signed the Protocol on Pollutant Release and Transfer Registers (PRTRs) to the

Aarhus Convention that was adopted in Kiev in 2003. It is presently attempting to establish a national PRTR for the energy sector. Preparations for the protocol ratification need to be intensified by involving key monitoring institutions, compliance authorities, sectoral ministries, business and industry, and NGOs in the development of a plan of action to set a legal, institutional and technical framework for the establishment of a national PRTR.

3.5   Environmental education

The Republic of Moldova is promoting environmental education covering pre-school, primary and secondary, and higher education. The Ministry of Education, Youth and Sports (MoEYS) is playing an active role as it elaborated and is presently implementing a plan of action for the development of environmental education strategy. The MENR is responsible for the organization of environmental education. Both the MoEYS and the MENR cooperate when preparing teaching manuals and organizing extra-curriculum environmental events at schools.

Pre-school and school education

In pre-schools courses are given to make children aware of environmental problems. In early 2000 a comprehensive and well-thought system of environmental education was established for elementary, primary and secondary schools. The MoEYS rejected the option of introducing a self-standing course on Ecology. Instead, it integrated environmental issues into mandatory curricula such as natural science (Biology, Chemistry, Physics, and Geography) and others (e.g., Man and Society, Civic Education and Skills for Life). Instruction books were published. Optional curricula include Environmental Education, Human Ecology, and Man and Nature.

Each school year starts with an ecological hour. Such hours are also held in April close to the Day of the Earth. Also some schools give specific environmental lessons with the assistance of NGOs.

Professional and higher education

The Ecology College in Chisinau trains junior environmental engineers and laboratory staff. Fifty students graduate from it annually. The College consults the MENR when preparing its education plans. Courses on air, soil and water pollution and

its impact on health are delivered to students from the Medical College.

Many higher educational institutions used to include environmental subjects in curricula for different disciplines (botany, zoology, geography, chemistry). The Economic Academy of Moldova introduced specific curricula like energy and environment, environmental monitoring and expertise, environmental economics, environmental insurance, and environmental standards. The State Agrarian University provides curricula in ecology and environmental protection, eco-toxicology and agro-ecology. The State University of Moldova has curricula for ecologists, environmental lawyers, meteorology engineers and hydrology engineers. The Technical University of Moldova has a curriculum for ecological engineers.

There is no system for teacher training in the field of Environment. The pedagogical weekly journal "Faclia" publishes environmental teaching materials on the environment. The REC is organizing, with the financial support from the National Environmental Fund, training courses in environmental geography for teachers in rural areas. Some NGOs, like Guta Club, organized environmental training for teachers under international projects.

Expert training

There are no continuous environmental training courses for experts working in public authorities. In 2004, the MENR organized ad hoc training for environmental inspectors and for heads of rayon divisions dealing with environmental control.

Tasks ahead

The former Ministry of the Environment drafted a law in 2001 on environmental education. The Ministries of Economy and Finance blocked the adoption of this law asserting it would have significant further budgetary implications. The lack of an environmental education law or provisions for such a law in the current legislation has negative consequences for the promotion of environmental education. For instance, it impedes interested secondary schools from getting the legal status of a college specialized in environmental education. No public authority is made clearly responsible for the non-formal and informal education of adults. There is no research either on environmental education or on education for sustainable development in the country.

The *Economic Growth and Poverty Reduction Strategy Paper* (EGPRSP) prescribes the MENR and the MoAFI to prepare in 2005-2006 a national strategy on environmental education. The MoE, which is promoting environmental education in the country, should become an active player in the preparation of the strategy. Mass media and civil society associations should be involved in the process and broader issues of education for sustainable development might be addressed.

3.6   The decision-making framework

Since 1998, the Republic of Moldova has adopted a series of laws and regulations setting or amending the decision-making framework for environmental information, public participation and education. The main documents are presented in Annex IV.

A number of policy documents on environmental information, public participation and education have been elaborated over the past seven years. Few of them set clear objectives or envisage concrete measures with responsible institutions, deadlines and sources of financing. Policy objectives and measures are frequently expressed in a very general or ambiguous way. As a result, it is hardly possible to assess progress in the achievement of policy objectives that were formulated in such way as to: (a) extend monitoring activities and undertake monitoring of biological resources (1995 *Concept of Environmental Protection*); (b) review and improve the environmental monitoring system (EGPRSP); or (c) improve legal mechanisms to ensure public participation in and access to justice on, environment-related matters (Human Rights Action Plan).

However, there was some progress in the achievement of a few policy objectives, in particular, the monitoring of POPs in the air (*National Action Plan on Environmental Health*), the preparation of an inventory of POPs and PCB (EGPRSP) and the creation of local environmental information centres (1995 *Concept of Environmental Protection*).

On the contrary, there is no evidence that several policy objectives had been or were being implemented, including:

- The development of a database on environmental quality and the state of natural resources, and the elaboration of programmes for monitoring surface and ground water quality, and of a national investment programme for improving the monitoring

system (1995 *Concept of Environmental Protection*);

- The creation of a groundwater monitoring programme and the improvement of forestry inventory (EGPRSP);

- The establishment of a coordinating committee and a secretariat to monitor the implementation of the National Action Plan on Environmental Health, and the harmonization of water standards with EU standards (*National Action Plan on Environmental Health*); and

- The creation of a national centre and databases for environmental education and training, and the launching of TV and radio programmes, e.g., "Ecological safety: realities and prospects" (*National Programme on Environmental Safety*).

Some objectives even regressed. For instance, the Environmental Information Centre of the MENR that was to expand its activities according to the 2001 *Concept of Environmental Policy* actually squeezed its activities due to drastically reduced staff numbers.

Overall, the existing systems of environmental information, public participation and education could function significantly more effectively if strategic planning and monitoring of progress made in achieving policy objectives were more effective. A substantial investment is urgently needed in staff expertise and capacity-building within the relevant public authorities to improve strategic planning and management skills.

3.7   Conclusions and recommendations

The Republic of Moldova has made some progress in observing its environment. It increased its surface water quality observation network and started monitoring some heavy metals and POPs in sediments, soil and in the atmospheric precipitation. It reactivated its only transboundary air-monitoring station. Nevertheless, the current monitoring networks remain insufficient to meet the requirements of the national legislation and international obligations of the Republic of Moldova. Monitoring does not cover several important point sources of groundwater pollution, diffuse pollution of surface waters is not measured and there is not a single background monitoring station in the country.

The lists of ambient quality parameters have not been revised or harmonized with international standards since Moldova received independence, except the drinking water quality parameters that are under revision to meet WHO requirements. An excessively large number of regulated pollutants impose unrealistic monitoring and enforcement requirements on public authorities. Some of the Moldovan standards are below the threshold of detection, so it is impossible to know whether they are being achieved or not. At the same time, some hazardous substances are unregulated.

No real progress was made towards the creation of a comprehensive nationwide monitoring programme. Individual ministries and departments develop their own, while decentralized databases of relevance to the environment follow their own technical protocols and procedures. The integrated environmental monitoring system is not operational in spite of the adopted regulation and the donor support provided.

Some institutions in the Republic of Moldova enlarged their environmental databases and improved environmental information management and reporting. For instance, today, statistical data collection covers 17 environment-related areas. Important databases, however, especially those on emissions and discharges, water quantity, groundwater quality, forests and environment statistics, are not managed by modern information technologies and are not easily accessible to decision-makers and the general public. The environmental reports are largely descriptive.

The Republic of Moldova was among the first States to ratify the Aarhus Convention. It adopted a series of legal and regulatory documents broadening the rights of citizens to have access to environmental information and to ensure public participation in environmental decision-making. It has still to elaborate its legal and regulatory framework further to more effectively implement the requirements of the Aarhus Convention.

Procedures are not sufficiently detailed enough to make general legal provisions that ensure public participation in environmental decision-making concerning laws, regulations, standards, permitting, plans and programs applicable in practice. The public does not generally participate in the State ecological expertise. The Regulation on public participation in the preparation and adoption of environmental decisions of 2000 is not being enforced.

The MENR frequently invites the public to participate in decision-making on policies, plans and programmes. An NGO representative, elected by NGOs themselves, is sitting on the Administrative Council of the Environmental Fund. The Environmental Fund provides NGOs with financial support, although the artificial limitation of the amount of grants to individual NGOs restricts considerably the true potential of this financial source for supporting civil society's environmental initiatives. The public is not represented in the Inter-Ministerial Committee on Sustainable Development and Poverty Reduction and in the National Commission on Environmental Policy.

The Republic of Moldova signed the PRTR Protocol to the Aarhus Convention that was adopted in Kiev in 2003. It is presently attempting to establish a national PRTR for the energy sector. Preparations for the protocol ratification need to be intensified by involving key monitoring institutions, compliance authorities, sectoral ministries, business and industry, and NGOs in the development of a plan of action to set legal, institutional and technical frameworks for establishing a national PRTR.

The Republic of Moldova is promoting environmental education covering the pre-school, primary and secondary, and higher education. A comprehensive and well-thought system of environmental education has been established for schools by integrating environmental issues into mandatory curricula. There are no permanent environmental training courses for public officials and judges, however. Non-formal and informal environmental education of adults is practically absent in the country.

Therefore, the following recommendations are addressed to the Republic of Moldova:

Recommendation 3.1:
The Ministry of Ecology and Natural Resources, jointly with the Ministry of Health and Social Protection and in cooperation with the Department of Standardization and Metrology, should review the national monitoring parameters and environmental quality standards:

(a) To limit substantially the number of regulated parameters by making the remaining ones consistent with international standards and guidelines;

(b) To introduce additional parameters and standards monitoring that are required by multilateral environmental agreements and EU environmental directives, and to set time schedules

for phasing in those new parameters and standards that could not be introduced immediately; and

(c) To focus on a core set of parameters and standards when planning the upgrading of monitoring stations, equipment and devices, and analytical laboratories including relevant staff retraining.
(See also recommendation 1.3)

Recommendation 3.2:
The Ministry of Ecology and Natural Resources, in cooperation with the Ministry of Health and Social Protection, the Ministry of Agriculture and Food Industry, the National Bureau of Statistics, the Agency for Forestry "Moldsilva", the State Water Concern "Apele Moldovei", the Agency for Geology "AGeoM" and other institutions concerned, should review the achievements and failures in the implementation of the 1998 Regulation on Establishing of an Integrated Environmental Monitoring System. On the basis of this review they should prepare a decree for Government adoption for the establishment of an institutional structure for inter-ministerial coordination on environmental monitoring and information. The proposal should envisage, among other things:

a)   A leading role for the Ministry of Ecology and Natural Resources in this institutional structure together with operational support by a monitoring centre to be established by the Ministry on the basis of its existing observation and information units and additional resources, as appropriate; and

b)   The preparation by this institutional structure, taking into account environmental monitoring and information provisions in various national strategies and programmes and international commitments, of a time-bound and consistent set of practical actions aimed at expanding observation networks and the number of parameters measured; improving data collection and exchange; harmonizing reporting with international requirements; and facilitating public access to environmental information.

Recommendation 3.3:
The Ministry of Ecology and Natural Resources, in cooperation with the National Bureau of Statistics,

the Agency for Forestry "Moldsilva", the State Water Concern "Apele Moldovei", the Agency for Geology "AGeoM", should re-assess the effectiveness of their environmental reporting policies to ensure the publication and uploading onto the Internet of environmental information collected by these institutions, and to make them publicly accessible through Internet, free of charge on a regular basis and in a user-friendly form and

Recommendation 3.4:
To further improve the participation of public in environmental decision-making, the Ministry of Ecology and Natural Resources should initiate:

- *Implementing fully the 2000 governmental Regulation on Public Participation in the Elaboration and Adoption of Environmental Decisions;*

- *Supplementing the Law on Environmental Protection with including relevant detailed provisions on public participation in environmental permitting, environmental standards setting, and development of laws, regulations, strategies, plans and programmes affecting the environment, taking into account provisions of the applicable multilateral environmental agreements; and*

- *Including civil society representatives into governmental commissions or committees on environmental policy and sustainable development.*

Recommendation 3.5
The Ministry of Education, Youth and Sports, in cooperation with the Ministry of Ecology and Natural Resources and other stakeholders concerned, including NGOs and the mass media, should consider the establishment of a council on education for sustainable development. This body should help promote and facilitate the implementation, at the national level, of the UNECE Strategy for Education for Sustainable Development, paying particular attention to non-formal and informal education of adults (including education on citizen rights) and to the training of policy-makers and judges.

Chapter 4

INTERNATIONAL AGREEMENTS AND COMMITMENTS[1]

4.1 General framework for the international cooperation

Located in South-Eastern Europe, the Republic of Moldova is bordered on the west by Romania and on the north, south, and east by Ukraine. As Romania is expecting to join the European Union (EU) in 2007, the country should shortly become an EU neighbour country. This geographic location and expected new political context are key determinants for the current and further development of the country's international cooperation.

Political and legal framework

In 2002 the Republic of Moldova announced its strong aspiration to join the EU. Several steps have already been made including the preparation and adoption of the EU-Moldova Action Plan. The new Government formed in spring 2005 reaffirmed this intention and is preparing a National Programme for implementing an Action Plan that will set more concrete and precise actions, terms and responsible bodies.

The 2004 *National Report of the state of the Environment* identifies the following main principles of international cooperation on environmental and sustainable development:

- Strengthening the institutional capacity via participation in international and bilateral agreements;

- Approximation of the national environmental legislation to the requirements of the international conventions and the EU legislation in view of the accession to the EU; and

- Mobilizing technical and financial assistance for implementation of national environmental policies.

The 1995 *Concept of Foreign Policy* remains the main document identifying the priorities of the country in international cooperation. Firm compliance with undertaken commitments is one of the main principles stated in the Concept and foreign policy is oriented towards bilateral and multilateral cooperation. The country sees the G7 countries[2] as important strategic partners and cooperation with the United Nations and other international or regional organizations as key. Special attention, based not only on geographical proximity but also on historical and cultural ties, is being paid to the country's cooperation with Romania.

The 2001 *Concept of Environmental Policy* puts emphasis on:

- The EU approximation, strategies and programmes;

- The development of a concept for international relations in the field of environment, and mechanisms for ratifying and implementing conventions and other international documents relating to the environment;

- The signing of bilateral collaboration protocols with Romania, Ukraine, Belarus and the Russian Federation; and on

- The signing and ratifying regional agreements, such as the Convention on the Danube River.

The 2004 *Concept of Transboundary Cooperation for 2004-2006* has been developed in order to foster dialogue with neighbouring states, and international and European organizations. The earlier Parliament decision from 2003 "On development of transboundary cooperation in the framework of Euroregions" established the Commission on Transboundary Cooperation that is responsible for 1) establishing mechanisms of transboundary cooperation in the framework of Euroregions as

---

[1] The present chapter reviews progress since the 1998 UNECE Environmental Performance Review of Moldova.

[2] Canada , France, Germany, Italy, Japan, United Kingdom and United States of America

main elements of the European integration process; 2) approximation of provisions of legal acts on transboundary cooperation to the level of European standards; and 3) the creation of a system for implementation of conventions and agreements that the country is party to.

The Laws on acceding to any convention or protocol are an inherent part of the national legislation. The conclusions of all international treaties by the Republic of Moldova are determined by two main legal acts:

- 1999 *Law on International Agreements*; and

- 2001 *Regulation regarding the Mechanism of Conclusions of International Agreements*.

The leading role in concluding any new environmental treaties or acceding to conventions belongs to the Ministry of Ecology and Natural Resources (MENR). It prepares all necessary background documents, and consults the other ministries involved, e.g., the Ministry of Foreign Affairs and European Integration (MoFAEI), the Ministry of Finances (MoF), the Ministry of Economy and Trade (MoE) and the Ministry of Justice (MoJ). When an agreement is reached the documents are submitted to the Parliament. The Government signs its decision, which has to be further promulgated by the President and then enters into force. The choice of joining certain conventions may sometimes depend on their giving possible access to related financing for implementation, which often creates an opportunity to use these resources for solving environmental problems.

Institutional framework

Ministry of Ecology and Natural Resources (MENR)

The MENR, through its Division on Environmental Policy and European Integration (DEPEI), is a leading state body for international environmental cooperation. It plays an active role in "Environment for Europe" and "Environment and Health" processes at European level. It cooperates with the Global Environment Facility (GEF) (in 2004 the country became an alternate member in the GEF Council), the UNECE Committee on Environmental Policy, the World Meteorological Organization (WMO), the UN Commission on Sustainable Development (UNCSD) and the UN Environmental Programme (UNEP).

Other ministries

The role of the MoE in international cooperation, including environmental, consists of the coordination and monitoring of technical assistance projects and of providing the Government with a yearly evaluation on the effectiveness of this technical assistance. It is also responsible for cooperation with IFIs. The main function of the MoFAEI is to provide sectoral ministries with assistance when international or bilateral/multilateral agreements are concluded. The MoJ provides legal expertise on conformity of provisions of international agreements with national legislation. The MoF signs technical assistance projects including environmental projects when domestic resources are provided.

International technical assistance

The main aims of the technical assistance in the environmental field are identified in the 2001 *Concept of Environmental Policy*. The Procedure for receiving technical assistance from abroad is rather flexible. Projects are managed by the MENR with the support of IFIs or via IFIs with offices in the country. Before starting a project, MoE is consulted to ensure that there is no duplication with any other project. If no financial contribution from the Government is required, then the project may be signed by the MENR; when financial contribution is required, then it is the MoF who signs the project endorsement letter.

At the same time, there is collaboration at the scientific level. Support for scientific research is provided by foreign organizations to the scientific institute mainly in the form of staff support, providing necessary software products and consulting services.

4.2   International and regional agreements

Following Recommendation 3.3 made in the first Environmental Performance Review (EPR) the country has been actively joining international agreements. Since 1998 it became party to 11 more agreements. As of today, the Republic of Moldova is party to 19 international environmental conventions, four protocols and a signatory to five more. Each international agreement has its national focal point.

In 1996 there was an attempt to create a systematic approach by creating a National Commission on supervision of the implementation of different international agreements. Its composition and the rules of procedures had been established by

Presidential decree, and in the first EPR it was recommended to strengthen the role and resources of this Commission. However it never became operational.

Currently, an interdepartmental or inter-ministerial Working Group (WG) is being created for the implementation of every international agreement, and its composition will be approved either by order of the MENR or by the decision of the Parliament. These WGs neither have legal nor binding powers, nor any clearly identified plans, procedures or mandates for their work. These procedures are referred to as "non-written". The WGs meet no more often than once every two months. This does not provide any systematic approach for assessing the progress on agreements implementation. The Ministry's experts recognize that the enforcement section in conventions implementation is severely lacking and needs to be strengthened.

Numerous offices that do not directly belong to the MENR (although some were created by MENR order) were created for the development of activities under different conventions. There are offices for biodiversity, ozone issues and climate change. Plans to create a chemicals management centre that would deal with four international agreements, Basel, Stockholm and Rotterdam Conventions and Aarhus Protocol on POPs to the Convention on Long-range Transboundary Air Pollution (CLRTAP), are foreseen.

Global conventions

Convention on Biological Diversity

The country ratified the UN Convention on Biological Diversity (CBD) in 1995. The main national legislative acts concerning biodiversity conservation are the 1993 Law on Environmental Protection, the 1995 Law on Fauna and the 1998 *Law on the Fund of Natural Areas protected by the State*. Several provisions concerning biodiversity conservation were also included in the 1995 *Law on Protection Zones for Water Rivers and Basins*, the 1993 *Water Code*, the 1991 *Land Code* and the 1979 *Forestry Code*. The National Assessment of Implementation of CBD was prepared in 2000 by the World Conservation Monitoring Centre. This assessment showed that the country has established the institutions to carry out biodiversity conservation and is managing projects financed by donor organizations, but that it still lacks financing.

There were a number of international projects related to the biodiversity issues that were supported by GEF and realized via the International Bank for Reconstruction and Development (IBRD). The biodiversity office has also made attempts to develop various projects related to biodiversity conservation and to assist in their realization. Currently the country is preparing its third National Report on biodiversity.

The Country ratified the Cartagena Protocol on Biosafety in 2002. To fulfil its commitments the country developed the *National Strategy and Action Plan on Biological Diversity* and the 2001 *Law on Biosafety*. To enable the country to consolidate efforts towards the establishment of the national biosafety system, UNEP and GEF are providing technical assistance. The Government established the National Biosafety Committee with a mandate and functions to make decisions and authorize activities connected to genetically modified organisms (GMO) use. The regulations on authorization of activities connected with production, testing use and distribution of GMOs were approved. The National Biosafety testing centre was established by an MENR and the Ministry of Health and Social Protection (MoHSP) joint decision to ensure detection of GMOs and assess their potential risks for the environment and human health. The created national biosafety framework serves as a guidance specifying priority aims in the development of a national system for GMO regulation, control and monitoring in order to comply with the requirements of the Cartagena Protocol.

United Nations Framework Convention on Climate Change

The country ratified the UN Framework Convention on Climate Change (UNFCCC) in 1995. While preparing the First National Communication on climate change (1998-2000) the country made an inventory of greenhouse gases (GHG) emissions for 1990-1998. The Climate Change (CC) office deals with a) the identification and implementation of projects related to climate change, b) the gathering of necessary data and the provision of technology requirements for climate change, and c) the holding of a roster of national experts on climate change. It was involved as a project management unit in the realisation of the GEF funded project that was to ensure synergy and the meeting of the country's obligations under three UN conventions: UNFCCC, CBD and UNCCD. At the moment it is dealing with another GEF-project on improvement of the quality of greenhouse gas emissions. The CC office has also contributed to the understanding of the importance of the Kyoto protocol and provided the MENR with information and assistance for the preparation of the documents necessary for ratifying the Protocol.

With support of GEF funding via the UNEP the country is now preparing a second national communication until 2008, with an inventory of GHG emissions for 1998-2006. In the framework of the same project a project proposal called "National inventory system", which aims to establish a long-term strategy on GHG emissions inventory, will be elaborated. Also a National programme on reducing GHG emissions is supposed to be elaborated by the end of 2005 by the MENR. Its preparation is financed from domestic sources, e.g., the National Environmental Fund.

The Kyoto Protocol to the UNFCCC was ratified in 2003. The main reasons for the country to ratify the protocol were a) the possibility to realise the Clean Development Mechanism (CDM) projects in the country that would help solve acute environmental problems, b) the awareness of its importance for global environment and c) the belief in its positive influence on climate stabilization. For the implementation of the Protocol the country has signed and ratified a Memorandum of Understanding on cooperation for the implementation of CDM projects (see also section 4.3). A special National commission that serves as a National Designated Authority (NDA) responsible for implementation of the UNFCCC and the Kyoto Protocol, was created and approved by a Government decision in 2003. The NDA is responsible for developing a policy framework on climate change, proposing changes to the national legislation and assessing projects recommended as CDM projects, and is in charge of certifying chosen CDM projects in the UNFCCC Secretariat.

United Nations Convention on Combating Desertification

With 33.9 % of its agricultural land eroded and a further increase of 0.9% per year, causing about 3.1 billion lei (US$ 251.3 million) of damage costs per year, erosion is a key economic and social problem for the country, which ratified the United Nations Convention on Combating Desertification (UNCCD) in 1998. With international support it has put together an assessment of land degradation starting from 1998 (or the earliest available data) until 2000. Based on this assessment, maps with degraded, eroded areas and areas subject to drought were published. In the curricula of university

agriculture courses, aspects of sustainable land management and the subject of combating desertification were introduced. The country also benefited from technical and financial assistance for the development of the 2000 *National Action Programme to Combat Desertification* and the 2000 *National Report on Convention Implementation*. Each ministry has an assigned responsibility in the framework of this Action Programme. Economic agents are identified as financially responsible for implementing the provisions of this plan.

The means to solve the land use problems are distributed between different ministries and economic agents and there is no specific focus on the land degradation problem. Experts also mentioned that as a consequence of land privatization, land degradation problems have strengthened. This is mainly due to the lack of knowledge and willingness to apply sustainable land use practices. These together make compliance with UNCCD provisions very difficult.

Vienna Convention for the Protection of the Ozone Layer

The MENR is responsible for the Implementation of the Convention for the Protection of the Ozone Layer and its Montreal protocol ratified by the country in 1996. The Customs committee also plays an important role. The Republic of Moldova issues permits for importing products containing ozone-depleting substances (ODS) under the Convention's obligations. Being an Article 5 country of the Convention, it can use ODS until 2010. However, the country has undertaken commitments to phase them out before 2008. These commitments were identified in the 1999 *National Programme for gradual phase-out of ozone depleting substances*. To assist in meeting its commitments the country was provided with support from the multilateral fund of the Montreal Protocol. This project is still ongoing (in 2004 it was prolonged until 2006) and is being implemented jointly by UNEP and UNDP.

During the project so far, a number of by-laws and regulations have been approved, the licensing system for ODS-containing products has been improved, and awareness-raising campaigns on ODS and their influence on the ozone layer and environment have been organized. An Ozone office within the MENR deals with the project implementation and the development of further activities to raise funds for the country to meet its commitments. The Ozone office coordinates activities under the project that include the implementation of a *National Programme for Recovery and Recycling of Refrigerants*; and the submission of annual reports on ODS consumption, on the progress of national programme implementation, and on the facilitation of information exchange with other parties of the protocol. The country acceded to the London and Copenhagen amendments in 2001. The MENR's proposal to adhere to the Montreal amendment is currently being reviewed by the Parliament.

Basel Convention on the Control of Transboundary Movements of Hazardous Wastes and their Disposal

Following the recommendations of the first EPR the country ratified the Convention on the Control of Transboundary Movements of Hazardous Wastes and their Disposal in 1998. In 2000 the *National Programme on the Management of Industrial and Domestic Waste for 2001-2010* was developed according to the requirements of article 28 of the 1997 *Law on Industrial and Domestic Waste*. The Programme considers recommendations of the Basel Convention and EU legislation on waste management. In May 2003, the Government approved the Categorization of the hazardous waste and Regulation on the control of transboundary movements and disposal of wastes, establishing concrete implementation procedures using the Basel Convention.

Stockholm Convention on Persistent Organic Pollutants

After the Republic of Moldova signed the Convention on Persistent Organic Pollutants, it received GEF financing for assessment of its national situation with POPs. The main sources of POPs and their location were identified and mapped. After the ratification in 2004, the GEF supported a project that aimed to create an inventory of POPs, and to prepare the 2004 *National Implementation Plan for the Stockholm Convention on Persistent Organic Pollutants*. It was adopted in 2004, as well as the *National Strategy on Reduction and Elimination of Persistent Organic Pollutants*.

Rotterdam Convention on the Prior Informed Consent Procedure for Certain Hazardous Chemicals and Pesticides in International Trade

The country ratified the Convention on the Prior Informed Consent Procedure For Certain Hazardous Chemicals and Pesticides in

International Trade in November 2004 and is developing an implementation plan. MENR experts recognize the complexity of this convention, but consider it an important element in the context of the World Trade Organization, which the country joined in 1999.

Ramsar Convention on Wetlands of International Importance especially as Waterfowl Habitat

The Republic of Moldova ratified the Convention on Wetlands of International Importance especially as Waterfowl Habitat in 1999, a convention of importance for a country where most of the wetlands have been drained and where marshes represent only 0.2% of the territory. The country became a member of this Convention after a first wetland area, the "Lower Prut Lakes", had been recognized as of international importance. With an area of 19,000 ha, it is situated at the Lower Prut and includes wetlands, a natural lake and the Lower Prut reserve that is listed as 1st category by the World Conservation Union (IUCN). It is also situated at a corridor of migratory birds. A management plan for the whole area was developed and approved. However due to an insufficient consultation process that has not involved all land owners, the provisions of the plan are not being followed fully. Lower Dniester, or the estuary of the Dniester River, is the second Ramsar zone.

Convention on Conservation of Migratory Species of Wild Fauna

The country ratified the Convention on Conservation of Migratory Species of Wild Fauna (CMS) as well as both Agreements - on Eurobats and on Afro-Euro-Asian species - in 2000. There are 21 species of bat in the country, thanks to special protected areas of natural habitat for these rare species having been created. Every year a National Communication of Eurobats is sent to Secretariat of the Convention. The National environmental fund provides support for NGO activities for bat protection.

Convention on International Trade in Endangered Species of Wild Fauna and Flora

In 2001 the country ratified the Convention on International Trade in Endangered Species of Wild Fauna and Flora (CITES). The main work being done under the Convention is related to the development of adequate legislation to control illegal trading. As a guideline the country consulted similar legislation from Romania the Russian

Federation, Ukraine. The MENR acts as the management authority, while the scientific focal point for this convention is the Academy of Science and the National Institute of Ecology. Movements of CITES species across the border are controlled by the Customs Department. Other bodies are involved, e.g., the veterinary and phytosanitary services. Some eight different-level documents (laws, codes and procedures) regulate activities on implementation of the CITES. According to the MENR, these documents would imply stricter measures than those required according to the international legislation and the EU. The MENR issues special CITES permits for cross-border movements of species and reports on their number to the CITES Secretariat yearly. The lack of expertise and training of customs officers and their continual reshuffling prevent the comprehensive mechanisms in place from enforcing the Convention. Several amendments have been made to the 1995 Law on Fauna in order to adjust it to the CITES provisions.

UNECE regional Conventions

The country ratified the Aarhus Convention on the Access to Information, Public Participation in Decision Making and Access to Justice in Environmental Matters in 1999. Certain steps to inform the public about the state of the environment were made even before joining this Convention. However, the ratification of the Convention meant the country became more likely to attract international funding. In 2000 it helped to create an Environmental Information Centre under the MENR. See chapter 3 on Information, public participation and education.

The country acceded to the Convention on Long-range Transboundary Air Pollution (CLRTAP) in 1995 and its Protocol on Persistent Organic Pollutants and Heavy Metals Protocols in 2002. In 2002 it developed a yearly Action Plan on CLTRAP implementation that included as priority actions: measurements of air pollution at the border with Romania, an inventory of pollution sources, and measures on the re-establishment of the EMEP (Steering Body to the Cooperative Programme for Monitoring and Evaluation of the Long-range Transmission of Air Pollutants in Europe) analytical station. The country submitted two reports on POPs and Heavy Metals to the Secretariat, one in 2002 and one in 2003. It also signed the EMEP Protocol and the Gothenburg Protocol on Combating Acidification. The EMEP analytical station restarted work in 2004. At the

moment its measuring capacities are quite limited: it only measures POPs and heavy metals. There are plans to expand the number of pollutants measured.

In 1993 the country became party to the Convention on the Protection and Use of Transboundary Watercourses and International Lakes. To fulfil its obligation, the country has signed a range of bilateral agreements with neighbouring countries in the field of transboundary water resources protection. Most of the work under the Convention is being done jointly with the MoHSP. During recent years amendments have been introduced to the Water Code following the provisions of the Convention. The 2003 *National Concept for Water Resources for 2003-2010* identified possible actions to help advance efficient water management. In 2004 a plan for the preparation of a strategy for sustainable water resources use in 2005 was approved. A budget of 1.5 million lei (US$ 121,700) was allocated. The Strategy will be in line with the EU water legislation.

The country is also a signatory to the London Protocol on water and health. Its ratification is currently under consideration by the Government. Its National focal points are the MENR and the MoHSP. The *National Action Plan for Environmental Health*, consisting of long-term activities related to the implementation of the London protocol, was prepared and approved in the country in 2001.

The responsibility for the implementation of the Espoo Convention on Environmental Impact Assessment in a Transboundary Context is under the DEPEI. During the last three years the country used the mechanisms provided by the Convention twice. When Ukraine expressed the intention in 2003 to build a navigable channel (Bistrij Channel) in the Danube delta (Zhebrjanskaya bay) that could influence the state of the ecosystems and hydrological regime in the Danube River delta, the country requested Ukraine via the MoFAEI to provide information about the project and its expected impact on the environment. So far, Ukraine has not replied. The other case relates to Romania's project for exploiting a gold mine with the support of Denmark. The Romanian side informed the country that it was planning to carry out a chemical extraction of gold and that it could potentially lead to small rivers contamination. After analyzing the information presented, the country came to the conclusion that the location of the gold mine was too far from the Prut River to have an impact and made a decision not to take part in the EIA. However it requested to get the EIA conclusions.

The MENR actively participated in the elaboration of the Protocol on Strategic Environmental Assessment (SEA Protocol), signed at the fifth Kiev Conference in 2003. In order to proceed with SEA implementation, the country plans to identify criteria for SEA, to establish procedures for conducting a SEA, and to introduce necessary changes in the current legislation. This would be partially done in the framework of the UNDP/REC project of development of the Guidelines for the SEA.

The State Environment Inspection is the focal point for the Convention on Transboundary Effects of Industrial Accidents that was ratified in 1993. With support from Germany the country has (a) identified facilities that could be potential sources of environmental pollution, (b) elaborated criteria for evaluating the risks of five types of industrial activity, (c) created a database for major pollution sources and (d) elaborated a computerized framework and an information and notification procedure for environmental accidents.

Other regional conventions

Convention on Cooperation for the Protection and Sustainable Use of the Danube River

The country is bordered by the Prut River, a major affluent of the Danube River, which explains its interest in joining the Danube Convention in 1999. The *Action Plan for Implementation of the Convention on Cooperation for the Protection and Sustainable Use of the Danube River* (Danube Convention) is developed annually. In 1999 with Tacis support, the country received a mobile analytical laboratory and equipment for spectral analysis and chemical reagents for its analytical laboratories. In the framework of the Danube Pollution Reduction programme for the years 1997-2000, institutional capacities training and target-oriented workshops, were carried out. A number of project proposals aimed at lowering the pollution load of the Danube were developed and further supported by Tacis, such as the "Prut river water management" project. Since 2001, under the Programme, tariffs for nutrient discharge to the environment have been developed and a plan for the integrated management of the Danube River is being worked out. Through the Convention,

relations and cooperation with Romania on the protection and management of transboundary water resources have strengthened. Recently the country started to finance certain actions under the Convention from local environmental funds and economic agents' contributions.

Bern Convention on the Conservation of European Wildlife and Natural Habitats

The country ratified the Bern Convention on the Conservation of European Wildlife and Natural Habitats in 1993. Since then, a database comprising relevant information on areas subject to conservation activities has been created, Moldovan rare species have been included in the Convention's list of rare species, national experts have taken part in the elaboration of an action plan for the conservation of species included in the Convention, and the country has become a permanent member of the Convention Committee.

Convention on European Landscape

In 2001 the Republic of Moldova ratified the Convention on European Landscape, which came into force in 2004. For its implementation its national focal point, the National Institute of Ecology (INECO), did some scientific research on the state of natural representative ecosystems. This created a basis for argumentation for the introduction of a stricter protection regime and for the widening of state protected areas. The high population density and strong agricultural orientation of the country means that there is a need to coordinate the activities that could potentially lead to the disturbance of landscapes.

The country possesses a rich and diverse landscape and ecosystem; however, past natural disasters and the economic situation itself are a threat to the biological resources and ecosystems of the country. Interruptions in gas and electricity supplies and other economic shortages have led to the unsustainable use of natural resources, such as forests, because no alternatives were available. Land privatisation also has a strong impact on landscape and biodiversity. Natural fences and bushes were cut down by the current owners regardless of any sustainable forest management principles. Extensive drainage of wetland in the past also played its role in the negative pressure on the environment. For quite some time the country has been considering the creation of ecological networks and corridors as a means to preserve the biological and landscape diversity and restore ecosystems, a project still at the conception phase (See Chapter 7 on agriculture). Numerous attempts have been made to rehabilitate forest-protected belts and increase the area of protected zones. INECO is gathering information to develop a common strategy.

4.3   Bilateral cooperation

The Republic of Moldova has signed nine bilateral agreements, protocols and memorandums of understanding with six countries. Most of these are umbrella agreements related to cooperation on environmental protection. Some were concluded after the country became party to certain international conventions or protocols, as a means to fulfil its commitments. Along these lines, a trilateral Agreement on cooperation on bordering areas of the Danube Delta and the Lower Prut was signed with Ukraine and Romania in 2000; a bilateral agreement with the MENR of Ukraine, consisting of provisions for the creation of transboundary environmental corridors and networks, is being prepared at the moment.

In some other cases, proposals for the development of new sub-regional conventions were formed in the framework of existing agreements. For example, under the Protocol with the Ministry of Environmental Protection and Atomic Security of Ukraine, the countries created a commission that considered the possibility of drafting a Convention on landscape and biodiversity conservation and rational use of natural resources of the Dniester River basin. However, when assessing the strength of the bilateral cooperation, the lack of financial resources must be considered, as it means that country partners are not able to meet and discuss joint activities on a periodic basis. The 1994 agreement with the Republic of Belarus has remained almost non-operational for the last several years due to this problem. Action plans for implementing the bilateral agreements signed do not allow for more effective bilateral cooperation. It can be linked partially to the lack of resources, and partially to the frequent changes in Government.

The bilateral cooperation with country donors is organized mostly to get assistance to implement certain international conventions or protocols. For example in 2003 the country concluded the Memorandum of Understanding with Denmark on cooperation for the implementation of CDM projects based on the Kyoto Protocol. Collaboration with the United Kingdom in 2003-2004 was focused on biosafety issues. The British Foreign and Commonwealth Office provided a contribution to the preparation of a National Biosafety Framework in accordance with Cartagena Protocol on Biosafety provisions. Bilateral cooperation with the Czech Republic is focused on climate change, and water and biodiversity protection measures.

4.4.   Cooperation with international organizations

World Bank (WB)

The country joined WB in 1992 and worked with it through the Country Assistance Strategy (CAS). In 2004, when the *Economic Growth and Poverty Reduction Strategy Paper* (EGPRSP) was completed and approved, the new CAS set out the lending and non-lending support for the country for 2005-2008.

By providing technical assistance, WB contributed significantly to a) reducing the discharge of nutrients into the Danube River and the Black Sea through integrated land and water management, b) creating the ecological network of the Prut River basin, and c) enhancing welfare of the poorest rural population and medium-sized towns and cities by improving the quality, efficiency and sustainability of their water supply and sanitation services. With WB and GEF support, the country was enabled to make progress with its commitments on POPs under the Stockholm Convention. At the moment, in the framework of the PDF B (Project "Grant on Preparation of Sustainable Persistent Organic Pollutants (POPs) Stockpiles Management Project"), the country is preparing a loan for a US$ 11 million investment.

Organisation for Economic Co-operation and Development (OECD)

The Republic of Moldova is not an OECD member. However, it is in active cooperation with the OECD's "Non-OECD Member Countries' Division" and especially the "Task Force for implementation of Environmental Action Plans" (EAP TF). The main aims of cooperation between the country and OECD are to 1) participate actively in a dialogue in the field of environmental policy and partnership between EECCA countries, 2) build the capacity for the application of modern economic environmental instruments, 3) improve environmental financing, 4) cooperate in the framework of the "Environment for Europe" process, and 5) integrate environmental concern into other sectoral policies. In 2000 an evaluation of the country's national and local environmental funds was done in this framework, and gave birth to a series of recommendations that significantly increased efficiency of use of these funds.

Cooperation with UN organizations and programmes

Participation in the "Environment for Europe" and "Environment and Health" processes

The country actively participated in the fourth (Aarhus, 1998) and fifth (Kiev, 2003) Ministerial Conferences "Environment for Europe" and in all stages of their preparation. It participated in the development of the Environment Strategy for EECCA countries adopted at the Kiev Conference.

The country also participated in developing the Strategic Partnership on Water for Sustainable Development: the EECCA Component of the EU Water Initiative. At the Kiev Ministerial Conference it signed all three protocols. The MENR is responsible for following up conference decisions and for their implementation, including changes in legislation and integration into sectoral policies and strategies. The Republic participates in the work of the UNECE Committee on Environmental Policy.

The country is a member of the World Heath Organization Regional Office for Europe (WHO-ROE) and participated in the third (London, 1999) and fourth (Budapest, 2004) European Ministerial Conferences "Environment and Health." In the last decade the country has made significant efforts to improve and adjust the legislative and normative framework in the field of environment and population health protection. To date, about 50 legislative laws and about 80 by-laws and regulations, as well as strategies, concepts, programmes and action plans have been adopted.

United Nations Development Programme

The UN Development Assistance Framework for Moldova for 2001-2006 sees environmental issues as cross-cutting issues and its support is limited mostly to helping the country to implement commitments under international agreements (conventions and protocols).

The UNDP-Moldova began to work on Environment in 1998. The projects carried out related to climate change, capacity building, ozone depleting substances, land management, strategic environmental assessment, and energy efficiency. The majority of projects realized via UNDP have received GEF funding.

UNDP has also provided substantial help for activities under Agenda 21 and has helped to bring about a better understanding of sustainable development issues.

United Nations Environment Programme

With the support of the UN Environment Programme (UNEP), the country prepared itself to enter the Cartagena Protocol on Biosafety and the creation of the National Biosafety Framework into force. It also implemented a project on institutional strengthening for the implementation of the Montreal Protocol with GEF funding, and is now preparing a second national communication on climate change.

Cooperation with European Union

The Partnership and Cooperation Agreement (PCA), which forms the legal basis of EU-Republic of Moldova relations, was signed in November 1994 and entered into force in July 1998 for an initial period of 10 years. It was said to be a "road map" document in which the country assumes a range of self-commitments, and it was regarded as a possible "list of actions" for which the EU could provide support. It covers a wide range of areas including political dialogue, trade and investment, economic co-operation, legislative approximation, and culture and science. To foster political dialogue and to monitor the implementation of the PCA responsible structures, including the Parliamentary Cooperation Committee, the Cooperation Council and the Cooperation Committee, have been established.

EU-Moldova Action Plan

In 2004, the enlargement of the EU offered an opportunity to develop an increasingly close relationship with neighbouring countries. The EU-Moldova Action Plan is a document that encompasses strategic objectives and concrete

---

Box 4.1: EU-Moldova Action Plan: Priorities for Actions for the environment

Take steps to ensure that conditions for good environmental governance are set and start implementing them

- Strengthen administrative structures and procedures to ensure strategic planning of environmental issues, including financing strategies, and co-ordination between relevant actors
- Establish procedures regarding access to environmental information and public participation, including implementation of the Aarhus Convention, particularly by establishing structures and procedures for ensuring an acceptable level of service to those wishing to have access to information.
- Prepare regular reports on the state-of-the-environment
- Strengthen structures and procedures necessary to carry out environmental impact assessments, including in relation to transboundary issues; complete relevant legislation
- Further improve communication strategies on the benefits of environmental policy and environmental education, support civil society actors and local authorities

Take active action for prevention of deterioration of the environment, protection of human health, and achievement of rational use of natural resources, in line with the commitments of the Johannesburg Summit

- Continue with the adoption of legislation for key environmental sectors (water quality, waste management, air quality, industrial pollution), including the adoption of the legislation on wild flora and ecological networks.
- Enhance administrative capacities, including for the issuing of permits as well as for enforcement and inspection
- Develop sector-specific programmes and plans (water, waste, air, industrial pollution), notably by completing the plan on liquid waste and the plan on persistent organic pollutants

Enhance co-operation on environmental issues

- Implement provisions under the Kyoto Protocol and the UN Framework Convention on Climate Change
- Participate actively in the Danube – Black Sea Task Force to implement a transboundary approach to water management; ensure active participation in the Eastern European, Caucasus and Central Asia component of the EU Water Initiative
- Identify possibilities with neighbouring countries for enhanced regional cooperation in particular as regards transboundary issues
- Possible participation in selected European Environment Agency activities
- Strengthen administrative capacities for the implementation of regional and international agreements

Source: EU-Moldova Action Plan for Neighbourhood Policy, 2005

---

actions for their achievement. It is supposed to accelerate the implementation of the PCA provisions and completion of planned political, economic and institutional reforms. The implementation of the Action Plan would significantly advance the harmonization of the country's legislation with EU norms and standards, while fulfilling the objectives and actions included in the plan would create conditions for attaining a higher level of relations with the EU. Deeper integration into Europe will also imply the willingness to accept political reforms demanded by the EU and in particular the solving of the Transnistrian issue. The EU-Moldova Action Plan was approved by the European Union in December 2004 and ratified by the Parliament in February 2005. It is prepared for an initial period of three years – 2005-2008; the assessment of its results will coincide with the expiring of the PCA.

In order to ensure comprehensive implementation of the Action Plan, the Government gave a task to the Ministry of Foreign Affairs and European Integration to put together a National programme that would transform provisions of the Plan into concrete actions to be taken by all authorities involved. This National programme specifying actions, deadlines, responsible institutions and the

required assistance has been sent to the EU for feedback concerning the possibilities for technical assistance and financial support.

<u>Technical Assistance to Commonwealth of Independent States (Tacis)</u>

The Tacis indicative programme for 2004-2006 focuses on transboundary regional projects. The only environmental project that Tacis supports for the country is the Regional Environmental Center. Tacis has supported some actions, in particular the extensive training in matters related to the UNECE Aarhus Convention.

Tacis also provided support for the regional project for Armenia, Azerbaijan, Georgia and the Republic of Moldova with respect to their Global Climate Change Commitments. In the framework of this project the country will have the capacity built to be able to host CDM projects and will receive assistance in forming the institutional infrastructure required to support CDM projects. There will be actions implemented aimed at enhancing awareness among key policy makers, the business community and the general public on the issues related to the UNFCCC and the Kyoto Protocol, and at developing local capacity in GHG emissions forecast modelling and assessment of sectoral GHG mitigation potentials and options.

Other organizations

The Mission of the Organization for Security and Cooperation in Europe (OSCE) to the country was established on 4 February 1993 and started work in Chisinau in April of the same year. Even though the issues of the environment are not specifically included in the OSCE to the country mandate, it is supposed to facilitate the achievement of a lasting comprehensive political settlement of the Transnistrian conflict in all its aspects. Within this context, environmental issues, particularly those related to the Dniester River (which for a large part of its length provides the de facto boundary between Chisinau -controlled and Tiraspol-controlled areas) are of very high political and security importance.

4.5 World Summit on Sustainable development and Millennium development goals

World Summit on Sustainable Development

To fulfil its commitments in the implementation of the World Summit on Sustainable Development (WSSD) plan, in 2001 the Government approved the *National Strategy of Social and Economic Development for the medium term until 2005*. This document established priorities for the governmental economic policy, with the objectives and measures necessary for the implementation of a viable market economy and for sustainable development compatible with the principles, norms, mechanisms and institutions of economically developed countries.

In 2001 the country started to prepare a new strategic document: the *Economic Growth and Poverty Reduction Strategy Paper*, which was approved in 2004 for 3 years (from 2004 until 2006). It has a strong focus on economic growth and social security. WB provided the financial support for the EGPRSP development as a three-year project. The three environmental objectives are as follows: 1) to prevent and reduce the degradation of natural resources and increase efficiency of their use; 2) to maintain the quality of the environment as a factor that ensures health and quality of life; and 3) to create an effective natural disaster monitoring, prevention and damage compensation system. A thorough analysis of the state of water resources, forestry and land was done and eight

major areas for improvement were identified with related priority actions to be undertaken.

The three year timeframe supposedly should make its implementation more efficient and allow for quick estimation of the progress and main achievements and further building of the Strategy for the next three years on these results. In order to proceed with economic and social reforms stipulated in the EGPRSP the Government developed a National Programme on technical assistance for 2005-2006 that should provide a necessary basis for technical cooperation with countries, donors and IFIs and an identification of priority areas for such cooperation. Overall, this Programme includes: the EGPRSP objectives related to the environment that are described above, the priority actions identified in EGPRSP, the responsible authorities, the projects proposed to the IFIs that should assist in implementing the priority action, the budget allocated and the beneficiary body.

Agenda 21

Since 2001 Strategic Action Plans for sustainable development (Local Agenda 21 (LA 21)) have been developed for 15 localities: five small cities and ten villages with the support of the UNDP. The LA 21 project targeted three groups in particular: local communities, major community groups, and local governments. The major objectives of the LA 21 Moldovan Project were to a) facilitate the active participation of the civil society and private sector in local decision-making, b) promote inter-sectoral dialogue and sustainable partnerships among local governments, non-governmental organizations and the private sector, c) strengthen local governments' capacity in sustainable participatory planning, and d) facilitate access to information and citizens' participation in the planning process for sustainable development.

This was done by assisting partner localities in resource mobilization, supporting local initiatives targeting the development of small businesses, job creation and rural poverty reduction, and sharing and promoting LA 21 best practices. In every partner locality an LA 21 expert has been included in the local authority structure. This person serves as a local consultant who, where necessary, brings knowledge and experience to other neighbouring localities. Several villages located nearby those where an LA 21 project is running, started themselves to prepare their local agenda with the help of the LA 21 experts, but without any financial assistance from the project.

The choice of the localities where the LA 21s were to be developed, was not based any set of common criteria or indicators. A diagnostic analysis of the situation, which included environment as one of the areas to cover, was made for every locality. Main environmental problems were identified, although they were limited to illegal dumpsites, litter, landslides, surface water contamination, and quality of drinking water. At the same time, the solution of these problems was taken seriously; several small enterprises for waste removal on a commercial basis were created, registered as economic agents and are operating successfully.

Since the project was launched in late 2001, so far it has been mainly concentrated on organizational issues, development and approval of the LA 21 and local environmental action plans, and education and training for local authorities and the population. No formal evaluation of the results of these LAs and Local Environmental Action Plans (LEAPs) has yet been done. However, it worth noticing that local authorities are aware of the LA concept and recognize it as a valuable tool for regional development. Future development and implementation of the created LAs and LEAPs could be done through the National Programme "Moldovan Village" that aims to rehabilitate the rural area.

Millennium development goals

The last ten years in the country were characterised by a decline in the quality of life, a high unemployment rate, and slow and ineffective privatization; moreover, the country had to face the consequences of the military conflict in Transnistria. This has lead to a significant decline in the development of the country, which is still amongst the poorest in Europe. Serious efforts need to be put into eradicating poverty, bettering childcare, improving children's health, and combating HIV/AIDS. At the same time some progress has been made in the education field and in promoting gender equality. In September 2000 the Republic of Moldova signed the UN Millennium Declaration that includes *Millennium Development Goals* (MDGs), to be achieved by 2015.

The analysis "Achieving the Human Development MDGs in ECA" conducted by WB in 2003 classifies the country as a low income country and shows that it is unlikely to achieve the MDG 1, 4 and 6, is likely to achieve MGD 5, and that it is hard to tell whether MDG 2, 3 and 7 can be reached in the set timeframe. The findings showed that 60% of water sampled from supply systems did not meet standards. The quality problems were shown to be particularly bad in rural areas, where 30% of households lacked access to piped water. Many urban areas also needed urgent action to prevent the collapse of delivery systems.

In order to progress with the MDGs the country was advised to set up clear national priorities (national Goals) and concentrate on those that are key for sustainable development and the creation of favourable life conditions. These can largely be ensured by protecting the environment and using its resources wisely. Following this, the Government, with support from the UNDP, has initiated a series of studies and conducted workshops to analyze the methodology of adjusting the targets and indicators envisaged by the Millennium Declaration in the context of the country. As a result and a means to fulfil adopted commitments, the country developed the First National Report "The Millennium Development Goals in the Republic of Moldova" and set national Goals to be achieved by 2015. For each Goal a situation analysis was made and concrete targets and monitoring indicators were developed based on its findings.

Under Goal 7 (Ensure environmental sustainability) a number of key issues for ensuring sustainable development were identified. These are forests, biodiversity conservation, quality of air atmosphere, water supply, and waste management. The importance of every issue, their linkage to the Goal implementation and the obstacles for their implementation, were also addressed. The general targets, the country's target, the indicators to be used and the obstacles impeding the particular Goal implementation are presented in the Annex. Subsequent to the approval of the First National Report "The Millennium Development Goals in the Republic of Moldova" and national Goals, all authorities involved should develop and approve their own action plans and conduct measures that will enable the country to meet the goals set. The process will be supported by the UNDP and monitored by the MoE.

As a core goal derived from the MDGs and the mandate assigned to the UNDP at WSSD, the Multi-Finding Framework of the UNDP for 2004-2007 includes managing energy and environment

Box 4.2: Millennium Development Goals for environmental sustainability

MDG 7: Ensure environmental sustainability

Global targets	Moldovan targets	Indicators	Obstacles
Integrate the principles of sustainable development into country's policies and programmes and reverse the loss of environmental resources	Increase the relative size of • Areas covered with forest from 10.3% in 2002 to 11.0 % in 2006, 12.1 % in 2010 and 13.2 % in 2015; and • Areas protected for the conversation of biodiversity from 1.96% in 2002 to 2.1 % in 2006, 2.2 % in 2010 and 2.4% in 2015.	• Share of land covered by forest • Share of protected areas • GDP per 1 kg of fuel consumed (in lei) • CO_2 emissions by mobile and stationary sources (kg per capita)	• Insufficiency of forest resources for economic, social and environment needs of population • Forests are scattered, dispersed (discrete, detached) and distributed unevenly across the country • Low Sustainability of forest against negative factors • Illegal forests cutting and inability (unwillingness) of local authorities to fight against that • Scattering and degradation of natural ecosystems • Outdated technologies
Halve by 2015 the proportion of people without sustainable access to safe drinking water	Increase the share of population with sustainable access to improved water sources from 38.5 % in 2002 to 47.7 % in 2006, 57.0 % in 2010 and 68.5 in 2015	• Share of population having permanent access to the safe drinking water sources	• Scarcity of water resources, non-rational use of water resources
By 2020 to have achieved a significant improvement in the life conditions of at least 100 million slum dwellers	The share of population with access to improved sanitation is envisaged to increase from 40.0 % in 2001 to 56.0% in 2006, 73.3 % in 2010 and 90.0 % in 2015	• Share of population having access to the improved canalization and sanitation systems	• Technical equipment, water supply and canalization systems are old and do not provide adequate services

Source: First National Report "The Millennium Development Goals in the Republic of Moldova", World Bank, 2003.

for sustainable development. Some of the strategic services under this goal would be: effective water governance, framework and strategy for sustainable development, and conservation and sustainable use of biodiversity. Implementation of the national goals will require synchronization with other global and regional development priorities, especially with the integration process to Europe. Some of the MDGs adapted to the reality of the country's situation are presented in the EGPRSP along with indicative targets.

4.6 Conclusions and recommendations

Since the first Environmental Performance Review, the Republic of Moldova has made a tremendous

step forward in international cooperation. It has a) actively participated in most big international environmental events, b) ratified most of the environmental agreements of regional and global importance, c) tried to go forward in their implementation by preparing national contributions and adjusting existing or drafting new national strategies on various specific subjects, and d) hosted a series of international meetings and conferences that helped the country to raise its profile and attract international resources and assistance for solving national environmental problems.

At the same time, regardless of its efforts to fulfil all relevant obligations, the practical level of implementation remains rather low and efforts poorly coordinated. For implementing most of the ratified conventions and protocols, the country mostly relies on international support, which in many cases remains donor-driven and does not always address the real needs of the country. It is important that the MENR be organized in such a way that it can inform potential donors of the needs and priorities of the country for investments and assistance in environment, and follow the projects that are ongoing, keeping track of the situation.

The country is preparing for and considering the ratification of several more environmental conventions and protocols and is conducting some work to bring national legislation in line with international agreements, and the shrinking number of staff at the Ministry. However, the work is far from being complete, mostly due to the constantly growing number of different policy and strategy papers, action plans and national programmes that are requested for the implementation of these international agreements. The country should streamline its priorities and concentrate its efforts on those agreements, related documents and actions that can bring the most to the country.

Some attempts to become more focused and coordinated in international cooperation have been undertaken recently. First of all the EU-Moldova Action Plan has been approved, and second of all the corresponding National Implementation Programme is being put together. This will help to streamline future joint activities and target EU assistance to the country that better fits its real needs. Also the recently adopted EGPRSP is in line with provisions of the EU-Moldova Action Plan and it highlights European integration as a fundamental focus of the country's long term development objectives. Now, the challenge will be to ensure that the activities under these two programmes do not duplicate but rather strengthen each other.

In the review period the Republic of Moldova continued to participate and implement policy directions provided by international intergovernmental organizations such as UNEP, UNECE, UNDP, WHO, WB, OECD and the governing bodies of international environmental agreements. It also continued to develop bilateral relations with neighbouring as well as other, mostly European, countries. Since 1998, due to a lack of resources, a lack of coordination on different levels, and numerous changes in the Government and in the Ministry, earlier bilateral agreements have not

been very successfully implemented. However, after the recent elections and the reconfirmation of the Government of its strong aspiration to approximate EU practices, the Republic of Moldova hopes for closer cooperation with the EU and sees it as a way to increase momentum and move forward with other bilateral agreements.

Overall, the Republic of Moldova has to start thinking of streamlining its activities on international cooperation and should try to concentrate on those problems that are the most important for the country, and not necessarily just rely on what donors are proposing. The EECCA Environmental Partnership Strategy adopted in Kiev at the fifth Ministerial Conference "Environment for Europe" in 2003, is a good framework for deciding on priorities because it has been elaborated by the EECCA countries themselves. The seven goals spelled out in it are quite concrete and the country can choose those that are of highest importance for itself. The Strategy has strong political support from Ministers, and donors are increasingly requesting to use the Strategy as a benchmark. The donors' use of the Strategy is a good way to bring together the country's priorities and donor possibilities.

Recommendation 4.1:
In order to improve implementation of the ratified international agreements, the Ministry of Ecology and Natural Resources should:

- _Establish clear mandates to the Working Groups for agreement implementation, coordinate their work and report about their results to the Government;_

- _Strengthen synergies between relevant Working Groups and avoid duplications of activities developed under the agreements; and_

- _Seek resources necessary to fulfil obligations under these agreements by all means including organizing donors' meetings._

Recommendation 4.2:
The Ministry of Ecology and Natural Resources should analyze the results of implementation of environmental bilateral and multilateral agreements and other forms of bilateral and multilateral cooperation. Based on this analysis, it should identify the priorities for cooperation and concentrate its resources on them. It should integrate this analysis into its annual report on cooperation with international organizations to the Ministry of Foreign Affairs and European Integration.

PART II: MOBILIZING FINANCIAL RESOURCES FOR ENVIRONMENTAL PROTECTION

Chapter 5

ECONOMIC INSTRUMENTS AND ENVIRONMENTAL FUNDS

5.1 Economic instruments for environmental protection

Legal, institutional and policy framework

Economic instruments of environmental policy include environmentally-related taxes and pollution charges. The first Environmental Performance Review (EPR) was produced on the basis of the information available until March 1998. The then existing legislation related to the natural resource and land use taxes; the road use tax on international transport and payments for environmental pollution continued to be effective. The 1998 *Law on Payments for Environmental Pollution* introduced *ad valorem* levies on imported cars and fuels. Additional import levies on selected environmentally damaging products were legislated in 2002. The natural resource, road use and excise taxes are collected by the State tax service and customs administration while emission charges and fines are collected by territorial ecological inspectorates and allocated to local environmental funds. In some cases (*ad valorem* levies on imported fuel and other environmentally damaging products), the revenue is collected by the customs administration with the aid of officers from the State ecological inspectorate and earmarked for the National Environmental Fund (NEF).

Over the time period under review (1998-2004), economic instruments played an increasingly important role in relative price adjustments by internalizing more fully some environmental externalities. Prices to households and companies in some environmentally sensitive sectors such as energy, transport and municipal water services increased since 1998 through a combination of price liberalisation, price regulation and tax measures. The authorities have no comprehensive measures of the extent of price liberalisation. According to the European Bank for Reconstruction and Development EBRD (2004), the number of monitored goods and services with administered prices dropped from ten in 1998 to eight in 2001 and seven in 2002 and subsequent years, remaining however higher than in most transition economies. Aside from the prices administered by the State, the National Agency for Energy Regulation (ANRE) sets energy prices (see Box 5.1). Local governments mainly regulate tariffs pertaining to municipal water services and heat supply.

Since the 1998 EPR both political stability and fiscal discipline improved considerably. Policies continued to be driven by domestic concerns. Unlike in the EU-candidate countries from South-Eastern Europe, no strong policy disciplines have been imposed on the authorities from the outside. The importance of environmental issues in the policy-making process was enhanced noticeably by the creation of the then Ministry of Ecology and Natural Resources (MENR) in 1998. Since then, the Ministry played a leading role in the design and implementation of environmental policies. Although there is no Government body that focuses specifically on the development of economic instruments of environmental policy, the MENR contributed decisively to the adoption of the levy on environmentally harmful products.

Economic instruments in use

Taxes

The environmentally related tax revenue averaged 3.5% of GDP during the 1998-99 recession, fluctuating in subsequent years around 3 per cent of the rapidly expanding GDP and accounting for some 9 per cent of the general Government revenues including social-security contributions. Relative to GDP, environmental tax receipts are comparable to that of advanced ECE economies. Similarly as in EU countries, the energy and transport taxes account for the bulk of environmental revenue. The per capita environmental revenue remains significantly lower than in EU States due to the relatively early stage of productivity catch-up.

The natural resource and land use taxes continue to be specified by annual budget acts according to the rules described in the 1998 EPR.[1] Their combined revenue kept increasing at a lower pace than nominal GDP due to rather sporadic adjustments for inflation. The principal water use tax rate remained constant at the 1998 level of 1.8 lei per 10 m^3 until 2003 when it rose to 5 lei in 2003. Tax rates pertaining to the use of mineral resources remained fixed at the 1998 levels until 2004 when their minimum levels doubled. The tax rates payable for using timber were frozen over the same time period and nearly doubled in 2004. The land use tax per graded hectare increased from one lei in 1998 to 1.5 lei during the period 1999-2003. Then it rose to 1.85 lei but large discounts for prompt payment (15 per cent in 2004 and 10 per cent in 2005) reduced the revenue impact. According to Ministry of Finance calculations, tax revenue losses related to various land tax breaks declined from 0.3 per cent of GDP in 2003 to 0.2 per cent in 2004.

Aside from the standard Value Added Tax (VAT) (20 per cent), taxes on imported fuel include excises in the form of an *ad quantum* tax on aviation and road fuel (1200 lei per ton of petrol and 500 lei per ton of diesel). These rates did not change in recent years so that the associated excises fell in real terms, remaining nevertheless the most important source of environmental tax receipts (Table 5.1). Annual budget acts earmark a changing portion of the associated tax intake for the Road Fund (15 per cent in 2005), the remaining part contributing to general revenues. The *ad valorem* tax on imported fuel amounts to 1 per cent of the customs value of leaded petrol and diesel or 0.5 per cent of the value of unleaded petrol. The associated revenue is earmarked for NEF. A levy on imports of other environmentally harmful products, effective since 2003, also generates earmarked revenue for NEF.[2] Another tax differentiated with respect to environmental effects is imposed on road use by vehicles not registered in the country. Since 1998, there is also an *ad quantum* excise tax on

imported cars that increases with the motor size. A surcharge based on the age profile of imported cars became effective in 2003.[3] No excise taxes are levied on imported trucks and tractors.

Emission charges and other payments

Since 1998 the country continued to have a fairly extensive system of emission charges on 1000 air pollutants, 27 water effluents, and five different types of waste. In some cases, the emission limits, inherited from the Soviet era, are stricter than those obtaining in the EU. The nominal amounts of charges per unit of pollution remained unchanged since 1998. Although some air pollution charges are relatively high by standards of the Commonwealth of Independent States (CIS) region, they are well below western levels (e.g. in 2001, the SO_2 per ton emission charge amounted to about US$ 30 in the Republic of Moldova vs. US$ 1 in the Russian Federation but US$ 1,800 in Sweden).[4] In contrast, the water effluent and waste charges appear to be below the CIS norm. The amounts assessed are based on outdated technical norms and installed capacity rather than actual emissions.

During the first decade of transition weak collection resulted in comparatively low revenues so that effective charges were much lower than statutory ones. However, the collection rate improved somewhat in recent years (to about 50 per cent), in line with robust economic growth and improving profitability of firms. Non-compliance fines are set at low levels that correspond to 3-5 minimum monthly wages of 1998 (about US$ 4.50 - US$ 7.50) per incident and rise five-fold if maximum permissible levels are exceeded. Enforcement of fines was consistently weak, reflecting reductions of staff levels at the environmental inspectorate in recent years as well as informal payments.[5] Official receipts from pollution charges and fines remain marginal (Table 5.1). The environmental liability system tends to be used frequently by the environmental inspectorate; however, courts rarely award the damages requested (for details, see chapter 2).

---

[1] Natural resource taxes include charges on water abstraction and non-consumption that are levied on all firms; however, there is a 50 per cent discount on water for irrigation purposes. The authorities also levy forest tree and hunting charges as well as payments for the use of sub-soil and biological resources.

[2] The *ad valorem* levy on environmentally damaging products is collected by the customs administration. The products taxed at 0.5 per cent of customs value include new tyres, recording discs and tapes. Products taxed at 1 per cent include halogenated derivatives of hydrocarbons, compounds with ozone depleting substances, cigars, cigarettes and used tyres. Products taxed at 1.5 per cent include naphthalene, batteries and electric accumulators. Products taxed at 3 per cent include plastic packaging and lamps (halogen, mercury, sodium). Products taxed at 5 per cent include acrylic paints and varnishes. Black oil (mazut) is taxed according to sulphur content at 0.5 or 1 or 2.8 per cent.

[3] The surtax is positively related to the motor size and starts for the vehicles operating 3-5 years, increases for the 5-7 years category and reaches the maximum for the vehicles operating for more than 7 years. Imports of cars older than 10 years are prohibited since 1998.

[4] Analysis of economic instruments in transition economies, see OECD EAP Task Force (2003).

[5] According to a study "Transparency International Moldova (2003)", based on interviews with 630 enterprises, the amount of informal payments extorted from firms by State inspectors (including environmental inspectors) equals or even exceeds the fines paid officially.

Table 5.1: Environmental revenues, 1998-2004

million lei

	1998	1999	2000	2001	2002	2003	2004
Total environmental revenue	324.7	478.2	523.4	568.8	699.3	931.3	1011.4
1. Taxes	324.4	476.7	521.4	565.3	687.6	914.8	987.9
Natural resources tax	10.4	8.2	7.6	8.6	12.2	15.7	21.3
Land use tax	85.7	139.7	159.7	164.5	189.7	167.8	190.9
Excise tax on imported diesel and petrol	175.0	242.8	244.5	264.2	322.7	383.4	406.8
Motor vehicle excise taxes	30.4	40.7	61.9	74.3	105.1	260.1	217.7
Road use tax	22.6	41.5	40.4	46.5	49.9	73.1	127.9
Levy on imported diesel and petrol	0.3	3.8	7.3	7.2	8.0	10.7	18.2
Levy on environmentally harmful products	..	..	..	..	..	4.0	5.1
2. Pollution charges and fines	0.3	0.3	1.7	1.9	3.4	4.8	4.5
3. Grants and technical assistance	0.0	1.2	0.3	1.6	8.3	11.6	19.0

Memorandum items:

Share in GDP, per cent

	1998	1999	2000	2001	2002	2003	2004
1. Taxes	3.6	3.9	3.3	3.0	3.0	3.3	3.1
2. Pollution charges and fines	0.004	0.002	0.011	0.010	0.015	0.017	0.014
3. Grants and technical assistance	0.000	0.010	0.002	0.008	0.037	0.042	0.059
GDP (million lei)	9,122	12,321	16,020	19,052	22,556	27,619	31,992

Source: Ministry of Finance, Ministry of Ecology and Natural Resources, National Bank of Moldova; 2005.

Notes:

1. For a classification of environmentally related revenues, see European Commission, Structures of the taxation systems in the European Union, 2000 edition.

2. Item 3 includes environmentally related grants from the Balance of Payments statistics as well as the amounts of grants and technical assistance recorded by the Ministry of Environment and Natural Resources.

Other financial sources

Non-tax revenue from grants for environmental purposes increased from the negligible levels of the 1990s and surpassed the revenues from emission charges by a growing margin. However, even in 2004, when such grants reached record levels, their size was dwarfed by environmental tax receipts (Table 5.1). The available information on commitments indicates that the amount of grants is likely to double in 2005. According to the *medium-term expenditure framework* (MTEF) for the period 2005-07, the gap between the costs of and the funding available for the realisation of the *Economic Growth and Poverty Reduction Strategy Paper* (EGPRSP) development goals is to be reduced by a more efficient use of available resources and increasing international assistance in the form of grants and preferential finance. The MTEF assumes that the Government would sign a new agreement with the International Monetary Fund (IMF) in the second half of 2005. This should then trigger significant inflows of grants, bilateral assistance and preferential loans from international financial institutions in subsequent years.[6]

---

[6] The government's previous agreement with the IMF was cancelled in 2003 and the Republic lost access to preferential IMF and World Bank financing facilities.

An improvement of the environment for doing business targeted by EGPRSP could stimulate Foreign Direct Investment (FDI) inflows into underinvested energy and water utilities, providing that legal as well as informal barriers to foreign ownership disappear. Furthermore, if the financial situation of the business sector keeps improving, firms could finance a sizeable share of environmental investment from retained earnings or new bank loans.

Effectiveness of economic instruments

If evaluated on the basis of revenue performance, the effectiveness of the market-based instruments used in the country improved considerably since the 1998 EPR. Excise taxes on imported fuel and cars, and the road use tax accounted for 72 per cent of environmental revenues in the years 1998-2004; this share averaged 77 per cent in 2003-04. The revenue performance would be even better if the inefficient exemption of imported tractors and trucks from excise taxes were abolished. The motor fuel taxes and levies resulted in relative price adjustments and better incentives (see section 5.3). In contrast, the revenue raised by emission charges remained marginal over the period 1998-2004. Moreover, the system of emission charges is too complex to be administered efficiently while the levels of charges are too low to induce abatement. The allocation of earmarked receipts to the environmental and road funds tends to cement input-oriented budgeting practices, resulting in suboptimal use of public funds.

The experience of advanced ECE economies and new EU States from East-Central Europe suggests that market-based instruments (eco-taxes and permit trading) can complement effectively the emission limits and technology standards to achieve fuller internalization of environmental externalities in the prices faced by producers and consumers. Unlike in the Republic of Moldova, emission charges are used only sparsely in critical sectors with a few key industrial facilities where they can be accurately measured; however, their levels are sufficiently high to induce an adoption of abatement technologies and cleaner technologies. Further, cost-reflective tariffs in energy and water utilities provide the basis for the financing of infrastructure investment programmes. This policy mix has resulted in a broadly successful decoupling of environmental pressures from GDP growth in advanced economies.[7] The benign decoupling trend has also materialised in the new EU States from East-Central Europe.

There is no *a priori* reason why this tried approach should not work in the Republic of Moldova, providing that it reforms the existing system of emission charges radically rather than in a piecemeal fashion. For instance, in Armenia the number of charges on pollutants was reduced from 78 in 1998 to 29 at present. Nevertheless, the high number of emission sources and limited monitoring capacity mean that the reformed system remains administratively cumbersome and inefficient. To improve the reform outcomes, it would be necessary to further reduce charges to a few priority pollutants while the rates ought to be significantly increased to provide incentives for firms to lower pollution. Moldovan authorities could study the Armenian experience and 'leapfrog' to a system of a few, less than 10, environmental charges on stationary sources that could be monitored reliably at low cost.

5.2   Environmental impact of pricing in key economic sectors

Getting the prices right

'Getting the prices right' through eco-taxes or emission trading permits is the most efficient way of implementing the "polluter pays" and "user pays" principles. While it remains questionable whether permit trading could work well at the current stage of transition, it should be feasible to approximate efficient prices with the aid of corrective eco-taxes and cost-based pricing rules set by an independent regulator. Eliminating price distortions would provide incentives for a desirable decoupling of environmental and economic trends but political economy constraints complicate the matter at hand in sensitive sectors such as transport, energy and municipal water services. Price developments in these sectors since the 1998 EPR are discussed in the following sections.

Transport

The transport sector generates significant externalities that are not fully reflected in prices, resulting in a growing share of road freight and passenger transport in economic activity. Road transport was boosted by liberalization that bypassed the rail system. Nevertheless, rail transport activity started to recover in 2002, especially in the area of freight services. The State-owned monopoly "Moldovan Rail" is in the process of implementing a 2003-07 action plan that should reduce the adverse environmental impact of its activity through a number of technical measures.[8] However, its financial situation remains fragile due to a defective pricing mechanism. The Government continues to impose on Moldovan Rail the obligation to transport passengers at affordable prices without adequate compensation from the budget so that freight services have to cross-subsidise passenger services.

Road transport accounted for 86 per cent of air emissions in 2003 and an even higher share in large cities.[9] The authorities addressed the air pollution problem by a number of regulations, including restrictions on imports of old cars and stricter norms for imported fuels that promoted the use of unleaded petrol and desulphurised diesel. Although imports of automobiles older than 10 years have been illegal since 1998 and private car ownership expanded rapidly since then, about one-half of the current stock of vehicles is older than 10 years. Used cars from CIS countries still account for some 80 per cent of imports. Over the period 1999-2003, the share of unleaded petrol in imports rose from 70 to 99 per cent (National Institute of Ecology, 2004). In addition to the regulatory measures, the

---

[7] Successful decoupling was associated with the availability of cost-effective 'end-of-pipe' technologies. The two areas where environmental pressures have continued to rise are municipal waste and greenhouse gases. See UNECE Economic Survey of Europe, 2003 http://www.unece.org/ead/pub/surv_032.htm.

[8] These measures include recycling of oils and technical water, and monitoring the toxicity of emissions. See National Institute of Ecology (2004), p. 21.

[9] See *ibid.*, p. 26.

authorities also used the economic instruments discussed above, including excise taxes and levies on imported fuel (which accounts for nearly 100 per cent of national consumption), excises on imported cars, and road-use charges on non-resident vehicles. They also continued to support local and inter-urban bus and rail passenger services through VAT exemptions. In addition to diesel fuel and petrol, the Republic of Moldova also taxes aviation fuel, being ahead of most ECE countries where it is tax exempt.

Pump prices of unleaded petrol averaged US$ 0.60 per litre in March 2005, exceeding somewhat the average price of the environmentally more harmful diesel fuel (US$ 0.57 per litre). The *ad quantum* excise tax rate on diesel fuel is considerably lower than on petrol. Contrariwise, the *ad valorem* excise tax rate on diesel (1 per cent) is twice as high as that on unleaded petrol so that large price increases of imported fuel in recent years saw the petrol-diesel price differential decline from 23 per cent in 2002 to about 5 per cent in the first quarter of 2005. This beneficial trend has resulted however from the rising world market oil prices rather than from the tax design. If the prices of imported petrol and diesel fuel were to fall, then the corresponding price differential would increase again.

A successful decoupling of transport-related environmental pressures from economic growth may well pose a significant challenge to policy makers, as the ongoing catch-up of per capita income is likely to induce strong demand for cars and better public road infrastructure. A clear preference for public infrastructure investment in roads rather than railways is apparent in the EGPRSP. Internalising further the transport-related external costs could influence positively the level and modal structure of transport activities, reducing environmental pressures. The experience of OECD countries suggests that price-correcting taxes based on the distance driven and environmental performance of vehicles can encourage modal shifts and provide the revenue needed for the development of infrastructure and environment-friendly modes.

Energy

The 1998 *Law on Energy* created a legal framework for cost-reflective energy pricing. This enabled the ANRE (Box 5.1) to set electricity and natural gas tariffs at levels that cover operating costs, maintenance and capital investment. The pricing situation remains unsatisfactory in the heat-supply sector. The ANRE regulates only one district heating company while local authorities have since 1999 controlled tariffs at the remaining two heat supply facilities. Only the ANRE-regulated company charges cost-reflective prices. A comparable district heating company whose tariffs are set by the Chisinau municipality charges almost 30 per cent less. Household tariffs for heat and hot water increased by less than consumer inflation

---

Box 5.1: National Agency for Energy Regulation

The National Agency for Energy Regulation (ANRE) regulates at present the electricity, natural gas, and technical water supply prices. It was established by the Government resolution no. 767 in 1997. Another Government resolution (no. 41/1998) enabled the ANRE to regulate electricity, heat and natural gas tariffs. Competences of the Agency were further strengthened by the 1998 Energy, Electricity and Gas Acts. In 1999, the Government transferred tariff-setting powers for two district heat supply facilities from the ANRE to the Chisinau municipality and other local authorities. The 2001 Act on the petroleum products market provided the Agency with the right to issue licences and price-setting rules in this sector. The Government authorised the ANRE to regulate technical water supply prices and provide non-binding price guidelines for other water services as of 2005.

The ANRE has a status of an independent legal entity but its regulators are appointed by the Government for a six-year period while the Agency's expenditures are provided by the State budget. In comparison to energy regulators in new EU States, the ANRE has a broader mandate that includes the petroleum products market and selected water services. The rationale for the Agency's involvement in these two sectors is provided by the need to protect interests of consumers in the uncompetitive market for petroleum products and by the difficulty of establishing cost-reflective water tariffs. Despite the full-cost pricing guidelines established by the ANRE, the electricity, heat and gas prices for industrial users and households have not changed since July 2003, April 2004 and March 2004 respectively. In contrast, the wholesale and final prices of petroleum products, which are subject to ANRE limits on profit margins, change frequently. This asymmetry in price setting may well reflect the Government's reluctance to adjust politically sensitive prices in line with rising costs of electricity imports and domestic generation.[10] The ANRE has argued that the sharp increase in the price of imported electricity in 2004 has been largely offset by currency appreciation; however, its own price formula does not incorporate exchange-rate effects so that the associated risks are borne by the firms regulated.

---

[10] For instance, the largest electricity generator in the capital (CHP-2) was authorised by ANRE to increase its supply price as of April 2005 while final prices charged by distributors remained fixed.

Table 5.2: Consumer price indices for selected services, 1998-2004

						Percentage changes (December over previous December)	
	1998	1999	2000	2001	2002	2003	2004
CPI	18.2	43.8	18.5	6.4	4.4	15.8	12.5
Electricity	23.7	68.9	24.0	8.2	2.5	10.2	0.0
Water supply and sewerage	26.7	133.6	47.9	36.0	39.6	17.8	23.3
Gas	29.6	160.1	12.6	-2.0	-0.3	19.2	8.9
Central heating	102.9	64.1	64.1	0.0	7.5	0.0	0.0
Hot water	26.0	74.2	50.3	64.1	0.0	0.0	0.0

Source: Department for Statistics and Sociology, 2005.

since 2001 and 2002 respectively. Moreover, heat and hot water supplied to households are subject to the zero VAT rate rather than the standard rate of 20 per cent. Effective tariffs continue to be below statutory rates due to poor payment discipline, partly because natural gas and heat are supplied as joint products so that it remains impossible to disconnect them separately. District heating systems could be privatised in principle but their substantial arrears on payments for deliveries of gas, electricity and water as well as the inconsistent regulatory environment make them unattractive to potential investors.

In contrast, an introduction of cost-based price setting in the electricity sector created preconditions for FDI. In 2000, privatisation of the sector started with sales of three regional power distributors to a Spanish utility, Union Fenosa.[10] Since then, the Government's privatisation efforts have been unsuccessful, reflecting to some extent the still opaque business environment and adverse perceptions resulting from protracted legal disputes with Union Fenosa and some other foreign investors from Western Europe in recent years. The State continues to own two regional electricity distributors and three thermal power plants. The post-privatisation developments in the country's electricity sector suggest that foreign ownership can improve efficiency noticeably. Although cross-subsidies from firms to households were eliminated, households do not pay VAT for electricity consequently their consumption is subsidized implicitly. A special tariff scheme for low-income households is offered by both State-owned electricity distributors but not by Union Fenosa. Table 5.2 shows that energy prices for households grew faster than inflation until 2001 while the opposite tendency prevailed in subsequent years.

Water services

Since the 1998 EPR the municipal water supply and sewerage sector continued to generate losses while cross-subsidies to households remained significant. Municipal water utilities are theoretically allowed to set tariffs on the basis of partial cost recovery, including operations and maintenance but not capital investment (that is to be provided by the local or central governments). In practice, the majority of local governments used their right to approve tariffs to keep them below operating cost and failed to provide finance for fixed investment, just like in many other transition countries. Cross-subsidies persist at different levels across the country, with firms and public-sector entities paying significantly more than households (Box 5.3).

According to detailed estimates of the Danish Environmental Protection Agency (2001), by the end of 1990s the water supply and sanitation tariffs paid by Moldovan households were comparatively high in relation to reported per capita income levels. However, real wages rose by 92 per cent between 1999 and 2004, outpacing significantly real GDP growth of 34 per cent over the same time period. Another important source of household income are remittances of Moldovans working abroad that expanded phenomenally over the same time period, reaching some US$ 600 million per annum (about one-quarter of GDP in 2004) according to the balance of payments (BOP) data. Given the large size of errors and omissions in the BOP data, independent experts estimate that the inflow of remittances may have reached close to US$ 1 billion last year (about one third of GDP). Even this would not make of Moldova into a high-income country but actual household incomes are most probably higher than the levels estimated with

---

[10] For a detailed analysis of Moldova's electricity sector, see Energy Charter Secretariat (2004).

Box 5.2: The continued plight of water utilities

The water services sector was decentralised in 2000 when State water supply enterprises were transformed into municipal water utilities. The 1999 *Law on Drinking Water* excluded the possibility of privatisation; nevertheless 3 utilities (including Apa Canal Chisinau, the country's largest water services provider) were transformed into joint-stock companies owned fully by local governments. One small municipality signed a concession agreement. The 2002 *Law on Municipal Services* allows for privatisation of water utilities, conflicting with the 1999 Law. Municipal water utilities are expected to operate as profit-maximising firms while water tariffs are set by local authorities. According to the available information, water utilities continue to provide services to households at prices that are below operating costs and four times below the average charges paid by firms and Government entities (six times in Chisinau). Moreover, the installed metering systems are unreliable and prone to tampering by households. Although the household tariffs kept increasing faster than inflation (Table 5.3) and water consumption declined significantly (by 47 per cent between 2000 and 2003), production costs grew more rapidly so that the number of loss-making water utilities increased from 80 per cent of the total in 2001 to 100 per cent in 2003 when the average operating cost of US$ 0.50 per m^3 exceeded the average tariff of US$ 0.45 (Association Moldova Apa Canal (AMAC), 2004). Uninterrupted water supply continues to be assured in three major cities while being available to residents of other municipalities for 9-12 hours per day only. Due to insufficient levels of maintenance and replacement investment, the share of sewage treated by municipal water utilities declined to 35 per cent by 2003 while the associated environmental pressures increased rapidly (Figure I.3). The service density has remained practically unchanged since late 1990s.

Adjustments of water tariffs have not been uniform. According to the energy regulator (ANRE), tariffs in some municipalities converge towards levels that are consistent with the recovery of operating costs while remaining frozen since 2001 in Chisinau, the capital city whose residents now enjoy, paradoxically, highest incomes as well as lowest water tariffs in the country. The decision of the Chisinau municipal government to keep the tariffs fixed violated provisions of the 1997 agreement with the EBRD that provided a State-guaranteed loan of US$ 30 million for partial rehabilitation of water supply and sewerage infrastructure. At present, the Chisinau tariffs are as follows: Households pay 2.62 lei per m^3 (water supply and sanitation) while firms and public institutions pay 14.90 lei per m^3 for the same services and 9.82 lei per m^3 of technical water. According to ANRE calculations, the average cost-based tariff for water supply and sanitation is 8.63 lei per m^3 (close to the level implied by the EBRD contract) while that for technical water amounts to 4.46 lei per m^3. A growing number of firms in the Chisinau area (around 400 by April 2005) reacted to the excessive tariffs by terminating contracts with the local water utility and finding alternative sources of water supply (artesian wells).

Attempts to resolve the critical situation in the municipal water services sector included a Parliamentary resolution of 18 July 2003 that instructed the Government to submit to the legislature a document specifying economic instruments that would implement the "polluter-pays" principle in the water services sector. In the event, the task for developing cost-based tariffs was shifted to the energy regulator as of 2005. However, the ANRE methodology is binding only for technical water tariffs. This is likely to improve somewhat the financial position of industrial users while producing the opposite effect on the balance sheet of water utilities, undermining further their already precarious financial situation. Although the cumulated overdue receivables of municipal water utilities continue to exceed their rising payment arrears to employees as well as suppliers of energy and other material inputs, this notional 'surplus' (equivalent to some US$ seven million in 2003) is unlikely to materialise due to poor contract enforcement.

---

the aid of statistical surveys.[11] The affordability problem could be mitigated by appropriate (i.e. pro-poor) targeting of social assistance benefits, e.g. by a more comprehensive use of means testing. Only two benefits are means tested while the allocation of social benefits remains inequitable.

In 2002, the top quintile of the population received some 6½ per cent of social benefits while the upper quintile got 46 per cent. Meanwhile, low-income households are not targeted well by tax expenditure. It is dominated by VAT breaks pertaining to food, energy and water services that are significant in terms of the revenue foregone but benefit disproportionately the more wealthy who spend considerably more on these items than the poor. Cost-reflective pricing would help to make the water sector feasible but could provide no more than perhaps one half of the investment necessary to meet the relevant MDGs. The analysis presented in the financing strategy for the water services sector (Danish Environmental Protection Agency, 2001) demonstrates that even if households pay tariffs that cover operating costs, significant outside financing would have to be raised in order to achieve sustainable improvement in the quality and extent of water supply and sewerage services. It also shows that the cost of implementing the extremely stringent wastewater effluent standards of Republic of Moldova's post-Soviet legislation would be prohibitive. However, prospects for external financing have deteriorated due to the conflict with the EBRD on Chisinau water services

---

[11.] Although the household surveys conform to international methodology, the respondents' lack of trust in the confidentiality of information is bound to result in under-reporting of incomes. Experts at the Department of Statistics are aware of the problem but do not attempt to adjust the income levels reported by households.

rehabilitation project[12]. To address the problem of excessive effluent standards, the MENR prepared a draft Government resolution to relax them to less demanding levels of the EU wastewater treatment directive. However, the Ministry's initiative has not been successful and the old standards remain in place.

Assessment

Since 1998, significant advances towards cost-reflective pricing took place in the road transport and energy sectors. A more modest progress was achieved in the municipal water services sector. The incentive effect of the motor fuel taxation could be improved further by simplifying the current system of two separate (*ad quantum* and *ad valorem*) excise taxes. The authorities might want to accomplish this by abolishing the *ad valorem* fuel tax and adjusting the *ad quantum* tax as follows. First, the *ad quantum* rates should be differentiated according to the environmental characteristics of different types of fuel (such as the benzene, lead and sulphur content) and increased to the levels that are sufficient to compensate for the revenue loss from abolishing the *ad valorem* tax. This would result in a revenue-neutral outcome with the price of diesel exceeding that of petrol at the pump.[13] Second, given the considerable technical and political obstacles to setting up an optimal user-pay (toll) system for roads, it would be expedient to increase gradually the *ad quantum* excise tax rates until pump prices of diesel and petrol incorporate the full cost of emissions and road use.[14] Consequently, the current road-use tax on non-residents should be phased out. Further, excise taxes on imported vehicles should be also levied on tractors and trucks at levels that reflect the relevant externalities. In rail transport, the Government should subsidise passenger services from the budget, allowing Moldovan Rail to create an independent and financially viable personal transport division. This would enable the freight division to generate profits that could be used for overdue investment and create a more level playing field for modal competition.

In the energy and water sectors, further price adjustments should proceed on the basis of cost-reflective methodology elaborated by the energy

regulator while extending its competence to price regulation of all municipal water services. To make this approach feasible, the independence of the ANRE ought to be enhanced by shifting the responsibility for appointing regulators from the Government to Parliament and allowing the Agency to finance its activities through charges levied on regulated firms. Unless prices in the energy and water services sectors can be brought in line with costs without undue political interference, there will be significant efficiency losses and environmental damages associated with suboptimal resource allocation as well as negative signals to prospective investors from abroad.

In the critical water supply and wastewater treatment sector, the entry of foreign investors could provide additional financing for the long overdue investment. Therefore, the authorities should amend the 1999 *Law on Drinking Water* to allow for entry of private firms into the water services sector. This would be consistent with the water sector priorities of the EGPRSP that include a creation of the legal and regulatory environment conducive to participation of private capital in the operation of water utilities. Equity issues related to the abolition of subsidies ought to be addressed by well-targeted transfers to the poor with the aid of means-tested benefits.

5.3   Environmental funds

Introduction

Since the previous EPR, the system of environmental funds was improved by the 1998 amendment to the *Law on environmental protection* that created a two-tier structure, consisting of the National Environmental Fund (NEF) and four Local Environmental Funds (LEFs). A new regulatory framework for the funds was provided by two Government resolutions in the final quarter of 1998. The MENR controls the NEF while the Ministry's four territorial agencies control LEFs. Neither the NEF nor LEFs have an independent legal status, constituting extra-budgetary parts of general government that are financed with the aid of earmarked revenues. Their finances have been outlined since 1999 in the annex to the State budget and approved annually by Parliament in the budget act; however, they are scrutinised less intensely than regular programmes.

The operational capacity of the NEF has considerably improved since 1998, initially with some transfers of know-how from the Polish environmental fund. Since 2001, the selection and implementation of the projects funded by the NEF

---

[12] EBRD website (http://www.ebrd.com) and *Ekonomicheskoe obozrenie*, 15 April 2005, p. 6.

[13] In the majority of ECE countries automotive diesel fuel is cheaper than petrol, reflecting the influence of powerful road transport lobbies.

[14] Pump prices of petrol and diesel are close to one-half of the EU average. This implies that the transport fuel taxes are below the combined level of emission and road-user charges.

Table 5.3: Roles and responsibilities of the National Environmental Fund: A comparison with international good practices

Role/Responsibility	National Fund	International good practice
Internal policies:		
Preparation	Secretariat, Ministry of Ecology and Natural Resources	Management unit, external consultants
Approval	*Administrative Council*	*Supervisory Body*
Establishing spending priorities	*Administrative Council*	*Supervisory Body*
Budget:		
Preparation	Ministry of Ecology and Natural Resources	Management unit
Approval	Administrative Council, Parliament	Supervisory Body
Internal documents and external reports:		
Preparation	Ministry of Ecology and Natural Resources	Management unit
Approval	*Administrative Council*	*Supervisory Body*
External communications	Ministry of Ecology and Natural Resources	Fund Director, Fund's Communications Department
Project cycle management:		
Identification	Secretariat, Ministry of Ecology and Natural Resources	Management unit
Processing applications	*Secretariat*	*Management unit*
Appraisal	Ministry of Ecology and Natural Resources, consultants	Management unit, consultants
Ranking of projects	None	Management unit
Selection of projects	Administrative Council	Fund recommends, Supervisory Body decides
Contract preparation	*Secretariat*	*Management unit*
Signing of contracts	Administrative Council (all members)	Fund Director, Chair of Supervisory Body, Minister (in cases of strategic
Implementation/ monitoring of projects	Secretariat tracks expenditures, Territorial Ecological Agencies check projects	Management unit
Financial activities:		
Approval of expenditures (signing of banking documents and invoices)	Chair of Administrative Council (Minister)	Fund Director, Chair of Supervisory Body
Financial monitoring and record-keeping	Secretariat, Accounting Department in the Ministry of Ecology and Natural Resources	Fund's Financial Department

Source: OECD EAP, 2002.
Note: Where the role and responsibilities of the National Fund correspond to international good practices, the text is in italics.

is subject to the regulations approved by the MENR. The 2002 OECD EAP Performance Review of the National Fund and the Chisinau Municipal Fund concluded that both conformed only partly to good practices.[15] The 2002 review recommended a clear separation of the supervision and management functions of environmental funds. Another key recommendation was to increase the professional staff working for the NEF secretariat. It was also recommended that the NEF status and mode of operating be modernised in line with good practices of some central European funds. These recommendations remain to be implemented while the management practices still fall short of the standards recommended (Table 5.3).

---

[15] These practices are described in so-called St. Petersburg guidelines (OECD, 1995).

Revenues of national and local funds

Total revenue of the National Environmental Fund increased significantly since 1998, reaching however only 0.1 per cent of GDP by 2004 when it peaked. In dollar terms, annual current revenue of the NEF (total revenue minus carryover from the previous year) jumped from some US$ 70,000 in 1998 to about US$ 2 million in 2004 (Table 5.4). Since 1999, the earmarked *ad valorem* levy on imported fuel provided about two thirds of current revenue. Growth of revenue from this source has remained strong in recent years, reflecting the impact of economic recovery and rising import prices of oil products. The levy on environmentally harmful products accounted for almost one quarter of NEF current revenue in the period 2003-04.

Table 5.4: Revenues and expenditures of the National Environmental Fund, 1998-2004

million lei

	1998	1999	2000	2001	2002	2003	2004
Total revenues	**0.4**	**3.9**	**7.7**	**7.9**	**11.0**	**20.6**	**34.8**
Carryover at the beginning of the year	0.0	0.1	0.1	0.6	2.0	4.3	10.3
Transfers from local funds	0.1	0.0	0.0	0.0	0.9	1.5	1.1
Levy on imported fuel	0.3	3.8	7.3	7.2	8.0	10.7	18.2
Levy on pollution-intensive production	..	..	..	..	..	4.0	5.1
Other income	..	..	0.2	..	0.0	0.0	0.0
Total expenditures	**0.3**	**3.8**	**7.1**	**5.6**	**6.6**	**10.3**	**23.3**
Environmental priority projects	..	2.5	3.6	3.5	3.0	7.4	19.5
Research	..	0.2	0.6	0.6	1.1	1.0	1.0
Environmental information systems	0.2	0.3	0.4	0.2	0.4	0.3	0.6
Salary bonuses for government experts	0.1	0.3	0.4	0.6	0.5	0.4	0.4
International co-operation	..	0.1	0.5	0.2	0.5	0.5	0.7
Emergency clean-up	..	0.2	1.4	0.3	0.9	0.5	0.9
Grants to non-government organisations	..	0.2	0.2	0.2	0.2	0.2	0.2
Balance	**0.1**	**0.1**	**0.6**	**2.3**	**4.4**	**10.3**	**11.5**
Memorandum items:							
Projects in the water services sector, million lei	..	..	1.6	0.9	1.6	4.4	10.3
As a share of current revenue, per cent	..	..	21.1	12.4	17.9	27.1	42.1
NEF current revenues in US$ thousand	70.4	359.6	612.2	561.2	656.5	1169.1	1956.3
NEF expenditures in US$ thousand	55.6	361.9	572.6	434.1	485.3	741.0	1864.0
Average exchange rate (lei/US$)	5.4	10.5	12.4	12.9	13.6	13.9	12.5

Source: Ministry of Ecology and Natural Resources, 2005.

Transfers from the local funds were comparatively low until 2000 but picked up in the following years, averaging some 7 per cent of NEF current revenues in subsequent years. Revenue growth of the local funds in recent years reflects the rising number of firms that pay pollution charges (Table 5.5).

Expenditures and policy priorities

The NEF is required by its own statute to spend at least 70 per cent of its budget on projects that are related to national environmental priorities. This requirement has been fulfilled since 2003. Given the importance of the municipal water sector that figures prominently among Moldovan MDGs and in the EGPRSP process, the percentage of the NEF current revenue spent on water supply and wastewater treatment projects can be used to evaluate the overall effectiveness of NEF expenditure management. In fact, spending on such projects accounted for 21 per cent of the NEF current revenue in 2000 falling to 12 per cent in 2001 but then rising steadily to 42 per cent in 2004 (Table 5.4). The number of all projects financed by the NEF increased considerably, reaching 245 in

---

Box 5.3: Environmental Millennium Development Goals and the Economic Growth Strategy

Republic of Moldova's Millennium Development Goals pertaining to the natural environment include intermediate and long-term targets in four areas. (1) The percentage of population with access to safe water supply should grow from 38.5 in 2002 to 47.7 in 2006, 57 in 2010 and 68.5 in 2015. (2) The percentage of population with access to sewage treatment should rise to 56 in 2006, 73.3 in 2010 and 90 in 2015. (3) The area covered by forests should increase to 11 per cent of the country's territory by 2006 and 13.2 per cent by 2015. (4) Protected areas should expand to 2.1 per cent of the territory in 2006 and 2.4 per cent in 2015. These Millennium Development Goals are transposed into the corresponding priorities of the 2004 *Economic Growth and Poverty Reduction Strategy Paper*. However, the financing of such priority actions appears to be largely unsecured. For instance, only one fifth of the expenditure necessary to achieve the intermediate objectives for water supply and sanitation in the year 2006 was budgeted in the Government's medium term expenditure framework.

The EGPRSP elaboration started in 1999 when GDP bottomed out and poverty peaked. In the context of widespread poverty, it is not surprising that the three EGPRSP priority sectors chosen are education, healthcare and social protection. Their enhanced status has been reflected in the setting up of corresponding output-oriented budget programmes with assured long-term financing (Ministry of Finance, 2004). The Ministry of Economy and Trade that also monitors the fulfilment of key objectives plays the co-ordinating role in the EGPRSP implementation. No results of such monitoring are available to the Secretariat at the time of writing the 2005 EPR.

2004.[16] Although outside experts are regularly consulted, they are not required to use uniform methodology and quantitative indicators, consequently projects cannot be ranked properly. The actual selection continues to be done *ad hoc* rather than on the basis of comparable indicators that would channel spending to projects with highest net benefits. This is hardly surprising because the NEF Secretariat continues to include only one professional despite the 2002 OECD EAP Performance Review's recommendation that two additional staff members should be hired to make efficient decision-making possible. LEF project spending averaged about 15 per cent of their current revenue in the early 2000s. Like the NEF, local funds have no capacity to rank projects on the basis of efficiency.

The NEF sectoral spending pattern in the late 1990s was dominated by transfers to the general government (State administration, municipalities, schools, universities and hospitals) that accounted for 60 per cent of total expenditure in 1998 and 2000. A significant part of this spending (salary supplements, school supplies, etc.) would normally

---

[16] The number of the projects financed by local environmental funds also increased over time, reaching 100 by 2004. See also chapter 6.

be financed directly by the responsible line Ministries rather than through an extra-budgetary fund but the economic situation was exceptionally adverse at the time. NEF disbursements financed current expenditure only in 1998; however, the funding of investment projects rose to 8 per cent of total expenditure in 1999 and to 22 per cent in 2000. Over the period 2000-03, the NEF was unable to disburse a growing proportion of its current revenues. In 2004, its spending increased considerably, reaching 95 per cent of current receipts. However, the cumulated carryover amount kept growing and reached 44 per cent of annual spending (Table 5.5). The comparable figure for the LEF system rose to 38 per cent in 2004.

Assessment

Since the 1998 EPR, the revenue situation of environmental funds improved remarkably. The improvement on the expenditure management side was less pronounced; however, the number of projects supported by environmental funds increased noticeably. The available indicators imply that following a setback in 2001, the NEF focus on the support of environmental priority projects improved in subsequent years.

Table 5.5: Revenues and expenditures of local funds, 1998-2004

million lei

	1998	1999	2000	2001	2002	2003	2004
Total revenues	**0.3**	**0.4**	**1.9**	**2.2**	**4.1**	**5.5**	**6.2**
Carryover from the previous year	0.0	0.1	0.2	0.3	0.7	0.7	1.7
Charges and fines	0.3	0.3	1.7	1.9	3.4	4.8	4.5
Air pollution charges	0.2	0.2	0.4	0.8	1.4	1.3	1.4
Water pollution charges	0.1	0.1	0.4	0.7	1.6	2.7	2.2
Transport related charges	0.0	0.0	0.0	0.0	0.0	0.1	0.2
Waste charges	0.0	0.0	0.1	0.0	0.1	0.5	0.3
Non-compliance fines and damage compensation	0.0	0.0	0.0	0.2	0.3	0.2	0.4
Other fines	0.0	0.0	0.8	0.2	0.0	0.0	0.0
Total expenditures	**0.1**	**0.2**	**1.6**	**1.6**	**3.3**	**4.2**	**5.4**
Transfers to the National Environmental Fund	0.1	0.0	0.0	0.0	0.9	1.5	1.1
Local environmental projects	..	..	0.1	0.2	0.6	1.0	0.7
Nature conservation	..	..	0.1	0.2	0.4	0.7	0.5
Waste disposal	..	..	..	..	..	..	0.3
Sanitary measures	..	..	0.3	0.1	0.1	0.1	0.6
Environmental education	..	..		0.1	0.2	0.2	0.2
Emergency clean-up	..	..	0.8	0.1	..	0.1	0.1
Equipment of environmental authorities	..	..	0.3	0.8	0.2	0.6	1.2
Salary bonuses of environmental inspectors	..	..	..	0.1	0.2	0.1	0.3
Other	..	0.2	..	..	0.7	..	0.4
Balance	**0.2**	**0.2**	**0.3**	**0.6**	**0.7**	**1.3**	**0.9**
Memorandum items:							
Number of registered project applications	..	..	..	..	81	120	146
Number of projects financed by local funds	..	..	..	..	69	82	100
Number of firms subject to environmental charges	..	..	..	..	1453	1482	1700
Number of firms paying the charges	..	..	..	..	1093	1263	1651

Source: Ministry of Ecology and Natural Resources, 2005.

The current system of monitoring by the environmental inspectorates and evaluation of projects by external experts needs to be further enhanced to conform to good practices. The authorities have failed to implement key OECD EAP 2002 recommendations that would improve the managerial system and operational efficiency of the NEF in line with good practices. The large and rising carryover amounts in the NEF and LEF budgets coexist with the shortage of financing for environmental projects in priority areas. This implies that further improvements to the process of allocating the environmental revenue by the funds are of utmost importance.

The remarkable political stabilisation and financial consolidation in the post-1999 period of sustained economic growth provide the necessary precondition for qualitative improvements in the functioning of environmental funds. The country's fiscal reforms in recent years entailed the growing use of medium-term budgeting. This framework could provide the revenue stability desired for environmental programmes, especially if the Government adopts environment as a key priority in the EGPRSP context. The NEF provisions for the rollover of unspent funds could be easily transformed into similar provisions within a multi-year budgetary process. Both national and local environmental fund operations should be reviewed periodically to assure that the implementation of measurable targets proceeds well. In case of repeated non-performance, the authorities ought to pursue priority environmental goals with the aid of new output-oriented programmes.

5.4   Conclusions and recommendations

Since the 1998 EPR the authorities improved the environmental policy-making process, introduced new taxes on environmentally harmful products and applied the existing legislation more effectively. This progress was reflected in the partial decoupling of economic and environmental trends, especially during the 1998-99 recession. Real GDP growth continued uninterruptedly since 2000 while environmental pressures associated with air pollution by road transport and water pollution by insufficiently treated sewage increased. These contradictory trends reflect the peculiar nature of consumption-driven growth and institutional shortcomings, including inconsistent legislation and an opaque business environment that discourage stronger participation of foreign investors and international financial institutions in economic restructuring, particularly in the critical water services sector.

Aside from more effective regulation and law enforcement, further reforms of the existing market-based instruments are needed than hitherto for a more comprehensive decoupling of environmental pressures from economic growth. Abolishing numerous tax exemptions could further enhance the solid revenue performance of environmentally related taxes. In contrast, the system of emission charges remains inefficient while playing a negligible revenue role. The incentive function of environmental taxes could be improved by a closer alignment with international best practice, particularly in the area of excises on motor fuel. The incentives associated with pollution charges could be enhanced considerably by imposing them only on a few major sources with easily measurable emissions. Whereas significant advances towards cost-reflective pricing took place in transport and energy sectors, the pricing of water services remains less satisfactory. Given the unwillingness of many municipalities to authorise operating cost-recovery tariffs, the prices of water supply and sewerage services ought to be set by the independent energy regulatory agency. In order to reduce the political interference in price setting, the autonomy of the agency could be enhanced by reducing the Government's role in the appointment of regulators and allowing the regulatory agency to finance itself rather than relying on the state budget.

Last but not least, the chapter concludes that both the financing and the functioning of environmental funds have improved considerably since 1998. Nevertheless, the managerial system and operational efficiency still fall short of good international benchmarks. The rapidly rising carryover amounts in budgets of the national and local funds imply that an introduction of output-oriented budgeting could improve the allocation of the available financial resources to priority environmental projects, providing that environmental objectives of the nation's Economic Growth and Poverty Reduction Strategy Paper become real priorities rather than empty declarations.

The recommendations listed below should be implemented to consolidate the Republic of Moldova's significant achievements of integrating environmental costs into economic decision-making and to assure further progress.

Recommendation 5.1:
The Ministry of Finance in cooperation with the Ministry of Economy and Trade, and the Ministry of Ecology and Natural Resources, should assure the realization of the Republic of Moldova's

Millennium Development Goals objectives pertaining to sustainable development. The environment should be made a priority area in both the Government's medium-term budget framework and related annual budgets to assure financing of the key environmental actions specified in the national Economic Growth and Poverty Reduction Strategy Paper.

Recommendation 5.2:
The Ministry of Finance and the Ministry of Ecology and Natural Resources should increase the "ad quantum" excise tax rates on petrol and diesel while differentiating them according to environmental characteristics with the objective to

significantly increase the price of diesel versus petrol to reflect its environmental impact. At the same time, they should phase out the "ad valorem" excises on imported fuel.

Recommendation 5.3:
The Ministry of Ecology and Natural Resources and the Ministry of Finance should streamline the system of pollution charges, introducing a small number (less than ten) on measurable priority pollutants and eliminating all other charges. It should set the rates of the new charges at levels that will influence the polluters' behaviour significantly.

Chapter 6

EXPENDITURES FOR ENVIRONMENTAL PROTECTION

6.1   Introduction

The overall situation with expenditures for environmental protection in the Republic of Moldova since the first Environmental Performance Review in 1998 has improved. The main reason for this improvement was the increase in available funding that corresponded to high rates of economic growth and the resulting increase in revenues of the State Budget. The National Environmental Fund (NEF) and Local Environmental Funds (LEFs) became the main sources of environment-related expenditures beginning in 2000. The country has been working on improving its legal, policy and institutional framework in the area of environmental expenditures; however, its efforts were sometimes inconsistent. For example, recommendations of the *Performance Review of the National Environmental Fund of Moldova* and the *Chisinau Municipal Environmental Fund* done by OECD EAP Task Force Secretariat and the Danish Environmental Protection Agency in 2002 have been implemented only partially.

6.2   Decision-making framework

Legal framework

The 1993 *Law on Environmental Protection* provides the main framework for environmental expenditures. The Law identifies all major actors (central governmental bodies, municipal authorities, private persons, and legal entities, including enterprises) in environmental protection and specifies their responsibilities. To fulfill their responsibilities in environmental protection the above-mentioned subjects must allocate certain resources for environmental expenditures. However, in most cases this obligation is implicit in the Law. The Law explicitly specifies that the Government should only provide funding for the activities of the central governmental agency on natural resources and environmental protection,

currently the Ministry of Ecology and Natural Resources (MENR), and its units, as well as related scientific research. The Law also specifically lists the expenditures from extra-budgetary environmental funds. It lists activities that can be exclusively funded from environmental funds, defines in general terms the procedure for allocating finances for these activities and sets the minimum limit of 70 per cent of revenues of Local Environmental Funds to be used on prevention and mitigation of environmental pollution.

The annual *Law on State Budget* contains a line item on expenditures on environmental protection and hydrometeorology with a sub-item on environmental protection. Separately, the Law contains an annex on NEF expenditures (extra-budgetary).

The 1998 *Regulation on Environmental Funds* makes operational provisions of the *Law on Environmental Protection* on distribution of revenues of the National and Local Environmental Funds, types of expenditures that can be made, the mechanism for the management of funds and decision-making for selection of projects for funding. The weakest part of this regulation is the lack of clear rules for the assessment of effectiveness and the efficiency of implementation of approved projects.

The 2004 *Law on Investments in Entrepreneurial Activity* is intended to attract, encourage and protect investments in the Republic of Moldova. It envisions the creation of stable and equal legal, social and economic conditions for investment activity, ensuring equal guarantees for foreign and domestic investors and eliminating obstacles to investment activity. Investments must comply with national legislation, including environmental legislation. However, the Law does not have direct references to environment-related investments. Based on former practices it means that authorities responsible for making decisions regarding a particular investment may overlook certain environmental issues for the sake of purely economic benefits.

The 1998 *Law on Payments for Environmental Pollution* identifies pollution fees and charges as the main source of revenue for environmental funds.

Institutional framework

The MENR is responsible for developing and implementing the policy on expenditures for environmental protection. This includes developing strategies and programmes in the area of environmental protection and contributing to sectoral strategies and programmes developed by other ministries. The identification of sources of financing is an important part of this process. Funding for programmes approved by the Government is included in the State Budget. However, in many cases this funding is insufficient and makes implementation slow or impossible. The MENR and the four Territorial (zonal) Ecological Agencies (TEAs) are responsible for assessing and selecting projects submitted for funding to the NEF and LEFs. The Minister of Ecology and Natural Resources is the Chair of the Administrative Council of the National Environmental Fund that approves projects for funding. The LEF Administrative Council is chaired by the TEA director.

Other ministries and governmental agencies, in particular Ministry of Economy and Trade, Ministry of Finance, Ministry of Industry and Infrastructure, Ministry of Agriculture and Food Industry, and Ministry of Transport and Roads Management, cooperate with the MENR on funding programmes and projects with an environmental component. These are included in the State Budget. However, the sectoral ministries do not monitor environment-related expenditures separately.

After the governmental reorganization in 2005, the Agency for Regional Development is responsible for the implementation of the investment policy, in particular, investments in water supply and wastewater disposal for communal services. .

Local authorities (at the level of communes, municipalities and *rayons*) include environment-related expenditures in their annual budgets. However, these expenditures are limited. In most cases, local authorities rely on funding from the NEF and LEF for environmental projects.

Additionally, communal services enterprises, most of which are on municipal property, are responsible for expenses related to maintenance and development of infrastructure for public water supply, wastewater collection and treatment, and waste disposal.

Specialized funds that are not part of the governmental structure may also be a source of environmental financing. An example of this is Moldova Social Investment Fund (MSIF) whose mandate is not directly related to environment but a number of projects financed by it have an environmental component.

Enterprises, both private and state-owned, are also a source of environmental expenditures. Reporting by enterprises of operating expenses and capital investments for environmental purposes is discussed in Section 6.3.

Institutional arrangements related to foreign sources of environmental expenditures are discussed in Section 6.4.

Policy framework

Since 1998 the Republic of Moldova has developed a large number of national strategies, concepts, programmes and action plans in the area of environment protection (see Chapter 1 on Legal and policy-making framework and Annex III), including sectoral ones. They outline measures and activities consistent with the aim of improving the state of the environment in the country. The implementation of these activities is often hampered by insufficient funding, even though every national programme approved by the Government is supposed to have adequate financing from the State Budget. Among the reasons for this situation is the lack of a thorough estimate of the resources required to implement these policies, other Government priorities in allocating scarce public funds, and problems with raising funds for specific activities from international donors. The resulting effect is that the country has many policy documents with lofty environmental goals but in practice they lag behind in implementation. By the time a previous programme had expired, a new one in the same area would often contain many of the same objectives and measures because they had not been implemented previously. The sheer number of national policy documents related to environmental protection (over 20 in the last five years) also makes them difficult to monitor.

One of the important policy documents with an environmental component is the *2002 Investment Strategy*. Among the major strategic goals are: to expand investments intended for environmental protection, to increase the effectiveness and efficiency of use of natural resources, to reduce the negative environmental impact of economic activity, and to increase the volume of investments into innovative technologies. The Action Plan attached to the strategy lists related actions and responsible governmental agencies. However, a lack of clear measurable targets makes it impossible to estimate how well the Investment Strategy has been implemented.

The Government is trying to change its approach in developing and adopting new programmes and strategies. The notion that the funds should be secured or at least gaps in funding should be clearly indicated was applied at the time of developing and adopting the *Economic Growth and Poverty Reduction Strategy Paper* (2004-2006) (EGPRSP). Environmental protection and sustainable use of natural resources is one of the 17 policy areas included in the EGPRSP. The distinctive features of the EGPRSP are the:

- clear ranking of actions in order of priority by sector;

- provision of indicative costing figures for actions;

- linkage to the Ministry of Finance *Medium Term Expenditure Framework* (2005-2007) (MTEF); and

- clear distinction between actions with funding secured under MTEF and those for which financing is not secured and could be considered by development partners.

The EGPRSP admits that it is not realistic to expect that large flows of additional resources could be generated from either domestic or foreign sources. It also recognizes that new activities to support the EGPRSP will need to be financed partially by restructuring existing budgets and using savings from reduced costs on new priorities. The thorough and balanced analysis of the situation presents a good basis for seeking additional financing and can serve as an example to follow when developing new or revising existing policy documents.

To secure funding from outside sources in support of EGPRSP priorities, the Government adopted the *National Programme of Technical Assistance* for 2005-2006 (March 2005). The environmental protection priorities and projects are reflected under policy areas such as water supply and wastewater disposal and environmental protection and sustainable use of natural resources that correspond with EGPRSP areas. However, not all priorities have corresponding projects and therefore lack funding targets for some priorities, particularly in water management. Policies regarding the achievement of Moldova's Millennium Development Goals related to environment are also reflected in the EGPRSP. See Box 5.1 (Chapter 5 on Economic instruments and environmental funds) and Chapter 4 on Implementation of international agreements and commitments.

6.3   Domestic financial resources

State financing

Table 6.1 presents data on state financing for environmental protection and rational use of natural resources. The *Expenditures for environmental protection and hydrometeorology* are included in the annual *Law on State Budget*. Expenditures for hydrometeorology are excluded from Table 6.1. The expenditures for environmental protection are allocated exclusively to the functioning of the central and local governmental environmental protection authorities and payment of their salaries. The only exception is the contribution of the Republic of Moldova to projects, for which the rest of the funding is provided by international donors. An additional major source of State funding is the National Environmental Fund and Local Environmental Funds. Total expenditures of the consolidated state budget are included in the Table 6.1.

In 1998-2004, revenues and expenditures of consolidated national budget showed a stable growing trend. The overall trend in environmental expenditures was also growing, both in absolute and relative terms. As a percentage of consolidated budget expenditures, they increased from 0.12 per cent in 1998 to 0.41 per cent in 2004. In terms of the structure of these expenditures, most of the state funding in recent years has come from environmental funds, of which the National Environmental Fund is the main source. The funding from the State Budget for specific projects has no discernible trend, as it depends on case-by-case agreements.

Table 6.1: State expenditures on environmental protection and rational use of natural resources, million lei*

Year	1998	1999	2000	2001	2002	2003	2004
Environmental protection	3.0	2.1	2.1	2.1	3.2	3.3	3.7
Expenditures not included in other groups (for specific projects)			0.1	0.2	3.1	1.6	0.4
Administration authorities	0.4	0.3	2.1	2.1	2.1	2.6	2.8
Subtotal	3.4	2.4	4.3	4.4	8.4	7.5	6.9
Percentage of consolidated budget expenditures	0.1	0.1	0.1	0.1	0.2	0.1	0.1
Expenditures of the National Environmental Fund	0.3	3.8	7.1	5.8	6.6	10.3	23.3
Expenditures of the Local Environmental Funds		0.2	1.6	1.6	2.4	2.7	4.3
Total state environmental expenditures (including NEF and LEF expenditures)	3.7	6.4	13.0	11.8	17.4	20.5	34.5
Percentage of consolidated budget expenditures	0.1	0.2	0.3	0.3	0.3	0.3	0.5
Expenditures of the consolidated national budget	3,027	3,495	4,269	4,326	5,194	6,178	7,387

Source: Annual Law on State Budget (1998-2004), Statistical Yearbook 2004, Ministry of Ecology and Natural Resources (2005).
*Note: In current prices.

**Note: To avoid double counting, transfers from the Local Environmental Funds to the National Environmental Fund are not included in the Expenditures of the Local Environmental Funds.

The share of environmental expenditures as a percentage of national budget remains low. However, certain spending on environmentally related purposes under the responsibility of other ministries, such as capital investments for water supply and wastewater treatment, are not included in the expenditures on environmental protection (see also sub-sections *Other domestic sources of environmental expenditures* and *Methodology for data collection and accounting*). The current structure of the budget and the fact that the ministries often do not have a unit on environmental protection and do not monitor environmental expenditures separately makes it impossible to analyze or account for these expenditures.

Expenditures of the environmental funds

In 2000 the National Environmental Fund and the four Local Environmental Funds became the main and increasing source of environmental financing. The expenditures of the NEF and LEFs and their breakdown are presented in Tables 5.4 and 5.5 (see Chapter 5 on Economic instruments and environmental funds). In 2002, the OECD EAP Task Force Secretariat and the Danish Environmental Protection Agency conducted a Performance Review of the National Environmental Fund of Moldova and the Chisinau Municipal Environmental Fund, which provided a comprehensive analysis and suggested recommendations to improve its management. The analysis of the current situation does not show a significant difference in the way the funds function compared to the period when the Review was

completed, in particular in the procedure of identifying projects, providing financing for them and assessing their effectiveness.

The National Environmental Fund continues to be managed by a one-person secretariat within MENR, whose responsibilities include reviewing the project proposals for funding before submitting them to the Administrative Council for approval. In practice, the projects are sent on an ad hoc basis for review to experts, usually MENR staff, according to their area of expertise. There are no clear guidelines for experts to give a positive or negative assessment of the project proposal, no clear set of priorities for funding, and no formal mechanism for ranking projects in terms of potential benefits, cost-effectiveness or other criteria. The application form provides only basic information on a proposed project and its requested budget. Beneficiaries are required to submit a report (substantive and financial) after the project has been completed but the assessments of the work accomplished are rarely done, primarily because the Fund does not have the resources and capacity to do this (financial audits of companies and organizations are conducted regularly by the Accounting Chamber but they do not and cannot comprehensively cover the substantive part of a project). The process is similar for the four Local Environmental Funds, of which the Chisinau Municipal Environmental Fund is the largest.

The steady growth in environmental fund revenues allowed for an increase in disbursements from the funds. However, as may be seen from Tables 5.4 and 5.5, the growth in the level of expenditures is lagging behind the increase in fund balances. In the case of the Republic of Moldova the fact that expenditures are consistently lower than revenues means that there is a bottleneck at the NEF and LEF management, and that their capacity to identify environmental activities that should be funded is insufficient. Another worrisome trend is that only about lei 200,000 per year since 1999 has been transferred as grants to NGOs, showing a less cooperative attitude from environmental authorities towards NGOs in recent years. As a result fewer NGOs are submitting project proposals and getting them approved.

Methodology for data collection and accounting

The methodology for data collection and accounting of environmental expenditures was developed in the Soviet era and there have been no major changes in it since. Some modifications have been made, but only in the structure of statistical reports and tables. The existing system does not cover environmental expenditures comprehensively and makes it difficult to classify such environmentally-related expenditures as expenditures for the management of natural resources, expenditures on prevention and decrease of environmental pollution, and expenditures on environmental monitoring. It also does not effectively distinguish between the expenditures from a company or organization's own sources and from transfers from environmental funds for a particular project.

Capital investments in environmental protection, operating expenses and expenditures for capital repairs by companies and organizations are reported to the Department of Statistics and Sociology (as of April 2005 – National Bureau of Statistics) after approval by Territorial Environmental Agencies. Operating expenses include areas of protection and rational use of water resources, air protection, the protection of land from production and consumption waste pollution, and land reclamation. Operating expenses in forestry are not reported as environment protection expenditures, although capital investments for protection and rational use of forests are included in the reporting. The number of reporting companies has been increasing in the reviewed period. In 2003 the number of companies reporting on operating expenses and expenditures for capital repairs was 1,005 compared to 622 in 2000. According to MENR staff this increase mainly represents better

compliance with reporting requirements but may also reflect the actual increase in environmental spending by more companies. The total number of companies that submit some forms of statistical reporting in the Republic of Moldova is around 30,000 but most of them are too small to have environmental expenditures and/or report them.

Domestic sources of environmental expenditures

Companies of various forms of ownership are another major source of domestic environmental expenditures. The current accounting system for environmental protection expenditures includes the following:

- Capital investments;

- Operating expenses; and

- Expenditures for capital repairs of main production facilities intended for environmental protection.

Total environmental expenditures (including operating expenses in forestry) are presented in Table 6.2. In nominal terms, they have been steadily increasing and reached lei 226.2 million in 2003. However, as a percentage of GDP, they were in fact decreasing until 2002, and this trend was reversed only in 2003. This may serve as an indicator that environmental protection has not been an increasing priority for the country in recent years. This is also confirmed by the fact that while environmentally related tax revenue in the country was over 3 percent of GDP for most of the reviewed period (see Chapter 5 on Economic instruments and environmental funds) environmentally related expenditures were in the range of 0.8-1.0 percent of GDP. The former figure is comparable to that of OECD countries, while the latter is significantly lower.

The increase in the share of capital investments, which grew from 4.5 per cent in 1998 to 9 per cent in 2002 and reached 18 per cent in 2003, is a positive trend. The structure of capital investments by purpose of investment (Table 6.3) has also changed. Until 2002, over 70 per cent of these were directed at the use and protection of land resources and under 30 per cent at the use and protection of water resources. In 2003 the proportion was reversed, but this does not indicate a change of

Table 6.2: Total environmental expenditures by type of expenditure and as percentage of GDP in current prices, million lei

Year	1998	1999	2000	2001	2002	2003
Capital investments in environmental protection	4.3	5.9	6.1	12.2	14.8	41.0
Operating expenses for environmental protection (excluding forestry)	60.7	76.2	85.5	96.1	93.9	102.1
Capital repairs of environmental protection equipment	5.8	4.1	4.1	4.2	5.4	5.8
Operating expenses in forestry	23.2	29.0	40.1	46.0	60.7	77.2
Total environmental expenditures	94.0	115.2	135.8	158.5	174.8	226.2
GDP	9,122	12,321	16,020	19,052	22,556	27,619
Total environmental expenditures as percentage of GDP, %	1.0	0.9	0.8	0.8	0.8	0.8

Source: Department of Statistics and Sociology, 2004.

priority areas in environmental protection for the country. The sharp increase in capital investments for water protection is explained by a one-time investment of approximately lei 27 million by the Chisinau municipal water utility Apa Canal. Investments for other purposes were marginal. As a source of financing of capital investments, state financing remains predominant. A relatively high figure for 2003 for financing from other sources is also explained by the above-mentioned investment of Apa Canal, a joint stock company fully owned by the Chisinau municipality.

Table 6.4 presents operating expenses for environmental protection (excluding forestry). These expenses were overwhelmingly directed at the protection and rational use of water resources.

In the period under review, environmental expenditures in the Republic of Moldova remained low both in absolute terms and as a share of GDP, although there was a modest nominal growth. In per capita terms, they also remained extremely low. Nominal per capita environmental expenditures (in lei) grew consistently from about 25 lei per capita in 1998 to over 60 lei per capita in 2003. However, when converted into US$, they plunged from just under US$ 5 per capita in 1998 to US$ 3 per capita in 1999 and 2000 (following a sharp devaluation of Moldovan currency in late 1998), and then grew

to US$ 4.5 per capita in 2003. The National Environmental Fund and Local Environmental Funds became the main sources of funding for environmental activities. It remains unclear to what extent the projects financed by the NEF and LEFs reflect the most urgent needs in environmental protection and how effective and efficient the implementation of these projects is. The insufficient capacity of the secretariats of the national and local funds also results in a consistent significant excess of revenues over expenditures and thus the underutilization of available resources for environmental protection.

6.4   Use of foreign financial resources in environmental expenditures

In the reviewed period, the Government did not include environmental protection as one of the main priority areas when requesting international technical assistance. As a consequence, country assistance strategies or their equivalents of international financial institutions (International Monetary Fund (IMF), World Bank, and European Bank for Reconstruction and Development (EBRD)), international organizations (European Commission and United Nations Development Programme (UNDP)) and bilateral donors that are active in the country do not list environmental protection as a priority.

Table 6.3: Capital investments in environmental protection and rational use of natural resource by purpose of investment in current prices, million lei

Year	1998	1999	2000	2001	2002	2003
Total	4.289	5.893	6.060	12.151	14.788	40.974
For protection and rational use of water resources	1.461	1.719	1.315	3.257	4.248	28.705
For protection and rational use of land resources	2.816	4.161	4.723	8.894	10.540	12.687
For air protection	..	0.007	..	..	..	..
For protection of forestry resources and reproduction of wildlife	0.000	..	..	..	..	..
For treatment and disposal of toxic waste	0.007	0.006	0.022	..	..	..
From State (national) and local budgets	3.617	4.578	5.118	10.284	11.636	13.494
From other sources	0.673	1.315	0.942	1.968	3.152	27.480

Source: Department of Statistics and Sociology, 2004.

Table 6.4: Operating expenses for environmental protection in current prices*, million lei

	1998	1999	2000	2001	2002	2003
Total	66.5	80.3	89.6	100.3	99.3	108.0
For protection and rational use of water resources	51.5	65.4	66.9	74.2	76.3	79.4
For air protection	5.3	5.3	9.1	10.1	6.6	8.3
For protection of land from pollution by waste of production and consumption	2.0	1.9	2.7	2.7	3.7	5.0
For land reclamation	0.3	0.6	0.6	0.7	1.9	0.1
Other	7.4	7.1	10.3	12.6	10.8	15.2

Source: Department of Statistics and Sociology, 2004.

*Note: including capital repairs of environmental protection equipment; excluding operating investments in forestry.

Neither the MENR nor the Ministry of Economy and Trade collect and analyze information on the amount of foreign financial resources used for environmental protection (regarding the procedure of receiving foreigntechnical assistance see Chapter 4 on Implementation of international agreements and commitments). In certain cases, projects and programmes with a different primary purpose (e.g. social support or infrastructure development) contain an environmental component or could be viewed as environmentally related, but singling out the "environmental share" is difficult. The country also benefits from a number of regional environmental programmes; however data on the amount of the country-specific funding are not always available.

The United Nations Development Programme has been supporting environmental activities in the Republic of Moldova since 1998 and included environment as a cross-cutting issue in its Development Assistance Framework for 2001-2006 (see Chapter 4 on Implementation of international agreements and commitments). Funding for UNDP projects is provided in the form of grants. The purpose of most of these projects is for the country to implement global and regional conventions and the source of their funding is the Global Environmental Facility (GEF). The total UNDP funding for environmental projects in 1998-2002 was approximately US$ 0.55 million (all projects are completed), approved funding for 2003-2006 is about US$ 0.48 million (projects are under implementation). Average annual funding from the UNDP can be estimated at approximately US$ 0.11 million.

The United Nations Environment Programme (UNEP) has been providing financial support in the period 1999-2006 for two projects (both with GEF funding) related to the implementation of global conventions with the total amount of approximately US$ 0.3 million.

World Bank has recently become one of the most important partners for the Republic of Moldova as a foreign source of environmental financing. World Bank provides financing in the form of loans (some as International Development Association (IDA) credits) and grants (mostly for projects with GEF funding). Until early 2000 environmental financing from the World Bank was limited. Among the completed projects, only Moldova Social Investment Fund Project (discussed below) and Energy Project (1996-2001) had an environmental component. The situation began changing in 2002, and several of the projects in the current portfolio can be classified as directly related to environment. The largest among them are the

- Agricultural Pollution Control Project (2004-2009, grant amount US$ 4.95 million: total project cost US$ 10.74 million);

- Soil Conservation Project (started 2004, grant amount US$ 5.18 million: total project cost US$ 14.42 million); and

- Pilot Water Supply and Sanitation Project (2003-2007, IDA loan amount US$ 12 million: total project cost US$ 14 million).

Funding for several smaller environmental projects (for the period 2002-2006) is provided in the form of grants for a total amount of approximately US$ 1.75 million. Several more major projects with GEF funding (Energy conservation and emissions reduction, Environmental infrastructure, and Sustainable persistent organic pollutants stockpiles management) are in the pipeline. Some other projects contain an environmental component. Of particular interest for this review is the Moldova Social Investment Fund (MSIF) Project (see Box 6.1). Certain MSIF experiences, particularly on Fund management and on selection of micro-projects (which have to be requested by communities), could be used to improve the effectiveness and efficiency of the environmental funds in Moldova.

Box 6.1: Moldova Social Investment Fund

Moldova Social Investment Fund has been established within the framework of the World Bank Social Investment Fund Project. The objective of MSIF is to improve living conditions of the rural population, especially the poor. MSIF funds demand-driven micro-projects (funding ceiling is US$ 75,000, average funding – US$ 48,000) through providing grants to communities. Proposals for micro-project funding may be generated by communities or by community level organizations, as well as local NGOs and local government.

MSIF typology includes projects on Sanitation and Environmental Infrastructure. They include: a) Rehabilitation and expansion of local/community level sewage networks, and pumping stations; b) Disposal and treatment of solid and liquid waste in the communities; c) Environmental improvement and rehabilitation through tree planting and a clean up effort; and d) Erosion control activities (tree planting, terracing, drainage canals) on public lands. These projects represent a relatively small share of the total portfolio (6-7 per cent), which is understandable because social and economic infrastructure is often seen as higher priority in poor communities. MSIF has recently introduced internal reporting on the environmental component of all projects. A selective survey of completed projects and analysis of the current portfolio estimates that the total share of the environmental component in all projects is close to 30 per cent.

The Project is in its second phase. The first Social Investment Fund (SIF) Project started in 1999 and was financed by a World Bank loan (on IDA terms) to the Government of the Republic of Moldova in the amount of US$ 15 million. It was completed in May 2004. In 2004 SIF II Project began, this time with US$ 20 million World Bank loan. In addition, MSIF has attracted over US$ 7 million as grants from international donors, including Germany, Japan, the Netherlands, Sweden, United Kingdom and United States. In SIF II, small towns (population under 20 thousand) are also eligible for funding (US$ 125,000 ceiling). In addition to the fact that all micro-projects are demand-driven (the community has to decide what are its priority needs), another distinctive feature of MSIF is that a grant to a community for any project is provided at a maximum of 85 per cent of total project budget. At least 15 per cent of the project budget has to be contributed by the community. The combination of these approaches appears to have been working very well to bring a sense of ownership of the results of the project to the community and ensures the sustainability of completed projects. In the first five years 479 projects in 415 villages have been completed.

Source: Moldova Social Investment Fund website http://www.msif.md; interview with MSIF staff.

It is not among the country's priorities for the European Bank for Reconstruction and Development to provide financial resources for environmental protection. Of the 31 active and completed EBRD projects, only one – Chisinau Water Services Rehabilitation Project (approved in 1997) – can be considered environmentally related. For this project, a US$ 22.8 million loan was provided to the Chisinau water utility Apa Canal to finance investments in improving the drinking water supply and wastewater treatment. Certain conditions of the loan, in particular the increase in service fees for clients, were not fulfilled by Apa Canal, and there are currently no plans for a similar project in the near future. All EBRD operations in the country are subject to the Bank's Environmental Procedures.

Financial assistance from the European Union is directed through its European Commission Tacis Programme. One of the major Tacis activities is promotion of environmental protection and management of natural resources. However the Country Strategy Papers and the National Indicative Programmes for 2000-2003, 2002-2006 and the latest for 2004-2006 mention environmental issues but do not focus on them specifically. Most of the funding for environmental protection is

provided in the form of grants to the Regional Environmental Centre-Moldova (REC-Moldova). Some funding is available through regional and cross-border programmes, in which the specific Moldova share is difficult to distinguish. REC-Moldova was established in 1998 according to the agreement between the Government of Moldova and the European Commission. From 1999 to 2003 (latest available data at the time of the mission), REC-Moldova received approximately € 2 million and its expenditures in the same period were around € 1.5 million. REC-Moldova currently is the only organization through which grants are provided to environmental NGOs for small projects within the framework of the NGO Support Programme. In addition, REC has been administering the Environmental Policy Programme, the Local Initiative Programme and the Information and Communication Programme, and implementing a number of environmental projects.

Denmark was the main bilateral donor in the environmental area in the reviewed period. It has financed a number of investment projects related to improved water management, water supply, and wastewater treatment in several localities in the country. Total funding provided by Denmark from 2001 to 2005 was over US$ 3.6 million. For all projects, a substantial local co-financing is a prerequisite.

The contribution of financial resources from other countries to the Republic of Moldova (including Germany, Japan, the Netherlands, Norway, Sweden, United Kingdom, and United States) for activities related to environmental protection was relatively small, as they focused on other priority areas.

The above analysis shows that the Government has not made environmental protection one of its priorities when applying for external funding. Main areas for the use of external financial resources for environmental purposes in the reviewed period were water supply and wastewater management, environmental protection in agriculture and land management, and implementation of international conventions ratified by the Republic of Moldova. In general, this reflects the environmental priorities of the country and corresponds with the priority areas in environmental expenditures from domestic sources (with the exception of the implementation of conventions where external financing dominated). If EBRD and World Bank projects, whose primary purpose was other than environmental protection, are excluded, the total amount of external financial resources in the country for the period 1998-2003 could be estimated at around US$ 7 million compared to the domestic expenditures of around US$ 81 million. While this corresponds to the trends in other countries in the Eastern Europe, Caucasus and Central Asia (EECCA) region where domestic environmental expenditures are significantly higher than foreign ones, the Republic of Moldova has the potential to attract more external sources of financing. A step in the right direction is the National Programme of Technical Assistance for 2005-2006, which was developed in support of the EGPRSP (2004-2006). The projects outlined in the Programme corresponding to EGPRSP priority areas have a better chance of attracting attention from potential donors.

6.5   Conclusions and recommendations

Since the first Environmental Performance Review the Republic of Moldova has improved the situation with expenditures for environmental protection. This progress, however, was inconsistent. The country has developed new and modified existing laws and elaborated numerous strategies, concepts, programmes and action plans aimed at improving environmental management and the state of the environment. Unfortunately, many of the policy documents do not contain clear measurable targets and do not indicate the necessary financial resources to achieve their objectives. In some cases, when the funding requirements are identified, the Government has other priorities and does not provide all the necessary funding, which hampers implementation of the programmes. The 2004-2006 *Economic Growth and Poverty Reduction Strategy Paper* lists environmental protection as a priority and sets clear funding requirements for it. It may serve as a good practice example when elaborating new or revising existing policy documents.

State funding remained prevalent in the country's environmental expenditures. Environmental funds (National Environmental Fund and four Local Environmental Funds) became the main source of funding in 2000 due to a substantial increase in their revenues. Unfortunately, insufficient capacity and sub-optimal management practices make their performance less effective than it could be. Environmental expenditures have increased in the reviewed period but remain low in absolute and per capita terms, as well as share of GDP compared not only to OECD countries but also to many other countries with economies in transition. At the same time environmental fund revenues continue to be significantly higher than their expenditures, which means that even existing resources are not fully utilized. Assessment of implementation of projects funded by the environmental funds is usually based on self-reporting by the grantee. The actual evaluation of their effectiveness and impact is rarely done.

Total expenditures for environmental protection may also be underestimated because of the existing methodology for data collection and reporting. Certain expenditures that may be considered environmentally related, such as for developing water supply and wastewater disposal systems are not included in this reporting. Sectoral ministries and other governmental agencies may have expenditures that include an environmental component but they do not account for them separately. Neither the National Bureau of Statistics (former Department of Statistics and Sociology), which collects and processes statistical reporting forms on environmental expenditures, nor the Ministry of Ecology and Natural Resources attempts to identify all environmentally related expenditures.

Foreign financial resources constituted a relatively small share of all environmental expenditures (less than 10 per cent). Environmental protection has not become one of the main areas for which international funding is requested. The Ministry of Ecology and Natural Resources does not have comprehensive information on financing for environmental protection from international sources and capacity to analyze their utilization. This limits the potential to attract additional resources as well as to coordinate the use of available resources with domestic funding on similar activities. The positive experience of some projects, such as Moldova Social Investment Fund, could be applied to such domestic institutions involved in expenditures for environmental protection as National and Local Environmental Funds.

Recommendation 6.1:
The Ministry of Ecology and Natural Resources should identify the priority environmental issues among the already approved national strategies, programmes and action plans. These issues should be consistent with the relevant priorities of the 2004-2006 Economic Growth and Poverty Reduction Strategy Paper, the EECCA Environmental Partnership Strategy and the EU-Moldova Action. The Ministry should set clear measurable targets with related actions for their realization and provide justification of necessary financial resources. The Ministry, in cooperation with other relevant ministries and other governmental agencies, should identify sources of financing that may include the State budget, the National Environmental Fund and external funding by development partners.

Recommendation 6.2:
The Ministry of Ecology and Natural Resources should restructure the management of the National and Local Environmental Funds in line with the recommendations of the 2002 Performance Review of the funds. In particular:

- The *capacity of the secretariats of the funds should be expanded to assure proper assessment of the project proposals and evaluation of the quality of implemented projects. The expanded secretariats should be funded from the revenues of the funds.*

- *The Administrative Councils of the environmental funds should set guidelines for appraisal of project proposals, ranking in accordance with priority and expected environmental benefits. The Administrative Councils should ensure that the funds' available resources are utilized to the maximum possible extent, and that annual expenditures of the funds are equal or close to annual revenues; and*

- *The Ministry should consider introducing best practices of the Moldova Social Investment Fund into the management of the National and Local Environmental Funds and into the procedure of selecting projects for funding.*

- *The Administrative Councils of the environmental funds should increase the capacity of the National Environmental Fund to prepare project proposals for external funding, coordinate fundraising activities, and monitor project implementation.*

Recommendation 6.3:
The National Bureau of Statistics, in cooperation with the Ministry of Ecology and Natural Resources and other relevant governmental agencies, should review the current system and methodology of defining and accounting for environmentally related expenditures in the context of best international practices. The improved accountability might serve as a basis for the Ministry to solicit the Government to increase the level of state environmental funding.

PART III: INTEGRATION OF ENVIRONMENTAL CONCERNS INTO ECONOMIC SECTORS AND PROMOTION OF SUSTAINABLE DEVELOPMENT

ENVIRONMENTAL MANAGEMENT IN AGRICULTURE AND FORESTRY [1]

7.1   Background

Current context for agricultural production

The landscape of the Republic of Moldova is shaped by agriculture. Chernozems, which are typical types of steppe soil, cover almost three quarters of total land area. These fertile soils are the main natural resource of the country and give a good basis for crop production. As much as 75 per cent of total land is used in agriculture and 73 per cent of agricultural land is arable land (Table 7.1). Almost nothing of the natural steppe vegetation remains and forests cover only 10 per cent of the land, a low figure in the European perspective.

As much as 59 per cent of the population live in the countryside and the rural population relies heavily on subsistence production. Nearly all families have access to a small household plot (0.1-0.3 ha) in addition to field plots and most of the households own their own livestock.

The agricultural sector employs 24.2 per cent of the labour force and is still important in terms of its contribution to GDP, which was 19.2 per cent in 2003. Processing of agricultural products is also an important sector. Food and vegetable products accounted for 51 per cent of export in 2003. Production and processing of agricultural products in the informal sector may add more than 50 per cent to the official figures in real terms.

All agricultural land was privatized in the 1990s, with the notable exception of pasture, four collective farms and some land and animal production units for agricultural research and breeding. There are more than 1.3 million landowners. Most of the processing industry has also been privatized. From an environmental perspective there are aspects of the privatization that are causing problems. For example, parts of the forest protection belts are now private. Also water protection zones are often in private hands.

Environmental objectives were as a rule not taken into account during the land privatization.

The privatization process resulted in an average landholding of 1.4 ha, often divided into two or more plots. It is in many cases not possible to use these small plots efficiently. Production of crops such as grain and sugar beet is dependent on mechanization, and therefore can be performed only on plots of bigger size. In addition, the new farmers and owners lack experience, technical skills and finances to develop their production successfully. The restricted access to credits is an additional bottleneck.

While 40 per cent of the land is under farms of one to ten ha, larger farms of 10-200 ha cover another 40 per cent. About 20 per cent of the land is under farms larger than 200 ha. The larger farms are set up in different ways: it is common that one or a few farmers lease land from many landowners in a village, paying them for the lease but also giving the same landowners opportunities to work on the farm. In other cases the landowners have established cooperatives.

A land market is developing and agricultural land as well as production is being consolidated. More than half the land is leased and the number of land transactions is increasing rapidly. But the lack of alternatives for employment and economic opportunities in rural areas is a negative factor for an overstaffed sector. Foreign investments in Moldovan agriculture and the food processing industry is limited as a result of restrictions and the hesitance of investors.

Agricultural production

Agricultural production in 2003 was 15% less than in 1996. It is now less than half of its 1989-91 level and has been decreasing continuously since that time. Production of high-value crops such as fruits and vegetables, dependent on inputs such as irrigation, fertilizers and pesticides, has decreased substantially. Declining use of costly inputs and the disintegration of management, production and land

---

[1] The present chapter reviews progress since the 1998 UNECE Environmental Performance Review on Moldova

structures, and migration of skilled workers have halved labour productivity. Many of those involved in agriculture have a negative view on the privatization and how it was managed and on the present situation in Moldovan agriculture. Nevertheless, since a few years ago agricultural production has been stabilizing and shows signs of recovery due to the consolidation of production, the development of farmers' skills and the improved marketing of agricultural products.

While agricultural production is generally not very profitable, the situation in the processing industry seems to be better. Winemaking is a major branch of the Moldovan economy and contributes significantly to the State budget. Along with grapes, the main fruit and vegetable crops processed in the country for export are tomatoes and apples. Processing of tobacco is also important.

There is considerable scope to increase fruit and vegetable production, and there are some developments of production, marketing efforts and in the processing industry. Eastern European countries are still by far the main markets for Moldovan processed products such as wine. It is a challenge to get access to and develop markets in the West.

Plant production

With a favourable climate and fertile soils, a wide range of crops can be cultivated. The most frequently grown crops are presently winter wheat, maize for grain, sugar beet and sunflowers (Table 7.1). Yields are generally low, and with the still low inputs of fertilizers, pesticides and irrigation that were already prevalent in 1996 (Figures 7.3 and 7.4), production is very dependent on external factors such as winter climate and precipitation during the growth season.

The application of balanced crop rotations has decreased, which is detrimental for soil fertility. Row crops such as sunflower and maize cover an increasing proportion of arable land, while the proportion of forage crops such as perennial grasses or lucerne has decreased. Production of vegetables, tobacco, fruit and grapes, and key high-value crops is still important but has decreased.

Table 7.1: Statistics on agriculture and land, 2003-2004

Total land (ha, 2004)	**3,384,600**
Agricultural land (ha, 2004)	**2,528,300**
of which arable land (ha, 2004)	1,845,400
of which perennial crops (ha, 2004)	298,000
including orchards	134,800
including vineyards	153,000
of which pasture (ha, 2004)	374,100
of which irrigated agricultural land (ha, 2004)	300,000
Sown area (ha, 2003)	**1,484,000**
Cereals and leguminous crops (ha, 2003)	896,600
of which wheat (ha, 2003)	202,000
of which maize for grain (ha, 2003)	553,500
Industrial crops (ha, 2003)	417,100
of which sunflower (ha, 2003)	352,400
of which sugar beet (ha, 2003)	37,800
of which soja (ha, 2003)	1,200
Potatoes, vegetables, melons and gourds (ha, 2003)	6,100
Forage crops (ha, 2003)	5,400
Animal production	
Cattle (1000 heads, 2004)	**373**
of which cows (1000 heads, 2004)	256
cows, milk yield (litres per year, 2003)	2,493
sheep (1000 heads 2004)	817
goats (1000 heads, 2004)	121
pigs (1000 heads, 2004)	446
poultry (1000 heads, 2004)	15,756

Source: Statistical Yearbook of the Republic of Moldova 2004.

Animal production

With the collapse of the previous economic system, production and consumption of meat and dairy products have changed significantly. The cattle, pig and some of the large poultry farms have been dismantled and individual households now own most of the livestock. Agricultural companies own less than 10 per cent of animals. The 1-2 cows held by the individual households are very important for the subsistence of families. In each village there are milk collection sites for small producers.

After a sharp decrease in the 1990s, animal production is now stabilizing, and productivity somewhat increasing. Profitability of animal production is improving resulting in investments in pork production, for example. Poultry production has been increasing significantly for some time. A continued consolidation of animal production is a likely perspective for the near future.

However, animal production is still inefficient. Insufficient quantities of feed, low emphasis on genetic improvement and low quality of veterinary services are a few reasons. The low status of the collective pastures owned and managed by municipalities is an additional important reason that will be explored below.

Forests

Presently 10.7 per cent of the land is covered by forest (Table 7.2), which is a very low figure for Europe[2]. Pressure from a long history of intensive agriculture and the exploitation of valuable forests are reasons for this low acreage of forests. Oak species and acacia are the dominating species, covering 40 per cent and 36 per cent of the forest area respectively. Beech, hornbeam and poplar are other common species. The ambition is to increase afforested land to 15 per cent and significant steps have been made during the past few years towards this. The percentage of afforestation differs between different parts of the country: 8.1 per cent in the north, 14.2 per cent in the centre and 7.7 per cent in the south. The Codrii Hills in the central parts have the highest concentration of forest. The acreage of rapidly growing but also rapidly aging species such as acacia is increasing.

Forests are an important stabilizing factor for the environment. They should be managed well and the acreage of forests should be increased in order to preserve biodiversity and to stabilize land threatened by erosion and landslides. Cutting of forests may be done for maintenance, regeneration, clearing and sanitary purposes. Clear-cutting of more than two ha is prohibited. Forests make up 95 per cent of protected areas, the total area being 63,000 ha. Forest protection belts planted to combat soil erosion covered, at its maximum, 20,000 ha in 1970. This acreage has declined significantly due to illegal cutting for firewood.

The responsibility for forestry management has remained essentially the same since the first Environmental Performance Review (EPR). The Agency for Forestry "Moldsilva" manages 89 per cent of the forest fund[3], the municipalities nine per cent and other authorities two per cent. Only 400 ha of forests are private. None of the forests in the Republic of Moldova are certified. Tree and secondary products from the forests are important for the official as well as unofficial economy.

The total volume of wood in Moldovan forests has been estimated to be 45.3 million m³. Forest cuttings increased from 374,000 to 439,000 m³ between 1997 and 2003. Annually 3,000-4,000 ha of forest is being regenerated. As a result of declining protection efforts the problem of forest pests and diseases has increased significantly over the past ten years.

7.2   Environmental concerns in agriculture

Soil fertility

Fertile agricultural land is the country's main natural resource, a fact that is reflected in national policies and programmes. Soil fertility is a complex condition and depends on several factors such as humus content and level of plant nutrients. An institute under the State Agency of Land Relations and Cadastre maps the soil quality of agricultural land, and a recent study reports that the applied average soil quality indicator has decreased over the past 30 years from 70 to 65 per cent. Among the reasons for this degradation are the drastic decrease of fertilizer use and the decreasing humus content of soils, which is difficult to stabilize. Instances of humus loss are seen in the increased cultivation of row crops[4]; sunflower cultivation has increased from 13 to 24 per cent of sown areas and maize for grain increased from 22 to 37 per cent between

---

[2] The European average of land covered by forest is 29 per cent.

[3] Forest protection zones on agricultural land, along roads, rivers and lakes are not included in the forest fund.

[4] Cultivation of row crops implies frequent cultivation of the soil during the growing period, which leads to humus loss.

1996 and 2003. The application of balanced crop rotations that include perennial grasses or lucerne has decreased, which is a negative factor for soil protection.

There are different ways to supply organic matter to the soil. The addition of manure, sludge from wastewater treatments and organic waste from different types of production are different options. Increasing the acreage of forage crops, in particular perennial grasses, is another. In spite of considerable opportunities, none of these options are broadly used in Moldovan agriculture presently. The acreage of forage crops has decreased and the use of organic fertilizers has decreased by as much as 94 per cent since 1996.

Erosion

Soil erosion is a significant problem. It is a widespread natural phenomenon that is due to the relief and climate of the country, and the very high proportion of arable land is an amplifying factor. Poor land management practices, such as overgrazing, excessive cuttings of forests, shrubs and bushes, and crop cultivation on steep slopes accelerate erosion. Water erosion is a major problem on the two million ha of agricultural land that is situated on hillsides. Pollution and sedimentation in rivers, lakes and water reservoirs are secondary effects of erosion.

In total 859,000 ha are eroded: 504,000 ha slightly, 253,000 ha moderately and 102,000 ha severely eroded. The acreage of eroded land has increased significantly over the past 35 years (See Figure 7.1). The most severely affected districts are Cahul, Calarasi, Hincesti and Ungheni. According to the National Environmental Action Plan (NEAP) of 1995, total annual economic losses from erosion were estimated at lei 2,432 million (US$ 197 million). Areas affected by landslides are also increasing, and annual economic losses are estimated at lei 83 million (US$ 6.7 million). The highest risk areas for landslides are found in the region between Chisinau and Balti.

Land privatization is also modifying the scope of erosion. Privatization resulted in a decrease in the size of fields, a factor usually favourable to a reduction of erosion. The practice of cultivating the soil across the slopes and applying optimal crop rotations, both of which are anti-erosion measures, are less applied than earlier. The distribution of long and narrow land plots along slopes during privatization is a negative factor, as the new owner has no other opportunity than to cultivate the land along the slopes, thus accelerating water erosion in particular. The current increasing trend for the cultivation of row crops and the destruction of forest protection belts along fields are also negative. It is claimed that the less than careful planning in the construction of roads and houses, which prevails at the moment, is contributing to a negative trend with regard to erosion.

Pastures and about 11 per cent of total land have not been privatized and are owned and managed by the municipalities. Livestock owners pay a fee for the collective use of pastures. The low production of forage crops and bad pasture management by the municipalities result in over-intensive grazing of pastures. Over-grazing is common and sometimes leads to erosion. Efforts are needed to protect this land from further deterioration and to improve yields.

Erosion is still a major concern, and it is likely that the problem is worsening. However, no systematic monitoring has been made to follow the evolution of the process.

Biodiversity of crop plants and domestic animals, genetically modified organisms

With a long history of intensive agriculture on most of the Moldovan territory, biodiversity and landscapes are thoroughly shaped by man. There are very few if any remaining old and domestic plant varieties and animal species in agricultural production. There are still, however, among crops such as fruits, nuts and grapevines, important collections that are threatened by extinction due to the limited resources available to scientific institutions to perform their conservation work. Biodiversity has been impoverished due to these intensive agricultural practices and the continuity of ecosystems that is vital for biodiversity conservation has ceased to exist. Re-establishing an ecological network in the country is an important objective that is not sufficiently taken into account in agricultural and forestry policies.

Figure 7.1: Soil erosion, 1965-2003

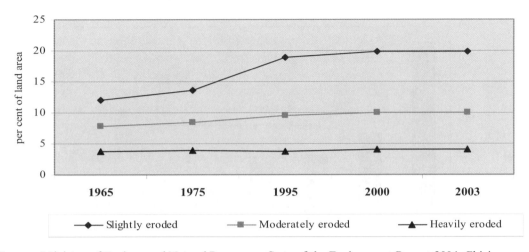

Source: Ministry of Ecology and Natural Resources. State of the Environment Report 2004. Chisinau, 2004.

In 2002-2004 a Global Environmental Facility (GEF) project developed a national biosafety framework for the Republic of Moldova to protect it from the uncontrolled introduction of genetically modified species, but the implementation of it has been weak. It appears that new genetically modified varieties of, for example, soybeans remain undetected.

Irrigation and drainage

Acreage that is possible to irrigate has decreased drastically from a maximum of 193,000 ha in 1990 to only 16,200 ha in 2004 and it is mainly in large farms. In 2005 this will increase to at least 24,000 ha. In parallel, water use for irrigation has shrunk and has continued to do so since 1996 (see Figure 7.2). The collapse of irrigation is an immediate result of the land reform which caused a total disorganization in the use and ownership of all heavy equipments and infrastructure, leaving them without maintenance. In the renewed development of irrigation, smaller-scale irrigation is applied. 124,000 ha are included in a rehabilitation programme to be concluded in 2008.

Larger farms or water user associations sign agreements on irrigation with the State Water Concern "Apele Moldovei". One bottleneck is that the development of water users' associations is slow. Costs for water deliveries are calculated for each agreement, with energy costs being subsidised by the State.

Irrigation and drainage are important for efficient agriculture, but can also have negative effects on

the environment and soil fertility. Erosion, salination and soil compaction are important negative effects of large-scale irrigation. 13,000 ha of previously irrigated land have been damaged due to salination and compaction. Monitoring of irrigated land, a responsibility of "Apele Moldovei", is presently not performed.

The previously drained riverbanks used for intensive agriculture are now left increasingly flooded as it is too expensive to pump the drained water. Only 17 per cent of the drained riverbanks are presently suitable for agriculture. The planned establishment of the national park "Lower Dniester" will build to some extent on this recovery of the wetlands.

At the moment, irrigation is not a significant environmental problem, as it is not seriously tapping into water resources. It is likely that irrigation will increase again, and water and soil management problems may arise as a result.

Use of pesticides and fertilizers

Pesticide use has been high, especially in wine, fruit and vegetable production, leading to soil and water contamination. But since the 1980s the annual use of pesticides has decreased from more than 38,000 tonnes to 3,100 tonnes in 1996 and 2,700 tonnes in 2004, a level which has been stable since 2000 (Figure 7.3). Although quantities are low, it is likely that the lack of training and information for farmers makes their selection and proper use of pesticides questionable.

Figure 7.2: Water used for irrigation, 1996-2003

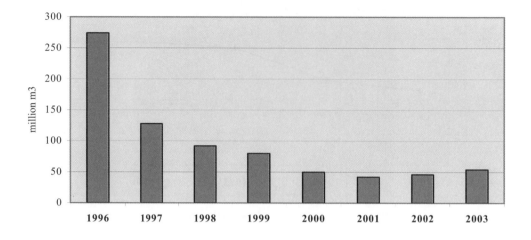

Source : Department for Statistic and Sociology. Statistical Yearbook of the Republic of Moldova 2004.

Only low levels of organochlorinated and other compounds have been found in soils and food products in recent investigations. One important exception is residues of copper-based fungicides in vineyards where the soil locally is literally poisoned.

In the past few years, the Republic of Moldova has been a pioneer in using biological and integrated methods to fight crop pests. However, today, only one per cent of the plant protection used is biological and systems to predict the outbreaks of plant diseases, a basis for integrated plant protection, are not applied. Such systems are needed to optimize the use of pesticides.

There is no production of pesticides in the country. Imports are a licensed activity, with regulations developed by the Ministry of Agriculture and Food Industry (MoAFI) and the Ministry of Ecology and Natural Resources (MENR) according to the 1999 *Law on Plant Protection*. Reportedly no persistent organic pesticides have been imported during the past decade.

While pesticide use is not an immediate threat, residual stocks of obsolete and banned harmful chemicals are a real problem. Some of the pesticides have been accumulated in a landfill in the southern part of the country, but there are still large quantities remaining all over the country. Former warehouses for pesticides are in some cases

only ruins, which leave the already damaged packages unprotected from rain and snow. Soil contamination, including from dichlorodiphenyltrichloroethane (DDT), is found around most of the facilities. Sixty per cent of the total amount of obsolete pesticides, which are estimated at 6,600 tonnes, has been buried at the designated landfill. After several unsuccessful attempts to solve the problem, the National Environment Fund (NEF), using a work force from the army, recently repackaged and centralized the obsolete pesticides stocks. A project for a final solution is now under preparation with funding from the GEF and NEF.

In the 1990s the use of fertilizers decreased substantially, with the lowest levels in 1999 (Figure 7.4). Since then its application has increased, but 30 per cent of agricultural land exhibits a deficit of mobile phosphorus with serious consequences on yields.

Based on the current low use of both fertilizers and pesticides, their run-off from the fields is probably significantly lower than in the past, even if increased erosion may be a side effect. However, with the very high proportion of arable land, fertilizer and pesticide run-off is one reason why it is important to establish water protection zones along rivers and lakes. In spite of the decisions taken, this process is too slow.

Figure 7.3: Pesticide use, 1990-2003

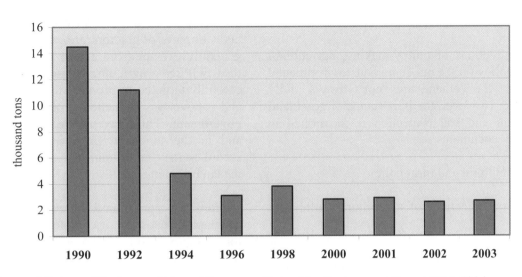

Source: Ministry of Ecology and Natural Resources. State of the Environment Report 2004. Chisinau, 2004.

Figure 7.4: Use of mineral and organic fertilizers, 1991-2003

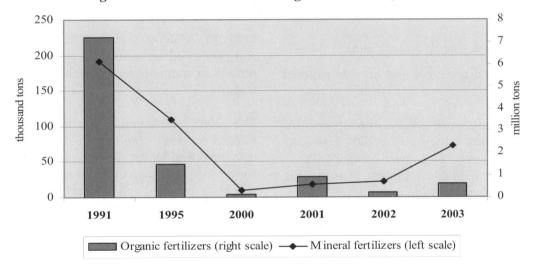

Source: Ministry of Ecology and Natural Resources. State of the Environment Report 2004. Chisinau, 2004.

Pollution from animal production

With the dismantling of 2000 large animal production units from soviet times, domestic animals owned by households, one or a few per family, have increased dramatically. Manure from animals living in crowded villages, as well as the general lack of sanitation and waste management, contributes significantly to the pollution of drinking water from wells. About 50 per cent of the population uses drinking water from wells that are frequently shallow. According to the Ministry of Health and Social Protection (MoHSP), which analyses all public wells[5] once a year, 76 per cent of the monitored wells do not have potable water[6]. Nitrate levels are increasing and it is being found deeper in the ground. There are attempt to solve the manure handling problem on the municipal level, but with limited success.

___

[5] There are in total 150,000 wells and fewer than ten per cent of these are public.
[6] Parameters included in the MoH analysis are microbiological contamination, nitrate and fluoride content.

7.3　Policy objectives and management in agriculture

The Policy Framework

The two directions of policy-making, agricultural and rural policy on the one hand and environmental policy on the other, are not always fully coordinated. However, the importance of good land management and soil protection is mentioned in most policy documents.

Agricultural and rural policy

The strategic objectives of agricultural policy are to:

- Promote efficient production, processing and marketing of agricultural and food products in a way that improves incomes and the welfare of farmers;

- Ensure the competitiveness of Moldovan agricultural and food products on world markets;

- Contribute to economic growth; and

- Protect natural resources and provide national food security.

Three policy documents of importance for agricultural and rural policy are the 2004 *Economic Growth and Poverty Reduction Strategy Paper* (EGPRSP), the EU-Moldova Action Plan and the presidential programme "*Moldovan Village*".

Consolidation of land and agricultural production is a clearly expressed objective of the MoAFI. So far farmers are driving the consolidation, but there have been attempts to make it possible for the authorities to introduce a more active administrative consolidation policy with State-appointed management and centralized provision of key inputs. However, according to the EGPRSP the Republic is going to promote a liberal agricultural policy including the strengthening of landowners' rights and the creation of free land markets.

Cash subsidies have averaged one per cent of GDP or three per cent of government expenditure in recent years, similar to levels in other transition countries. Cash subsidies reduce input costs for farmers by providing a partial refund of the excise cost on motor fuels, subsidized financing for the acquisition of tractors, and interest subsidies on bank loans, investment grants and other production-related payments. The price-distorting impact of cash subsidies is amplified by subsidies on energy costs for irrigation, subsidies on tax expenditure, preferential VAT rates (five per cent instead of 20 per cent) on inputs and an exemption from profit tax. Imports of tractors are, as another example, generally exempt from excise taxes. According to the EGPRSP agricultural subsidies should be carefully targeted to promote the economic growth and poverty reduction objectives of the government. This may not be the case at present and in the longer term several of the existing subsidies may contribute to increased pressure on the environment.

Markets for agricultural inputs and products are developing, but are not completely free. There are for example administrative limits on profit margins for certain basic foodstuffs. State control and trade intervention for exports of grain have increased. All export deals should be closed via the "Universal Commodity Exchange of Moldova", which is making it more difficult for the farmers to get the best price for their products.

In the EU-Moldova Action Plan, rural development is a priority along with sanitary and phytosanitary actions to improve food safety and conditions of trade.

The 2005 presidential programme "*Moldovan Village*" was built on proposals from municipalities. Under the programme, water supply and sewage systems as well as natural gas networks will be constructed and modernized. Environmental protection is another objective of the work with activities including destruction of obsolete pesticides and establishment of forest protection belts. It is not clear how this expensive programme – US$ 3.6 billion over ten years - will be funded.

The development of extension services is essential to respond to the needs of the new private farmers. Significant steps have been taken in this direction. Several donor programmes support the development of extension services, and help to overcome an important financial bottleneck for agricultural production in supplying credits.

The European Union supports the State budget within the framework of its Food Security Programme (FSP), which is designed to address poverty, improve food security, and give technical assistance to the MoAFI. After a discontinuation of the funding in connection with the International Monetary Fund (IMF) default, the FSP is now developing support for irrigation, rural water supply, animal breeding and animal health.

The United States Agency for International Development (USAID) works through its Private Farmers Assistance and Private Enterprise Development programmes. British and Swedish development agencies are engaged in work on sustainable rural livelihoods, rights to land, access to markets and decreasing environmental degradation.

The Agricultural revitalization project funded by a concessional loan of US$ 15 million from the International fund for agricultural development include land improvement, support to agroservices, processing and development of marketing channels, and improvement of village infrastructure.

Two World Bank loans are funding the Moldova Social Investment Fund. The Fund supplies municipalities with grants for projects, in some cases related to environmental activities such as planting of forests and erosion protection work. The World Bank Rural Investment Support Project offers credits for agricultural enterprises as well as individual farmers (See chapter 6 on Expenditures for Environmental protection).

Environmental policy to reduce agriculture adverse effects

Implementation of organic agriculture and prevention of erosion, landslides and other forms of soil degradation are important items in the 2001 *Concept on Environmental Policy*. Decreasing the rate of soil degradation is one of the main environmental strategic objectives of the MENR. A number of programmes have been established with the aim to improve land management, but their funding and implementation is often weak. Involved organizations are generally unwilling to cooperate between themselves. The lack of a common digital map for spatial planning purposes is an additional bottleneck.

The *Complex Programme for Protection of Soils against Erosion 2003-2012* is being funded by the State and implemented by the State Association for Soil Protection. The Programme also includes funding for forest planting by "Moldsilva".

The 2003 *National Programme on Utilization of New Land and Improvement of Soil Fertility for 2003-2010* is not very detailed and the responsibility for its implementation is shared between the Agency for Land Relations and Cadastre, the MoAFI, the MENR, "Moldsilva" as well as district and municipal authorities. The Programme is to be funded by extra budgetary and other sources.

The 2000 *National Action Plan to Combat Desertification* is an ambitious programme including a broad range of measures but the implementation of it has been weak. A recent analysis, after five of the ten years of the programme, shows that only a minor part of the action plan had been implemented. The 2001 *National Strategy and Action Plan for Protection of Biodiversity* includes several components related to land use in agriculture as well as forestry.

The Moldova Soil Conservation Project is a project funded by the Prototype Carbon Fund and developed in cooperation with "Moldsilva". Its aim is to promote soil conservation in and around degraded agricultural areas by planting trees and shrubs on 14,494 ha. The total budget for 2002-2012 is US$ 13.34 million. As an exception to most other programmes on similar issues, this project is being implemented according to its plan

The MoHSP plans to raise the awareness of the population of the links between pollution and water quality, to improve the coverage of water monitoring and to direct the inhabitants to the wells where the best water can be found. According to the MoHSP, municipalities should have the responsibility of establishing appropriate sanitary zones around the wells to inform the population on the water quality in individual wells.

The Agricultural Pollution Control Project is a US$ five million project funded by the Global Environmental Fund with co-funding from the Republic. The overall objective is to reduce nutrient pollution from agriculture. It includes the promotion of environmentally friendly farming practices by subsidising efforts by farmers to decrease nutrient run-off from manure. It also aims to help introduce EU legislation in the field of environmental pollution control.

A planned GEF project "Integrated and Sustainable Land Management through Community Based Approach" is a commendable response to the lack of an integrated approach and coordination between authorities and stakeholders. This project is in contrast to the high number of similarly-oriented but underfinanced land management and soil protection programmes and action plans. The project aims to address inconsistencies in the national legal framework and consolidates cooperation between the main actors. The development of an interagency information management system for land management is a particularly important component in this project. A uniform spatial reference of the underlying core data would make it easy to combine datasets from different sources of planning or authorities and help them in arriving at complex planning decisions.

Legal Framework

Overall, the legal framework for protection of agricultural land and environmental protection is well developed while its implementation is in many cases weak.

The 1991 *Land Code* (and subsequent amendments) is a Law where important provisions, in particular the framework for land privatization, have been implemented. It defines the different categories of land such as agricultural land and the forest fund. According to the code, land and soil protection is a priority, and it includes mechanisms that make it possible to waive the right to use land in situations where land use causes land degradation. Landowners can also be sanctioned or even lose their ownership on the land if agricultural land is not used. The Land Code severely restricts any possibility of changing the category of agricultural and forest land. Foreign private persons or companies cannot own but are allowed to lease agricultural land.

The 1999 *Law on Plant Protection* and the 2004 *Law on Fertilizers and Products for* Phytosanitary *Use* regulate the use of fertilizers and pesticides.
The 2001 *Law on Biosafety* regulates the production, testing, and release into the environment of genetically modified organisms. The government adopted a regulation on 25 September 2003 to implement this Law.

The 1995 *Law on Water Protection Zones and Belts along Rivers and Water Bodies* and the *2001* Regulation *on Activities to Establish Water Protection Zones and Belts along Rivers and Water Bodies* aim to decrease diffuse run-off and increase water quality in rivers and lakes. Important components are the regulations on activities that are allowed in the water protection zones and the establishment of forest belts or hayfields along the watercourses. Delimitation of water protection zones has been made, but the process of establishing the zones as was recommended in the first EPR is in practice very slow.

A 2005 *Law on Ecological Agricultural Food Production* harmonized with the corresponding EU-directive includes provisions for certification of organic products. It also includes the establishment of a fund to support development of organic agriculture. There is a draft Regulation on Pasture and a draft Law on Soil Protection, but these have not yet been presented to the Parliament.

Institutional framework

The Ministry of Agriculture and Food Industry (MoAFI) has the primary responsibility for the development and implementation of agricultural policies. After the privatization of acricultural land it has not been directly involved in its production. Further restructuring of the MoAFI seems to be needed in the adaptation to a privatized and market-oriented agriculture.

The Agrochemical and Ecology Division of the MoAFI supports the development of organic agriculture and regulates imports and use of pesticides. "Apele Moldovei" is responsible for irrigation and drainage infrastructure. Farms enter into agreements with "Apele Moldovei" on the delivery of irrigation water. The State Agrochemical Service under the MoAFI that previously dealt with soil analyses and mapping, does not have the capacity or resources to take on any serious responsibility in this area.

The MoAFI is represented on the district level. District offices of the State Service for Plant Protection are responsible for pesticides being traded and used according to regulations. They should also provide plant protection prognoses, but this practice is not well developed. At district level there are also inspectorates for selection and reproduction for animal production, as well as for seeds and sowing material.

The district councils include Agriculture and Food Departments covering land use, and plant and animal production. Their activities are directed towards increasing efficiency of agriculture including facilitating the consolidation of land plots. Support to the farmers in developing marketing mechanisms is important. The district departments are further involved in the control of land use. According to the Land Code, municipalities have broad responsibility for land management. Municipalities establish land commissions that decide on demarcation of land for pasture and other purposes. They are further in charge of any distribution of municipal land to other owners. Municipal and district administrations employ land surveyors. They are involved in resolving land disputes, implementing anti-erosion work and other land use issues.

Only one person is responsible for soil protection in the MENR. Under the MENR, the Agency for Geology "AGeoM" monitors and makes prognoses on the risk for landslides. The State Ecological Inspection (SEI) has broad responsibilities including enforcement of the 1991 Land Code. At district level, one of three inspectors is responsible for forestry, agriculture and land use issues.

The Agency for Land Relations and Cadastre works directly under the government and is responsible for land administration, cadastres and also programmes to improve soil fertility. Two institutes dealing with land surveying, cartography and geodesy work under the Agency. The State Association for Soil Protection under the Agency is responsible for anti-erosion work and protection and improvement of soil fertility. The Association includes 12 regional soil protection companies. Their funding comes from the profits of land sales from the State, presently lei 17 million (US$ 1.4 million) annually.

The State Hydrometeorological Service operates a soil-monitoring programme. Samples are collected in ten districts all over the country in the spring and in the autumn, and analysed for pesticides and heavy metal contamination.

Cooperation and coordination between different authorities are not always smooth and the cooperation between the MoAFI, the MENR and the Agency for Land Relations and Cadastres could be improved. Information flow between the authorities is limited and the regulations issued by the different authorities are not fully streamlined. Each organization tends to focus on its own programmes and plans with little concern for finding opportunities to synergize funding and manpower for their more efficient implementation.

In comparison with other EECCA countries, probably due to the importance of agriculture and the small size of the country, extension services have developed well and are available in most of the country. Several independent organizations provide advisory and other services to the farmers. The National AGROinform Federation unites Regional Information and Consultancy Centres with their main funding from donor projects. They organize seminars and provide consulting on various themes. AGROinform publishes manuals

and brochures, and has programmes providing credits for development of marketing and storage.

The National Rural Extension Service (ACSA) was formed in 2001 by partners such as the National Federation of Farmers and the Union of Association of Agricultural Producers within the framework of a Tacis project, and is now funded mainly by a World Bank loan and the MoAFI. It has advisory centres in all districts and 350 local part-time advisors in the municipalities. The ACSA also produces publications for farmers on different subjects and has grant programmes.

The National Federation of Farmers is developing dynamically and has about 30,000 members. Its main objective is to support the rights of the newly established farmers. Exchange programmes for farmers and development of farmers' cooperatives are other aims of their work. There is a great need to develop organizations for cooperation in the marketing and processing of products.

Various institutes under the MoA have considerable capacity for research but these institutes are under severe financial constraints. The Nicolae Dimo Research Institute of Pedology and Agrochemistry focuses its research on soil fertility and land protection. The Institute for Plant Protection is one of the pioneer institutes dealing internationally with biological plant protection. For an agricultural country like the Republic of Moldova, it is essential to have a well functioning structure for applied science with close links to extension services. This is the key to the development of efficient and environmentally friendly agriculture.

The State Agrarian University in Chisinau educates students in a whole range of agricultural specialties, and has a consulting centre. They recruit 2,500 students annually. In a recently developed programme environmental specialists are being trained. All students have to take an obligatory course on environmental protection.

Environmental awareness of farmers and organic farming, involvement of local authorities

Guidelines for Good Agricultural Practice (GAPs) are the result of cooperation between the MoAFI and the MENR. Further joint efforts are needed to promote the guidelines. Not only do GAPs respond to the need to integrate economic and environmental concerns, but in the longer term they are also a positive factor for penetrating exports markets.

Organic agriculture is developing with the support of the MoAFI and international donors and is another area where cooperation between the MoAFI and MENR yields positive results. A study prepared by the government concluded that the conditions in the Republic are suitable for the introduction of organic agriculture. Experiences of biological treatment of plant pests, integrated pest management and production of substances for biological treatment of plant pests are positive. Low labour costs also give the opportunity to minimize the use of pesticides. After the approval in 2000 of the *National Concept on Organic Farming, Production and Marketing of Organic and Genetically Unmodified Products*, an Action Plan was approved to implement the Concept as well as a national standard for organic agricultural production.

The Association for Organic Farming EcoProdus promotes development of organic farming. Together with the Institute for Field Crops it has elaborated technical regulations for organic products. Certified products from 11,300 ha of land, including 5,000 ha of vineyards, are finding a market. The most important products are vegetables, dried fruits and wine. Only a minor part of this production is exported.

The local population and decision makers are not sufficiently involved in land management programmes. Dialogue with the local population is hindered by a lack of integration of information on land management and planning. For example, there is no consolidated Geographical Information System (GIS) map for the different authorities' use. Local authorities are not always well informed about legal acts and programmes. Often, municipalities are too small to have a sufficient capacity for land use and spatial planning. A positive development is that the environmental fund and some donors are increasingly funding plans and activities on the initiatives of municipalities.

7.4   Environmental concerns in forestry

It is a matter of dispute between environmental activists and authorities, and "Moldsilva" whether the permitted cutting of forest damages the environment, or whether it is sustainable. According to statistics less than 40 per cent of forest growth is harvested at present. Cuttings could most likely be increased in municipal forests and

new procedures are being worked out with the environmental inspectors to enable licences to be given to the municipalities for cuttings.

The volume of illegal cuttings is also disputed. High energy prices and the poverty of the population are main causes of illegal cutting for fuel all over the country. For this reason and also due to privatization, the forest belts protecting against erosion have suffered. However, official statistics indicate a decline in illegal cuttings from 14,000 m^3 in 1997 to 3-5,000 m^3 after 2000.

Protected areas are forest areas and are managed by "Moldsilva". There is an unresolved conflict between the MENR and "Moldsilva" on the definition and management of the four reserves: they are scientific reserves according to the MENR and protected areas according to "Moldsilva". In the case of the planned 55,000 ha Lower Dniester nature reserve, forestry interests have interfered and have at least temporarily stopped the process of setting up the reserve. Overall the area under protection in the country is low (1.96 per cent of the territory) and has not increased since the first review (See Introduction).

There is a need to increase the proportion of afforested land in the country, in particular to alleviate the widespread erosion and runoff of nutrients from agricultural land. The acreage under forest, which was stable during the 1990s, has been increasing since 2000. This is a positive development even if there are difficulties in this process. The resources available for planting are small and it may be difficult to reach an agreement on planting forest on land belonging to municipalities, the second largest landowner. The increasing number of private livestock contributes to the damage of newly planted forest areas.
There is a debate on which species should be used for forest regeneration. The introduction of alien species such as acacia and boxelder (*Acer negundo*) is an issue in forestry management. Acacia is a species commonly used to stabilize eroded land; but on the regeneration of more stable forests such as oak forest, not enough resources are spent. This is a rather complicated and expensive process.

The lack of economic resources obstructs the establishment, regeneration and protection of forests including protected areas. "Moldsilva" cannot manage the forest in a sustainable way under the present regime of self-financing. The opportunities for supervision and inspection are restricted. The fines for illegal cuttings are low and a significant part of these fines is not collected.

7.5 Policy objectives and management in forestry

According to State policy, the main function of forests is the protection of land and biodiversity. They are a stabilizing factor for the environment. Moldovan forests are divided into five subgroups according to their function with half of the acreage designed to protect against negative climatic factors and industrial pollution. Protection and increase of afforested areas and protected areas is one of the main environmental strategic objectives of the MENR as defined in the 2001 *Concept of Environmental Policy*. The Parliament approved on 12 July 2001 the *Strategy of the Sustainable Development of the Forest Fund*. The objectives of this Strategy are to:

• Improve existing forests,

• Conserve biodiversity in forests,

• Enlarge forest areas,

• Improve protection of forests, and

• Integrate forest management with other sectors.

The Strategy can be seen as a response to one of the recommendations of the first EPR, even if it is weak with regard to biodiversity aspects such as the creation of a National Ecological Network. It sets the ambitious objective to increase forests to cover 15 per cent of the land from the previous level of 10.7 per cent. This would include tree planting on 25,000 ha, facilitation of natural regeneration on 39,000 ha and natural regeneration on 32,000 ha until 2020. According to the Strategy a total of 128,000 ha of land will be afforested.

Implementation of the Strategy is promising. In 2002-2004 forest was planted on 24,000 ha. Most

of this land is outside the State forest fund and owned by municipalities. Presently "Moldsilva" has difficulty in finding land where the municipalities will agree to plant forest, as municipalities want to keep as much pasture as possible. "Moldsilva" is developing a *Concept of Agro-forestry* as a response to this problem.

The National Ecological Network of Moldova (NENM) aims to extend the existing areas of forests to establish a more coherent network of natural areas. It will further identify critically degraded areas for restoration and define land management practices for these areas. It is being developed by the MENR as a unifying component of the 2001 *National Strategy and Action Plan for the Protection of Biodiversity*, and the 2000 *National Action Plan to Combat Desertification*. The establishment of the network is at the concept stage, and there is presently no funding available. Implementation of the NENM will be particularly difficult when the land to be included in the network is private.

The prototype Carbon Fund finances the Moldova Soils Conservation Project, which is a key project for afforestation. The Japan Trust Fund finances a community forest development programme linked to the Soils Conservation Project, with the main aim to help municipalities and communities to develop their forest and land management.

The 1979 *Forest Code* gives a framework for the management of forests with the sustainable development of forests and protection of its biodiversity as a cornerstone. The code defines the responsibilities of the State forest authority, other authorities and stakeholders and sets up rules for the use and protection of forest resources. It states that forests in the Republic of Moldova are owned by the public.

Table 7.2: Forestry statistics, 2004

ha

	Forest fund	Area covered by forests in the forest fund
Total	403,400	362,700
managed by "Moldsilva"	359,300	318,600
managed by other state authorities	9,200	9,200
managed by municipalities	34,500	34,500
private forests	400	400

Source: "Moldsilva", 2005.

Legal framework

The 2000 *Law on Amelioration of Degraded Territories through Afforestation* defines procedures for afforestation of public or private degraded land. "Moldsilva" was responsible for the implementation of the Law, including expropriation of private land in cases of non-compliance with the Law. If landowners take the appropriate steps according to the Law, they are exempted from land tax for 25 years.

The 2004 *Regulation for Agreeing on Cuttings in the Forest Fund and Forest outside the Forest Fund* establishes that the cutting plan of each forest company shall be agreed upon by the environmental authorities. Regeneration of forests only in the forest fund should be agreed upon by the MENR.

Institutional framework

Management of forests is following the same patterns as set out in the first EPR. Its recommendation to separate policy authority and exploitation of forests has not been implemented. The Agency for Forestry "Moldsilva" with 5,500 employees is in charge of 359,300 ha or 89 per cent of the forest fund. "Moldsilva" works directly under the government and has the task of regulating, coordinating and controlling the management of forests in the forest fund. In 1990, "Moldsilva" was 90 per cent financed by the State budget but now it is self-financed at more than 96 per cent, even though the contribution from the State budget has increased significantly since 1998.

"Moldsilva"'s office in Chisinau supervises 18 forest companies, four forestry-hunting companies, and four offices for protected areas responsible for protection as well as economic activities in different forest ranges. The central office in Chisinau is also responsible for the monitoring of forests.

The Institute for Forestry Research and Planning is under "Moldsilva", and is responsible for the development of ten-year forestry management plans for the forest companies that are the basis of all management activities in the State forests. The forestry management plans are not under any expertise or Environmental Impact Assessment (EIA) by the MENR. If the environmental authorities would approve the forest management plans, the balance between protection and use of forests might be improved. The Forestry Institute is

also responsible for statistics on forests and forestry.

Local authorities and other landowners manage the remaining ten per cent of the forest fund. Only 400 ha of forests are private property.

The MENR's Division on Natural Resources and Biodiversity has two people dealing with forestry issues and is responsible for developing legislation for the management of forest resources. It is a weak counterweight to "Moldsilva". The SEI has further important roles in the protection of forests, issuing licenses, inspecting forest cuttings, and making sure that afforestation programmes are implemented. One inspector in each regional agency of the SEI, mostly with training in forestry, is responsible for forestry protection and the permitting/inspection of cuttings. In 2001 the SEI, following one of the recommendations in the first EPR, established a special department in Chisinau with 14 inspectors to fight illegal cutting and poaching.

The dialogue between the MENR and "Moldsilva" is difficult. Although there is intensive interaction between them with regards to licensing and control, there are no formal joint structures or programmes for cooperation such as working groups or projects. Environmental authorities and activists often express concern about the way that Moldovan forests are managed. The conflict between "Moldsilva" and the MENR on the definition and management of the four protected areas is a point of concern. Attempts are still being made to increase the influence of the MENR. "Moldsilva" has to get the approval of the MENR and the SEI for most of its activities, such as cuttings. SEI inspectors are also responsible for inspection.

7.6   Conclusions and recommendations

Agriculture and land use

Agricultural production in the Republic of Moldova is in a difficult situation. With very restricted resources at its disposal, the sector has to adapt to a dramatically changed structure of production and new markets. Nevertheless efforts are being made to minimize negative environmental effects from agriculture. The awareness of the importance of land and soil protection in the country, its only real natural resource, is high. Several of the steps that were taken with the support of donors can be commended:

•   The development of extension services,

- The projects aiming at decreasing diffuse pollution from agriculture,

- The promotion of organic agriculture, and

- The promotion of Good Agricultural Practice.

In the current difficult economic situation, and in the perspective of an ongoing consolidation of agricultural production, it is not easy to introduce elaborate schemes on environmental protection in the agricultural sector. New or changed practices are only likely to be introduced successfully if they also contribute to improved production and an improved standard of living in the countryside. More productive agriculture with an improved economy would have a positive impact on soil and land management and on the efficiency of the use of agricultural inputs.

In the development of agricultural policies, the size and design of agricultural subsidies can have serious effects on the environment. Product and price subsidies are almost always negative for the environment in the long term, and should be avoided also for economic reasons. The review of agricultural subsidies, which is planned, should take into account their possible adverse effects on the environment.

Extension services and training are key instruments in the development of private agriculture, and should help to communicate the cause-effect linkage between agriculture, environment and health. An important task for the extension services is to promote agricultural practices that will decrease erosion, and a safe and efficient use of pesticides and fertilizers. To do this, they need a solid scientific basis and an educational capacity, and increased financing. Applied agricultural research is a weak area that needs to be developed. Good Agricultural Practice should always be the core of attention for the extension services.

For all land management, the local population and decision makers should be involved in the design and implementation of programmes. Efforts are being made, but this work needs to be intensified. It is a drawback that the municipalities are too small and poor in resources to take on greater responsibility for environmental issues and land management.

No single institution is able to carry out measures to combat land degradation successfully. Only joint and integrated efforts, based on good information, can promote cost-efficient measures and achieve

their targets. The development of a national Geographic Information System is one important step to facilitate planning and cooperation. The planned UNDP-GEF project "Integrated and Sustainable Land Management through Community Based Approach" is an opportunity to find synergy in the coordinated action of several authorities and administrative levels, and to stop the propagation of non-funded and unrealistic programmes and action plans.

There are two categories of land that need particular attention: the pasture owned by the municipalities and the water protection zones. Two draft legal acts, both important as a basis for improved land management, a Law on Soils and a Regulation on Pasture, have been developed but are not yet approved by Parliament. Improving management of pasture will provide economic as well as environmental gains. It is crucial that a country with as high a proportion of arable land as the Republic of Moldova actively protects its waters by establishing water protection zones. The National Ecological Network of Moldova will provide another important aspect of land management – the establishment of ecological corridors. This is a difficult challenge in a landscape so dominated by agriculture.

Drinking water quality is a serious problem in the countryside. Efforts by the MoH to improve the information available on water quality are important, and should lead to a better awareness in the municipalities on the action needed. Improved handling of manure and other waste, and improved protection of the wells used are key measures.

Forestry

Moldovan forests are under considerable pressure. The present work to increase the acreage of forests is important as it serves to improve land and soil protection. It further prevents diffuse pollution and protects biodiversity.

As in many other countries there is a heated debate and a frequent lack of understanding between the forestry sector and environmental authorities and activists. There are two aspects of this lack of understanding. On the one hand, efforts must be made on both sides to improve the dialogue. On the other hand, based on other countries' experience, it takes a long time of joint work in projects, working groups, seminars, to create a better understanding, a basis for an improved dialogue and ultimately better forestry and environmental policies.

Afforestation of water protection zones, NEMN and the new GEF project on sustainable land management are opportunities to establish joint work and a constructive dialogue.

The other aspect is more serious. At present "Moldsilva" is an agency that is essentially self-regulating. The key instrument for its economic activity is the ten-year forestry management plans developed by its own Institute for Forestry Research and Management. These management plans are not assessed by any outside authority. The management of four scientific reserves according to the 1998 Law on Protected Areas also demonstrates the shortcomings in the regulation of the forest sector. This issue needs to be resolved urgently and in the short term.

Recommendation 7.1:
The Ministry of Agriculture and Food Industry in cooperation with the Ministry of Ecology and Natural Resources should, as a priority, develop a programme for implementing Guidelines for Good Agricultural Practices that should be used as a key instrument to guide policy development and extension services in the agricultural sector. Advising farmers on how to counteract erosion efficiently and effectively should be one of the central components of this implementation programme.

Recommendation 7.2:
The Government should delegate the lead role to the Ministry of Ecology and Natural Resources for, in coordination with the Ministry of Agriculture and Food Industry, the Agency for Forestry "Moldsilva", the State Water Concern "Apele Moldovei" and the Agency for Land Relations and Cadastre with the active involvement of farmers, NGOs, and municipal and district authorities, elaborating all ongoing and planned land management and afforestation programmes. These

efforts should in particular focus on achieving the following important objectives:

- *Improvement of the management and protection of pasture;*

- *Establishment of water protection zones according to the existing laws and regulations; and*

- *Establishment of the National Ecological Network of Moldova.*

Recommendation 7.3:
The Agency for Land Relations and Cadastre and the Agency for Forestry "Moldsilva" should develop a national Geographical Information System (GIS) in order to provide uniform presentation of topographic information and information on real estate (cadastre), which would facilitate all spatial planning purposes and related decision-making.

Recommendation 7.4:
The Ministry of Agriculture and Food Industry should ensure long-term financing under the aegis of scientific institutions with the objective to using the results of applied research and introducing environmentally friendly technologies and practices in agriculture.

Recommendation 7.5:
The Government should make a proposal to amend the Forest Code in order to give to the Ministry of Ecology and Natural Resources the authority to approve the forestry management plans, transferring to it the structure responsible for developing them. It should improve the supervision of forest exploitation and should be authorized to impose higher fines. Capacity building and its staffing should be adjusted adequately.
See also Recommendation 1.1.

Chapter 8

ENVIRONMENTAL MANAGEMENT IN INDUSTRIAL ACTIVITIES

8.1   Current situation in industrial activities and environmental impact

Industry

From 1990 to 1999 industrial production dramatically declined but picked up steadily afterwards (Figure 8.1). It grew 8 per cent in 2000, 14 per cent in 2001 and 16 per cent in 2003. During the 1990s the country's economic structure changed significantly. The industrial sector's share declined markedly and in 2003 supplied 18 per cent of GDP. In 2003 the processing industry's share in GDP was 15.7 per cent and accounted for 9.4 per cent of total employment. More than half of this is due to food, beverage and tobacco production (Table 8.1), which is a strategic sub-sector for the country.

In the Republic of Moldova, the main industries are food processing (55 per cent of industrial production), paper and cardboard, furniture, leather, and heavy machinery. Construction materials are also an active sector. Moldovan industry suffered a sharp decline in the 1990s, with an absolute minimum in 1999, and started its revival in 2000 (Table 8.2). A major share of industry is private. Out of 674 big enterprises in 2003 just 64, i.e., less than 10 per cent, were public. Foreign companies or joint ventures account for 26 per cent of industrial production.

In general, the situation in the sector remains complicated. Most industries did not reach the production level of the pre-transition period and industrial capacities are far from being fully used. Lack of investments led to a degradation of fixed assets. Depreciation of the value of capital reached 80-90 per cent in a number of enterprises. Industrial equipment has a high level of depreciation and huge investment is necessary for modernization.

Figure 8.1: Trends in GDP and industrial output, 1995=100

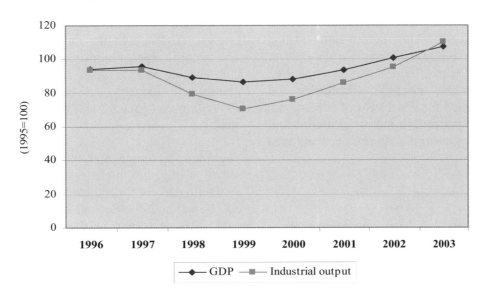

Source: Department of Statistics and Sociology. Statistical Yearbook 2004. Chisinau, 2004.

Table 8.1: Structure of industrial production, %

	1995	1996	1997	1998	1999	2000	2001	2002	2003
Industry total	100.0	100.0	100.0	100.0	100.0	100.0	100.0	100.0	100.0
Manufacturing	83.6	84.7	78.8	70.1	68.1	82.1	80.4	82.9	86.3
Food and beverages	52.8	54.2	52.4	45.9	40.8	48.1	49.3	52.4	53.6
Tobacco	3.8	5.3	4.2	4.1	6.2	6.1	5.2	3.2	2.8
Textile	2.3	2.4	1.9	1.5	1.8	2.1	2.3	1.4	1.4
Chemical industry	0.8	0.9	0.7	0.9	1.6	1.4	1.2	1.2	1.0
Paper and pulp industry	1.2	1.7	1.2	1.0	0.5	0.7	0.7	0.9	1.6
Non-metallic products	5.5	5.3	5.6	5.4	5.8	8.6	7.8	8.5	8.1
Machinery and metallurgy	9.0	7.9	6.4	6.0	5.1	5.7	5.5	5.7	6.2
Other	8.2	7.0	6.3	5.3	6.3	9.4	8.4	9.6	11.6
Mining	0.8	0.8	1.0	0.9	0.8	0.8	0.7	0.8	0.8
Electricity, gas and water supply	15.6	14.5	20.3	29.0	31.1	17.1	18.9	16.3	12.9

Source: Department of Statistics and Sociology. Statistical Yearbook 2004. Chisinau, 2004.

Table 8.2: Industrial production, annual change in %

	1995	1996	1997	1998	1999	2000	2001	2002	2003
Industry total	-4.0	-6.0	0.0	-15.0	-12.0	8.0	14.0	11.0	16.0
Manufacturing	-4.0	-7.0	-3.0	-17.0	-12.0	18.0	15.0	13.0	18.0
Food and beverages	4.0	-9.0	-2.0	-20.0	-19.0	13.0	18.0	17.0	19.0
Tobacco	-26.0	12.0	-6.0	-7.0	25.0	-6.0	-3.0	-33.0	-0.2
Textile	-49.0	1.0	-17.0	-21.0	18.0	33.0	28.0	15.0	11.0
Chemical industry	-45.0	-29.0	-19.0	26.0	67.0	-1.0	27.0	8.0	-20.0
Paper and pulp industry	-17.0	-14.0	17.0	-12.0	-41.0	66.0	40.0	29.0	82.0
Non-metallic products	2.0	20.0	16.0	-9.0	-16.0	65.0	9.0	26.0	9.0
Machinery and metallurgy	-12.0	-20.0	-21.0	-13.0	-19.0	16.0	13.0	16.0	25.0
Mining	-21.0	-17.0	6.0	-13.0	-14.0	-2.0	9.0	24.0	26.0
Electricity, gas and water supply	-7.0	4.0	-0.2	-9.0	-14.0	-29.0	9.0	-2.0	3.0
GDP	-5.0	-5.9	1.6	-6.5	-3.4	2.1	6.1	7.2	6.0

Source: Department of Statistics and Sociology. Statistical Yearbook 2004. Chisinau, 2004.

The structure of industrial production is not sufficiently diversified. The investments in food and beverage enterprises accounted for the bulk of investment in the processing industry at around 62 per cent of the total in 2002. Machinery and equipment accounted for 3 per cent of investment, with a share of 6 per cent in industrial production. Sixty per cent of industrial activity is concentrated in Chisinau.

Energy consumption in industry

The transition period has been characterized by a significant decrease in energy use in the country, with 4.7 Mega-tons of coal equivalent (Mtce) used in 1997 and 2.7 Mtce in 2003. The economic and structural reforms in the country resulted in a substantial reduction in industrial production, which in turn resulted in reduced energy consumption. However since 2001 the final energy consumption in industry started to increase (in 1998

it amounted to 0.15 Mtce and in 2003 to 0.17 Mtce. Energy efficiency in the industrial sector is low. The specific energy consumption in processes is high and the energy losses are substantial. Energy intensity in industry has been decreasing since 1999; however since 2001 it has been increasing again.

The food, beverage and tobacco industry is the sector with the highest energy consumption, amounting to 54.5 per cent of the total industrial energy use in 2003. Second in energy consumption with 22.9 per cent is the group of industries including textiles, dressmaking, the leather industry and machinery. All other industry sub-sectors consume less than 10 per cent of the total energy consumption in industry. The energy consumed by industry in 2002 was primarily from natural gas (54 per cent), followed by electricity (20 per cent), heat (17 per cent) and oil products and coal (9 per cent). In 1997 and 1998 there was a shift from coal and oil products to natural gas; this has significantly reduced airborne pollutants emissions.

Environmental impact and trends decoupling

Data on industrial pollution are incomplete. Most often the emissions reported by enterprises are calculated on the basis of the input and technology process data instead of being directly measured, because all industrial laboratories were liquidated (more information about self-monitoring in Chapter 2), except for two thermal power plants in Chisinau.

There is a lack of integrated indicators of the industrial impact on the environment. Emissions of pollutants into the atmosphere and surface waters from industry are not reported in any official statistical data source. Industrial pollution is not being analysed and reduction targets are not established in industrial development programmes or environmental documents. Though enterprises must report annually on their air emissions, wastewater discharges and waste generation, industry is not always fulfilling its obligations. Only waste generated by industries is reported on a regular basis in official information sources. The lack of environmental indicators to monitor pollution in industry is related to the environmental standards inherited from the Soviet past. A gradual implementation of the Integrated Pollution Prevention and Control (IPPC) Directive (96/61/EC) would help improve the situation. The few existing data on industrial pollution, water and energy use show a slight increase in environmental efficiency from the decrease in air polluting emissions and industrial waste generation being sharper than the decrease of the total industrial output.

Atmospheric pollution

Stationary sources are responsible for 13 per cent of total atmospheric emissions (7 per cent in Chisinau). The energy and heat generation sector is by far the biggest contributor (about 80 per cent of total atmospheric emissions). The decrease in energy demand and the replacement of solid and liquid fuels in combustion units by natural gas also contributed to lower emissions. At present, 2,289 stationary sources are registered, including three power and heat generation plants, 40 regional, 28 inter-regional, and 1,645 local boiler houses, 529 gasoline and gas stations, and 24 big fuel storage sites. Figure 8.2 does not include emissions from the *Dnestrovsc* Moldovan Thermal Power Plant

(MTPP) located in Transnistria. If emissions from MTPP were included, they would double total emissions from stationary pollution sources.

Since 1998, SO_2 emissions have decreased more than four times from 12,000 tons to 2,500 tons in 2003. NO_x emissions have almost halved from 4,000 tons in 1998 to 2,500 tons in 2003. This decoupling between Total Primary Energy Supplies (TPES) and emissions of stationary pollution sources is related to the increased use of natural gas. At the same time, the air quality in the main cities (Chisinau and Balti) did not improve, mainly due to the increased number of (older) road vehicles in recent years.

Water pollution

As traditionally done in the former USSR countries, industrial facilities discharge their wastewater into municipal treatment plants. In 2003, 123 million m^3 of a mix of domestic and industrial wastewaters from municipal wastewater treatment plants were discharged into the receiving water bodies. Since 1999, there has been a relative reduction in the volume of wastewaters discharged, while industrial production has been increasing; but this is being offset by the increased concentrations of the pollutants these wastewaters contain. The data on concentrations of pollutants after treatment presented by Apa Canal Chisinau[1] (Figure 8.3) indicate an increase in all major compounds since 1998. Many of the industrial wastewater stations that are pre-treating (i.e., detoxifying) their effluents before discharging them into the municipal sewerage network are malfunctioning or do not function at all, and subsequently insufficiently pre-treated wastewater flows into the municipal sewerage system and badly affects the performance of the biological step of the waste water treatment plant (WWTP).

Moreover, of the 580 WWTPs with a biological stage that were built by the early 1990s with a total capacity of 650 million m^3/year, only half of them were still functioning in 1995 and 104 in 2003. In these plants, the biological step does not always function, so their performance is even more drastically reduced. Therefore the situation, which was already bad in 1998, has further deteriorated

---

[1] Apa Canal Chisinau: the public water supply company owned by the municipality of Chisinau which monitors concentrations of pollutants in waste-water discharges and collects payments for water pollution from enterprises connected to its sewage systems

Figure 8.2: Emissions into atmosphere from stationary sources, thousand tons

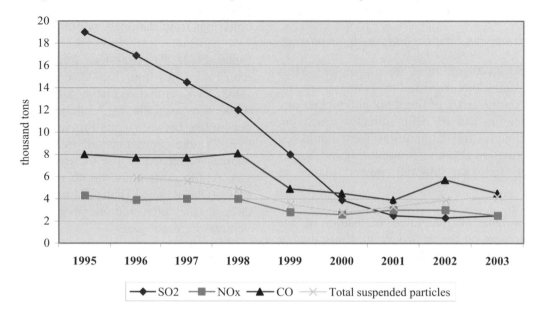

Source: Department of Statistics and Sociology. Statistical Yearbook 2004. Chisinau, 2004.

because of the lack of investments needed to maintain or improve these obsolete wastewater treatment infrastructures.

Apart from industrial wastewaters discharged through the MTPP, other potential major industrial pollution sources are the filtration beds of sugar factories. The environmental impacts of all these pollution sources are not monitored. The lack of data on water pollution indicators hampers the sound assessment of the situation and therefore makes it impossible to take adequate pollution mitigation measures to prevent further degradation of surface and ground waters by the industrial sector. According to the current legislation, water users must operate according to requirements set in the water use permits. These requirements stipulate the volume of water that can be used and set limit values for the discharge of pollutants contained in the wastewater. During the last decade, the number of water users decreased dramatically, following the general drop in economic activity (1,692 water users had permits in 1992, 600 in 1998 and 322 in 2003).

Solid waste

Large amounts of solid waste are generated by the mining industry, the food and beverage industry, and the energy sector. Industrial waste is stored on enterprise premises. The run-off from these sites is a big problem due to the insufficient precautionary measures taken by enterprises. If authorized,

enterprises can dispose of their waste in municipal landfills.

Enterprises report annually to regional authorities on their annual waste generation. Based on these reports, taxes are calculated and collected from enterprises, though enterprises do not need permits for solid waste generation (only an authorization: see chapter 2). In 2003, the total amount of generated wastes, about 3.7 million tons, was 30 per cent below the 1998 level, more than five million tons less. This significantly lower amount of wastes in 2001-2003 can be explained by the implementation of the 2000 *National Programme on the Management of Industrial and Domestic Wastes for 2001-2005*, i.e. the Waste Programme (See Recommendation 7.1 in the First EPR). However, Recommendation 7.2 of the first EPR on ensuring resources for the acquisition of waste treatment technologies, training of staff at all levels of waste management and developing an information system was not fully integrated into the Programme.

Industrial hazardous waste

The wine industry is responsible for the accumulation of ferro-cyanides, which are considered hazardous waste of Toxicity Category 1 (according to the Soviet system of waste classification, which is still applied in the country). About 7,000 tons of this waste is accumulated on the premises of wine industry facilities. The Waste Programme entails measures to tackle this problem

Figure 8.3: Concentrations of pollutants in treated waste water, mg/l

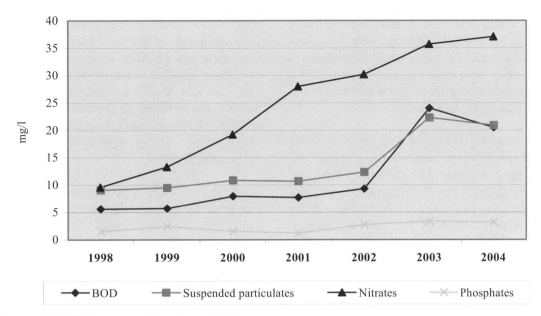

Source : 1998-2004 reports of Apa Canal,Chisinau

(Measure 17). Studies have been undertaken on the reduction of Persistent organic pollutants (POPs). See Chapter 4 on International agreements.

8.2 Environmental considerations and policies in industrial activities

Priorities of environmental protection in industry

According to the 2001 *Concept of Environmental Policy*, the environmental protection requirements will be integrated into the economic reform and sector policies. Environmental priorities in industry are: promoting cleaner production by using non-polluting technologies, encouraging enterprises to reduce their waste generation and to process wastes for use as secondary raw materials, modernizing and exploiting installations for the collection and treatment of toxic substances, and allocating funds from the proceeds of pollution charges to cover the costs of priority environmental protection measures.

The 2003 *National Programme for Environmental Safety* points out the main issues relevant to industries, i.e. the POPs and the dangerous industrial activities regulated by the 2000 *Law on Industrial Safety of Dangerous Industrial Activities*. The relevance of air, water and waste protection requirements for industries is stipulated in the 2001 *National Action Plan on Environmental Hygiene* (NEHAP). The NEHAP requests that national

programmes and territorial plans for the reduction of atmospheric emissions of major pollutants up to 2002 are prepared under the responsibility of the Ministry of Ecology and Natural Resources, the Ministry of Industry and the Ministry of Energy. However, these plans have not yet been elaborated. The 2000 *National Programme on the Management of Industrial and Domestic Wastes for 2001-2005* sets priorities and establishes the main actions for industrial waste management. The main general targets of the Programme are: waste disposal and utilization; reduction of waste accumulated; and implementation of separate waste collection principles. The improvement of the legal basis and the introduction of measures to stimulate waste recycling and usage of secondary materials are foreseen in the Programme, as are the introduction of profit tax exemptions for secondary materials collection and supply. Tax exemptions and soft loans for persons using waste as raw materials are proposed. However, the measures on fiscal instruments that were recommended in the first review, particularly preferential profit taxes and import duties encouraging cleaner technologies and waste recycling, were not implemented. Nevertheless, even if only partly implemented as of the beginning of 2005, the Programme has had a positive impact on waste disposal and many of the important actions foreseen have been implemented or started.

The main issues addressed in the Programme relevant to industrial waste are: disposal of hazardous waste (ferro-cyanides from wine industries, galvanic waste, and batteries), disposal of waste from mining and mineral industries; disposal of waste oils, and disposal of POPs. A programme for waste management in the construction sector has recently been elaborated.

Integration of energy conservation objectives into industrial sector policies

The former Ministry of Energy developed the 2003 *National Energy Conservation Programme for 2003-2010* in accordance with principles from the 1998 *Law on Energy*. The Programme sets priority areas for action and aims to increase energy efficiency, with a target of 2-3 per cent annual decrease of energy intensity. It also aims to utilize local and Renewable Energy Sources (RES) to substitute about 5 per cent of TPES by 2010. The Programme anticipated the development of sectoral programmes for energy efficiency, such as the 2003 *Programme for Energy Efficiency Improvement in Industry for 2004-2005,* elaborated in 2003 by the Energy Institute of the Moldovan Academy of Science. The annual energy saving target is 10-13 ktce or about 10 per cent of current industrial consumption. The Programme was developed by the Ministry of Industry and Infrastructure based on data on energy saving potential provided by enterprises. It covers the enterprises that are under the jurisdiction of the Ministry of Industry and Infrastructure but does not include food and beverage, construction materials, mining and other industries regulated by other authorities.

Though all these programmes are set out with established aims and targets, there are no adequate economic incentives in place to encourage implementation of the recommended measures. Neither energy prices, nor pollution taxes nor their offsets (an analysis of pollution taxes is presented in the following section) create incentives to increase energy efficiency or introduce RES. The current methodology for electricity pricing does not project any advantages for Combined Heat and Power (CHP) production or RES.

Polluter pays and user pays principle

Pollution charges were introduced in 1991 and remained in force until 1998 when the *Law on Payments for Environmental Pollution* was adopted. The actual charges for air and water emissions from stationary pollution sources are calculated at regional/city level. The

methodological instruction includes tables with rates per pollutant based on toxicity (there are 110 pollutant categories for atmospheric emissions) and coefficients for cities or regions that are applicable for emissions up to Maximum Allowable Concentrations (MAC). The atmospheric emissions exceeding MAC are charged at five times that rate. The law sets tariffs for air, water pollution and waste disposal based on the minimum wage (18 lei in 1998). The pollution charges for imported goods, which have negative impact, were established by the same regulation.

The total environment-protection costs in the industrial sector are still very small, under 1 per cent of the industrial added value. The environmentally related tax revenues make up about 3 per cent of GDP (See Table 5.1 in Chapter 5 on economic instruments). Though the minimum wage has increased more than 4 times since 1998, the environmental tariffs are still being calculated by applying the rate of 18 lei/month.

The atmospheric pollution charges are presented in Table 8.3. The tariffs have been stable since 1998 and indexation not applied. Consequently, pollution charges are now significantly lower than in EU countries although still higher than in some countries in the Eastern Europe, Caucasus and Central Asia (EECCA) region, having base rates close to nil like in the Russian Federation or Ukraine.

Standard charges for water supply and wastewater discharges have been set in each region. Using the same approach as with atmospheric pollution charges, toxicity coefficients have been established for 27 pollutants in wastewater. In Chisinau, enterprises connected to public sewage systems pay user fees for technical water supply and wastewater services to Apa Canal. The water supply tariffs for enterprises (regulated by municipalities) have been constant since 2001, at 14.9 lei/m^3, or more than 5 times higher than household tariffs (See box 5.3 in Chapter 5). These enterprises connected to the public sewage system also pay water pollution charges to Apa Canal. Payments are only due for specific pollutants exceeding limits. Enterprises that are not connected to public sewage systems pay water pollution charges for all specific pollutants within limits and also for emissions exceeding limits.

Table 8.3: Taxes for atmospheric emissions from stationary pollution sources, lei/ton, in Chisinau

	1995-1997	1998-2004
SO_2	242	396
NO_x	275	450
CO	22	18
Dust	220	360
V_2O_5	5,500	9,000

Sources:

1. Law on Payments for Environmental Pollution No. 1540, 25.02.98.
2. Ministry Ecology and Natural Resources. Provisional Instructions on the Application of the Standards Governing Payments for pollution. Chisinau, 1991.

In turn, Apa Canal pays water pollution tariffs for Biological Oxygen Demands (BODs) and Suspended Particulate Matters for discharges within limits and for discharges exceeding the norms of the State Environmental Inspectorate. For other pollutants Apa Canal just pays penalties for the emissions exceeding norms. The development of water pollution charges in Chisinau is presented in Table 8.4. Charges for water pollution are significantly lower than in all EECCA countries except for Ukraine.

Charges for waste disposal are applied based on the classification of waste according to Soviet standards. Rates are applied for the existing four classes of toxic and non-toxic waste. Different rates are established for waste that is disposed on enterprise premises and for those disposed in special waste disposal facilities (higher rate). As with other discharges, a limit value for disposable quantities of waste is determined and tariffs per ton

are applied. The waste exceeding limit value is charged at five times the standard rate (see Table 8.5). The tariffs have been stable since their introduction in 1998 and inflation has reduced their economic impact on polluters. Tariffs for waste disposal are lower than in East Europe and Caucasus but higher than in Central Asia.

The 1998 *Law on Payments for Environmental Pollution* included offsets for pollution taxes where enterprises can prove that they are investing in pollution abatement technologies (listed in Annex I of the Law), This measure has never been applied, as the pollution taxes are too low to have any incentive effect. The pollution tax system needs improvement to work effectively as an economic incentive to reduce pollution. However, such improvement needs to be undertaken in combination with the improvement of regulatory instruments such as setting standards for emission limits based on the IPPC approach.

Table 8.4: Charges for water pollution from stationary pollution sources, lei/ton, in Chisinau

	1995-1997	1998-2004
BOD	72	77
Suspended particulates	72	77
Nitrates	558	599
Phosphates	1,090	1,170
Sulphates	2.2	2.3
Chlorides	0.6	0.7
Oil products	4,370	4,680

Sources:

1. Law on Payments for Environmental Pollution No. 1540, 25.02.98.

2. Ministry Ecology and Natural Resources. Provisional Instructions on the Application of the Standards Governing Payments for pollution. Chisinau, 1991.

Table 8.5: Charges for waste disposal, lei/ton (disposed on the site of enterprise)

	1998-2004
1 class	104.40
2 class	32.40
3 class	10.80
4 class	5.40
Non-toxic	0.018

Source: Law on Payments for
Environmental Pollution No. 1540,
25.02.98.

Integration of environmental objectives into industry policies and strategies

The 2004 *Economic Growth and Poverty Reduction Strategy Paper (EGPRSP) for 2004-2006* sets the following medium term objectives for industry: a sustainable increase in industrial output; a diversification of industrial production in branches processing raw agricultural material; and an accelerated development of industrial production in regions so as to contribute to the recovery of regional economies. The EGPRSP is to develop a clear and efficient industrial policy to promote investment and innovation. Priority Actions for 2004-2006 include: accelerating the privatization and restructuring processes, drafting and implementing development programmes for selected industrial sectors to attract investments, creating the legal base for the creation of industrial parks, and developing the Programme of implementing integrated systems of quality management.

No less than 26 strategies and programmes have been elaborated for the industrial sector since 1998. In most of them environmental issues are addressed. The most important are the following programmes, which integrate environmental objectives in industrial policies:

• The *Programme "Quality and implementation of quality management system according to requirements of ISO 9000"* was implemented in 2004 by introducing quality management systems in 10 enterprises and creating preconditions for their implementation in 22 other enterprises;

• Industrial policy in the context of integration into the EU. This policy is based on the *EU-Moldova Action Plan* in the framework of the European Neighbourhood Policy of the EU;

• The *Sectoral Strategy for Industry Development for the short-term period up to 2006,* developed as an integral part of the

EGPRSP It foresees a four-fold increase of industrial output, maintaining an annual industrial growth of 17-20 per cent, and the creation of 25,000 new jobs. The Strategy was updated for 2004-2008 and harmonized with the EGPRSP targets and those of the industry policy for integration into the EU. It predicts an annual growth of industrial production of 18 per cent. It served as a basis for the elaboration of programmes for industrial sub-sector development;

• The 2004 *Programme for the Implementation of New Technologies in Industries* anticipates the enhancement of cooperation between scientific institutions and enterprises in the field of technological innovations and the creation of industrial parks and industrial clusters; and

• The 2003 *Programme for Energy Efficiency Improvement in Industry for 2004-2008*, which integrates energy conservation objectives into industrial sector policies.

8.3 Implementation and enforcement of policies to mitigate environmental impact from industrial activities

Implementation and enforcement issues such as permitting, environmental impact assessment and monitoring are covered in chapter 2.

Environmental management certification

So far there are no companies that have environmental management systems complying with ISO 14000 or eco-management and audit schemes (EMAS). The situation in this field is slightly improving because of activities of the Cleaner Production and Energy Efficiency (CPEE) Centre within the framework of the Moldovan-Norwegian long-term collaboration Programme on "Cleaner Production and Energy Efficiency". A combined training and system development Programme on Environmental Management

Systems (EMS) was held from April to November 2003 in Chisinau. The main goal of the Programme was to raise awareness among the Programme participants and encourage them to develop such programmes (following the requirements of ISO 14001) in their companies. During the Programme, 21 quality managers, environmental managers and environmental specialists from six manufacturing companies were trained in EMS principles. At the end of the Programme three companies had concrete plans to obtain ISO 14000 certificates during 2004 and have made contact with local representatives of international accredited certifying bodies for guidance and assistance (no accreditation body has been created in the country).

Preventive measures to reduce risks of industrial accidents

The *National Programme for Environmental Safety* sets the main priorities for industrial safety. The 2000 *Law on Industrial Safety of Dangerous Industrial Activities* regulates such types of activities. The Department of Standardization and Metrology is responsible for granting certification for hazardous industrial objects and regulates them (e.g., mines, gas storage facilities, chemical plants and boilers). Five hundred industrial objects dangerous for the environment are regulated and checked 1-2 times per year, although they are currently operating at very low capacity.

Cleaner production experience

The country has signed the UNEP Declaration regarding Clean Production (CP) promotion and developed the *National Declaration on Cleaner Production* in 2003 with the aim of implementing its main principles. Among them are: integration of environmental protection policies into industrial activities, pollution prevention, sustainable use of natural resources, energy conservation, and waste minimization. The Declaration foresees the development of sectoral programmes by relevant ministries for CP. However such programmes have not been elaborated.

Industrial cleaner production programmes have been implemented since 1999 with technical assistance from the EU and some non-EU countries. So far, 25 industrial operators have implemented such programmes. There are positive examples of implementation of cleaner production technologies at industrial enterprises such as SA Stejaur, SA Vitanta-Intravest, SA Carmez, SA Era-

Prim, SA Piele and Orhei-Vit. In the framework of the ongoing Tacis project *Cleaner Production in the selected countries of Newly Independent States (NIS) – Moldova, Georgia and Kazakhstan,* pilot projects were implemented at three enterprises (Avicola Rosa, Lactis and Macon). Avicola Rosa is a poultry factory, Lactis a diary produce factory, and Macon a construction materials company. The Tacis project implemented Recommendation 7.4 from the first EPR to launch a pilot project on CP for each of the main industrial sectors with an emphasis on low-cost measures. All three companies well represent Moldovan industry and their experience can be easily transferred to other similar companies.

The Project activity is supported in each country by its own Regional Environmental Centre (REC). The Tacis project has procured the necessary equipment at the value of € 1,415,000 and the calculated amount of benefit for the three companies will be around US$ 350,000 annually. These figures show that the implementation of CP strategy may result in bringing both environmental and economic benefits to companies.

Recommendation 7.4 of the first EPR of the Republic of Moldova also stipulated the necessity for creating a centre for clean production. In June 1999 the Centre for Prevention of Industrial Pollution, a non-governmental non-commercial organization, was established. In 2001, the Norwegian Ministry of Foreign Affairs and European Integration confirmed its willingness to support the long-term capacity building Programme *Cleaner Production and Energy Efficiency (CPEE) in Moldova*. Since 2001, a number of activities have been carried out by the Centre including four combined training programmes on CPEE in Balti, Chisinau, Comrat and Tiraspol during which 75 participants from 28 manufacturing companies completed CPEE programmes and identified 266 CPEE measures. Of these, 144 measures have been implemented, resulting in savings of approximately US$ 1,085,000 per year. A Revolving Fund was capitalized with US$ 30,000 from the Norwegian Ministry of Foreign Affairs within the CPEE Centre. The Fund offers loans to finance the most profitable measures developed by companies participating in CPEE programmes. By December 2004, three companies received financing from the Fund to implement CP measures. In December 2004, approximately 38 per cent of the total debt service costs were already repaid.

Box 8.1: The experience of Company "Macon" with Cleaner Production

Company "Macon" produces construction materials, bricks and ceramic. The annual turnover of the company is about € 50 million. The initial "Macon" technology of gypsum partitions production was very energy intensive. The products, gypsum partition panels, had limited application and limited markets due to their parameters, and were used only for internal partitions.

The Tacis pilot project "Cleaner Production in the selected countries of NIS – Moldova, Georgia and Kazakhstan" was implemented in "Macon" and the required equipment "Cutting complex" was installed. The overall cost for the project was € 159,800, of which € 93,870 was self-financed and € 65,960 was a grant from the Tacis project. New technology and new materials with standardized operational characteristics generated environmental as well as economic benefits. The environmental benefits were: the creation of a closed production cycle with savings of 15 per cent of process water, 45 per cent of natural gas, 45 per cent of electric energy, 69 per cent of solid oil and industrial oils; and a reduction of NO_x and CO emissions by 26 per cent. The project improved the company's image and provided annual economic benefits of € 65714 of which energy savings amounted to € 55,710 and savings on lubricants € 10,004.

Macon implemented some pollution reduction measures and having satisfied the criteria according to the *Law on Payments for Environmental Pollution* was entitled to receive offsets. However, the company did not attempt to negotiate these offsets with local authorities as they only pay US$ 4,000 pollution taxes per year and with such a high company turnover, what they would receive was not worth their while to negotiate.

8.4 Legal and institutional framework for environmental management in industrial activities

Legal framework

In addition to the 1992 *Law on Enterprises and Entrepreneurship* and the 1995 *Law on Standardization*, several laws were elaborated since 1998: the 1999 *Law on issuing licenses for certain types of activities*, the 2000 *Law on Industrial Safety of Dangerous Industrial Activities*, and the 2001 *Law on the Licensing of Certain Types of Activities*.

Institutional framework

Ministries and Institutes

The Ministry of Industry and Infrastructure is responsible for machinery, chemical, light, furniture and waste recycling industry except food, beverage and construction materials industries. The Ministry of Agriculture and Food Industry is responsible for the food processing industry except for the wine industry, which is under the Agro-industrial Agency "Moldova-Vin". The Agency for Regional Development is responsible for the regulations in the area of territorial development, construction and construction materials. It is driving the activities for raising the energy efficiency of buildings and has initiated the Programme for rehabilitation of the thermal conditions of residential buildings.

The Ministry of Economy and Trade is responsible for the regulation of all branches of the economy, including industries. It is responsible for the development of economic instruments for promotion of clean production, energy efficiency improvements, and waste recycling; and for the preparation and implementation of technical cooperation programmes. It has played an important role in the preparation, implementation and monitoring of the EGPRSP.

The Ministry of Energy[2] has the responsibility and executive authority for the development and implementation of energy policy. It supervises activities of the National Agency for Energy Conservation. Within the Ministry, the State Energy Inspectorate has the technical oversight of all power and heat companies, irrespective of their ownership and production capacity, to assure reliable, efficient and safe power generation and heat supply.

The Department of Standardization and Metrology is responsible for certification of industrial objects on quality and safety according the 2000 *Law on Industrial Safety of Dangerous Industrial Activities*. The Department is also providing the technical oversight for gas and petroleum products.

The National Institute of Ecology is the basic state institution for environmental research. The main research areas of the institute are: municipal and industrial waste management, development of the environmental norms and standards, and integrated ecological monitoring in order to evaluate quality of environment. Annually the Institute together with other institutions and experts elaborates the national report on the state of environment, but

---

[2] Since 2005, the Ministry of Energy is part of the Ministry of Industry and Infrastructure

these provide very limited information on industrial pollution.

The National Agency for Energy Regulation, established in 1997 as an independent authority to support the introduction of market mechanisms in the energy sector, issues licenses, regulates fuel and power prices, and establishes energy pricing principles and calculation methodology (See Box 5.2).

There is also a Chamber of Commerce and Industry (CCI), established in 1999, that represents the interests of private companies in various industries in the process of CP production. The Tacis project "*Cleaner Production in Selected Countries of the NIS – Republic of Moldova, Georgia and Kazakhstan*" recommended CCI to lead the overall process CP promotion in industry by organizing a trade fair of new environmental technology and cleaner production. The private sector dominates in industry and ministries responsible for industries have not developed appropriate tools to encourage cleaner production, such as appropriate economic incentives.

Other stakeholders are involved in the energy sector:

• The National Energy Council, an advisory NGO on energy and energy efficiency policies;

• The Energy Faculty: promotes energy efficiency and using of RES;

• The Energy Institute at the Academy of Sciences: does research in energy and energy efficiency issues;

• Tthe National Institute for Economy and Information, involved in reviewing the real economic costs of pollution and in helping to identify the appropriate levels of fees and fines;

• The Alliance to Save Energy Regional Office: provides support to design and implement innovative energy efficiency policies and identifies barriers to their successful implementation; and

• The Association of Energy Consumers: represents and defends energy consumers' interests in the regulatory process and in practical issues.

Specialized Centres

In June 1999 the Centre for Prevention of Industrial Pollution, a non-governmental non-commercial organization, was established (see section 8.3).

The National Agency for Energy Conservation was established in 1994 within the framework of the Tacis Programme. It worked mainly on projects for industrial enterprises on a contractual basis. Since its establishment the Agency has completed more than 80 audits in industry, mainly in the sectors connected with processing agricultural products. About 60 per cent of the measures prescribed by energy audits were implemented by the enterprises, but the real results in energy saved have not been monitored and assessed. Since 2002, the National Agency for Energy Conservation has been entrusted with the development and implementation of the energy conservation policies and programmes, with no corresponding extra capacities allocated. Currently, neither the Agency nor the National Fund for Energy Conservation, created in 2003 to secure the financing of energy conservation measures, can efficiently carry out their tasks.

The Moldovan Cleaner Production and Energy Efficiency Centre (CPEEC) is involved in many national and international activities and programmes and is continuously identifying new partners for its services. However, the national market for cleaner production is developing slowly and hence on a commercial basis the Centre's activities are barely self-sustaining.

Given the high qualifications of CPEEC staff and its large experience in CP activities, CPEEC would be able to advise the Ministry of Ecology and Natural Resources on the implementation of an integrated permitting system for all new installations, as well as for existing installations that intend to carry out changes that may have significant negative effects on the population or environment. For this, the State should provide CPEEC with some support for the consultancy and expertise in developing further EU approximation work in IPPC and waste management, a project initiated in May 2000 by REC. The project *Preparatory EU Approximation Work of the Republic of Moldova in Integrated Pollution Prevention Control and Waste Management* financed by EU DG Environment was finalized in 2001 by the study of 16 Directives/Regulations identifying gaps in the national environmental legislation and making concrete recommendations for the eventual modifications and completion of the national environmental law. Similar studies conducted in Lithuania and other Baltic States resulted in the implementation of the IPPC Directive. The outcome of these two projects in the country however was not applied for the improvement of the permitting system and for setting pollution limit values for air pollution, water sewage and waste disposal. It was recommended in the first EPR (Recommendation 2.3) to consider the IPPC Directive as a long-term target for pollution prevention and control and to include this issue in the EU partnership and cooperation agreement.

Inter-sectoral coordination

The country has many environmentally related programmes, strategies and actions plans. In almost all documents the integration of environmental policies into sectoral strategies is stated and a preparation as well as implementation of sectoral strategies for specific environmental programmes is foreseen. However the implementation of these environmental policies in the industrial sector is weak. This is because the same sector is regulated by several responsible institutions: the Ministry of Economy and Trade, the Ministry of Agriculture and Food Industry, and the Department of Agriculture, the Ministry of Industry and Infrastructure, and the Agency for Regional Development. The coordination among ministries in the implementation of important environmental policies including energy conservation, waste management, pollution reduction and clean production is insufficient. The monitoring of implementation and reporting is also very weak because of the lack of indicators expressed in clear measurable targets for policies and strategies. EGPRSP is an exception because the Millennium Development Goals (MDG) for the Republic of Moldova were formulated and addressed specifically in this strategy. The *National Energy Conservation Programme* has also established targets. However its implementation has not yet started, although it is considered to be a major priority by the Government. Only a few sectoral programmes on energy efficiency improvements have been prepared (for some industries and the energy sector) but the implementation is proceeding very slowly. The strengthening of inter-ministerial collaboration and coordination of responsibilities is necessary in order to integrate better environmental policies into sectoral programmes.

8.5　Conclusions and recommendations

The country has implemented almost all recommendations relevant to the industrial and energy sectors proposed in the first Environmental Performance Review. The most positive results regarding the industry sector were achieved by the elaboration and implementation of a waste management strategy, the establishment of a cleaner production centre and the implementation of pilot cleaner production projects for each of the main industrial sectors. Some of them for energy (liberalization of energy sector and getting energy prices right) had also a positive impact on energy efficiency and mitigated the environmental impact of the sector. However others were only partly implemented: improvements were anticipated in the elaboration of an energy saving programme and establishment of energy savings funds but there were neither economic incentives nor appropriate financing mechanisms in place, so the objectives were not fully realized

Not all results envisaged by these recommendations were successfully achieved. Some very important and still relevant recommendations were not implemented: the development of modern instruments for waste management, the development of relevant fiscal instruments, particularly profit taxes and import duties to encourage cleaner production, and the development of economic instruments (tax reduction, exemptions from profit taxes) for energy savings.

Since 1998 the country has elaborated various environmental strategies, action plans and programmes covering the most important issues relevant to industrial activities: waste management, water resources, POPs, environmental safety, environmental hygiene and clean production. In all documents the integration of environmental policies into sectoral strategies is stated and preparation as well as implementation of sectoral strategies for the implementation of specific environmental programme is being foreseen in these documents.

However implementation of sectoral environmental policies needs improvement. The sectoral programmes above-mentioned need to be further implemented. Some programmes in energy efficiency and waste management were elaborated. However, their implementation is being poorly monitored because of the lack of indicators and weak coordination between ministries responsible.

Information about the environmental impact of industries is very limited. Therefore it is difficult to analyze the situation in this sector or to set targets for emission reduction, or to identify priorities and measures needed to achieve these targets. The programmes for development of industries declare that environmental issues should be integrated but do not give any priorities or environmental impact reduction targets and do not provide any capacity for their monitoring. The environmental standards inherited from the Soviet past are too numerous and unrealistic. The IPPC Directive should be considered as the long-term target and its implementation should be started gradually but without delay.

Weak implementation of environmental policies in industries is also caused by an institutional framework for the regulation of industrial activities being shared between several responsible institutions. Clearly there is insufficient coordination. Nevertheless a positive trend can be noticed towards the promotion of cleaner production as a result of the establishment of Cleaner Production and Energy Efficiency Centre (CPEE) and its successful operation since 1999. The CPEE Centre could use the Polish Clean Production Programme as an example for its own involvement in the implementation of IPPC Directive requirements in the country.

However the main obstacle for a successful implementation of environmental policies in industries is the lack of economic incentives. Pollution taxes and user charges are low and imposed based on calculations instead of actual emission monitoring. They therefore do not stimulate implementation of pollution abatement measures. Economic measures for the promotion of cleaner production and the implementation of energy saving measures and waste recycling were not concretely introduced though they were stipulated in the relevant programmes.

The Ministry of Ecology and Natural Resources in cooperation with the Institute of Ecology and the CPEE Centre should elaborate emission limit values for the major pollutants (NO_x, SO_2, CO and particulates matters) starting with large combustion installations. Limit values should be implemented gradually for other sources and other pollutants, based on the experience of other countries that inherited similar systems from their Soviet pasts. The results of the Tacis project "Preparatory EU Approximation Work of the Republic of Moldova in IPPC and Waste Management" and other relevant studies should be used for the further work. The Ministry should initiate the revision of pollution taxes in combination with emission standards. Taxes should be increased and only principal pollutants should be taxed. Other pollutants can be grouped according their toxicity into the four toxicity classes and the same tariff per class should be applied. The studies elaborated by the Energy Institute and the State Institute of Economy and Information can be used for setting rates for pollution taxes. (See Recommendation 5.3)

Recommendation 8.1:
The Ministry of Ecology and Natural Resources in cooperation with the Ministry of Industry and Infrastructure and other relevant stakeholders should develop an integrated system of indicators for monitoring the environmental impact of industries. This system should enable the establishment of targets that would be used for setting priorities for environmental impact mitigation in industrial development strategies.

Recommendation 8.2:
The Ministry of Economy and Trade should coordinate relevant institutions more effectively, monitor the implementation of sectoral programmes, and ensure that environmental issues are integrated effectively into these programmes.

Recommendation 8.3:
The Ministry of Industry and Infrastructure should initiate the restructuring of the National Energy Conservation Agency and the National Fund for Energy Conservation based on the experience of other countries on energy savings and energy efficiency improvements.

Recommendation 8.4:
The Ministry of Economy and Trade in collaboration with the Ministry of Finance and the Ministry of Ecology and Natural Resources should improve economic incentives (for instance, reduction of profit taxes and other taxes for industrial production based on waste recycling and reuse, reduced charge rate for enterprises reducing their waste, etc.), elaborate measures for promoting recycling and disposal of waste; stimulate energy efficiency improvements; and enhance clean production methods based on related national programmes.

ANNEXES

Annex I: Implementation of the Recommendations in the First Environmental Performance Review

Annex II: Selected Economic and Environmental Data

Annex III: Selected Regional and Global Environmental Agreements

Annex IV: List of Environment-Related Legislation in Republic of Moldova

Annex I

IMPLEMENTATION OF THE RECOMMENDATIONS IN THE FIRST ENVIRONMENTAL PERFORMANCE REVIEW [1]

PART I   THE CONDITIONS OF ENVIRONMENTAL POLICY AND MANAGEMENT

Chapter 1:   Legislative and institutional framework

Recommendation 1.1:
The National Strategic Environmental Plan should be entirely overhauled in order to provide an integrated programme of linked and phased activities, which can easily be put into operation by ministries and departments in their respective sectors. Specific targeted policies should be meshed with current sectoral actions.

Implementation:
There was a need to implement a unified policy on the environment and use of natural resources that integrated environmental requirements into the process of national economic reform. This, coupled with the political desire for integration to the EU, has resulted in reviewing the existing environmental policy and developing a new policy concept.

The 2001 *Concept of Environmental Policy* replaced the action plans and concepts that had been in force since the mid 1990s. It covers the adjustment of the major environmental policy objectives to take into account social and economic changes, as well as incorporating regional and global programmes and trends to protect the environment. Environmental requirements have also been integrated into sectoral policies.

Since 1998 other environmental strategies and programmes have been elaborated, providing a basis for environmental protection and legislation. The very large number of these strategies, concepts, programmes and plans has not resulted in their practical implementation due to the lack of human and financial resources and administrative capacity. The list of these documents is given in Annex III.

Recommendation 1.2:
Lawmakers should focus on reviewing existing environmental laws to identify overlap, contradictions and gaps amongst them all; amendments should be proposed accordingly.

Implementation:
Although the Ministry of Ecology and Natural Resources (MENR) is reviewing legislation and amending legal acts, the existing legal acts are largely based on early 1990's principles and methodologies and some areas are still unregulated. The strictly sectoral (i.e., single-media such as air, water and waste) character of environmental laws and their prescriptive nature mean that there is no synergy between sectors and no holistic view of environmental problems, or of their solution. This is likely to increase difficulties in moving towards the implementation of an integrated pollution prevention and control system as there is still little experience of cross-media and cross-sectoral practice.

---

[1] The first Environmental Performance Review of the Republic of Moldova was carried out in 1998. Its report is available at the following internet address: www.unece.org/env/epr/studies/moldova/welcome.htm

Recommendation 1.3:
The DEP should be raised to the level of ministry as a result of the necessary restructuring and integration of governmental decision-making and management in the areas of environment, use of natural resources and, possibly, physical planning.

Implementation:
To take environmental decisions at a higher level the Department of Environmental Protection was lift up to a Ministry of Environment in 1998, and then restructured several times till becoming the Ministry of Ecology and Natural Resources in 2004 with extended rights and responsibilities. Four territorial environmental agencies have been created, with their own field laboratories.

Recommendation 1.4:
A national steering committee for sustainable development should be created with broad governmental and non-governmental participation. This committee should also ensure effective coordination and implementation of environmental policies across the sectors.

Implementation:
By the Decision of the President of the Republic of Moldova N 996-III on 3.12.2002, the National Council on Sustainable Development and Poverty Reduction was established in 2004 and a regulation on the Council was issued. In compliance with the regulation, the Inter-Ministerial Committee for Sustainable Development and Poverty Reduction was additionally set up to coordinate activities related to strategic planning in the socio-economic policy. This was intended to be oriented towards the sustainable development of the country and improvement of the quality of life of the population. However, as of early 2005, the Council has not been operational.

Recommendation 1.5:
The responsibilities of local authorities regarding environmental management should be reviewed, clarified and strengthened and the necessary resources allocated accordingly.

Implementation:
The 1998 *Law on Local Public Administration* established the competences of each territorial unit of the first and second level of administration, and gave them competences in environmental protection. After the 2003 revision, environmental functions were recentralized and the financial autonomy of local administrations reduced. As a result of the 2005 election, the environment management will be decentralized again.

Recommendation 1.6:
Environmental policies should be formulated, with authoritative support, at the highest government level to direct and coordinate the activities of the ministries, departments and agencies involved in agriculture, forestry, water and land use.

Implementation:
The main objective of the 2001 *Concept on Environmental Policy* is to coordinate the environmental State policy priorities with socio-economic changes in the country, in line with global and regional trends, programmes and plans. The 2004 *Economical Growth and Poverty Reduction Strategy* represents a key-factor in strategic coordination of different sectors of the national economy. The Government and the Parliament have also drawn up a number of other specific documents containing environmental policy objectives. For instance, the coordination with other relevant institutions is obligatory and foreseen in the following regulations: Government Decision № 699 *on approval of rules regarding the elaboration of the projects of normative acts,* of 1994, which describes the process of elaboration and coordination; Government Decision *on approval of Rules regarding the elaboration of departmental normative acts, which* covers the coordination of projects within an institution or interested organizations; provisions in the statute of the Ministry of Ecology and Natural Resources; and Law № 317-XV on normative acts, of 2003.

In spite of all these mechanisms, coordination can still be characterized as inefficient, because the Ministry of Ecology and Natural Resources is not involved early enough in the elaboration of plans, programmes and laws. The Ministry only receives final versions of documents, a step at which introducing some changes is becoming quite difficult.

Recommendation 1.7:
Capacity-building activities should be implemented in the "non-environmental" agencies to sensitize senior decision makers to environmental concerns and to train operational staff in appropriate environmental issues, approaches and techniques. Financial assistance for environmental capacity building should benefit not only bodies involved in environmental issues at the national level, but also local governments and the environmental NGO community.

Implementation:
The MENR introduced courses on environmental protection to the non-ecological profiles in university faculties. To improve the professional skills of office employees and local administration authorities in the Presidential Academy of Public Management, a course on environmental protection is envisaged. The National Environmental Fund (NEF) finances NGOs in the implementation of environmental education and public awareness projects. NGOs and specialists from other Ministries and Departments are invited by the MENR to be involved in the elaboration of strategic documents on environmental protection.

Recommendation 1.8:
Revised procedures of public involvement should include:

- *Announcing the commencement of State Ecological Expertise (SEE) and Environmental Impact Assessment (EIA) processes in the local press;*
- *Inviting individuals, organizations and communities to submit written comments and participate in public meetings relating to (i) identifying the issues to be considered in the SEE/EIA investigations; and (ii) the contents of SEE/EIA reports;*
- *Requiring all SEE/EIA reports to have non-technical summaries;*
- *Placing copies of reports in local libraries; and*
- *Specifying rules governing the conduct of public meetings and the methods by which the results are conveyed to the proponent and other decision makers and how they will be used in decision-making.*

Implementation:
To contribute to public awareness and to facilitate access to environmental information, the Environmental Information Centre was established within the MENR. Despite stipulations in the laws, the State Ecological Inspectorate (SEI) is not proactive in seeking public comments as part of the State Ecological Expertise (SEE), and usually disregards "public environmental review" (PER) conclusions. Project proponents themselves do not share their documentation with the public, using commercial confidentiality concern as an excuse.

Recommendation 1.9:
The instrument of environmental impact assessment should be more systematically used at all levels of government: national, regional and local. The official attitude to public participation in EIA projects should take into account the high value of such participation, as demonstrated in all European countries.

Implementation:
The Republic of Moldova signed the Protocol on Strategic Environmental Assessment (SEA) to the Espoo Convention at the Fifth "Environment for Europe" Ministerial Conference in 2003. Under the regional UNDP project "Strategic Environmental Assessment: Promotion and Capacity Development" (covering Armenia, Belarus, Georgia, Republic of Moldova and Ukraine), a manual is being developed for all governmental and non-governmental stakeholders on the implementation of this Protocol However, assessments of government programmes and strategies are not performed systematically, while the Environmental Impact Assessment (EIA) on projects is usually limited to the old-style formalistic State Ecological Expertise.

Chapter 2   Integration of environmental and economic decisions

Recommendation 2.1:
The scope, sources of finance and purposes of the national and local environmental funds should be reconsidered between all levels of administration involved and clearly delimited. Additional funds might be forthcoming for environmental protection, if percentages of economic aggregates like GNP were earmarked for environmental protection in national budgets. The strengthening of environmental funds operations should be extended also to training for local staff to manage local funds.

Implementation:
The legislative basis and financing of environmental funds have improved since the 1998 EPR. The NEF is financed mainly by levies on imported fuel (introduced in 1998) and other environmentally harmful products (since 2003). Local funds are financed by pollution charges, if they are actually levied. Some training for staff at territorial environmental agencies, which manage local funds, has been provided since the late 1990s but most local funds are in practice unimportant. Although environmentally related revenues were solid in recent years, averaging three per cent of GDP, the amounts spent from the NEF on environmental protection are significantly lower.

Recommendation 2.2:
Project assessment and monitoring of project implementation should be part of a transparent administration of the National Environmental Fund. Financial analysis should be integrated with environmental audit, impact assessment, and the work of the inspectorates. Successful experiences in managing environmental funds in other countries in transition should be retained.

Implementation:
The secretariat of the Administrative Council of the NEF was appointed in December 1998. It commissions outside experts to evaluate projects prior to funding. Some know-how from the Polish environmental fund was passed on with the aid of the Eco Fund Project. The SEI and territorial environmental agencies of the Ministry of Ecology and Natural Resources monitor the execution of projects. The State Ecological Inspection and territorial environmental agencies managed and controlled the implementation of projects. However, good practices for managing environmental funds were implemented only partly.

Recommendation 2.3:
The IPPC Directive of the EU should constitute a long-term target for pollution prevention and control. It should be included in the Partnership and Cooperation Agreement.

Implementation:
There have been several EU-sponsored attempts in recent years to study and plan a transition to integrated permitting. In 2001, a law on integrated environmental permitting was drafted but not approved by the government due to its poor preparation and opposition from key stakeholder ministries. However, permitting reform is part of the 2005 EU-Moldova Action Plan.

Recommendation 2.4:
Fines for environmental pollution should be indexed to quarterly inflation figures (CPI) as published by the Department for Statistics.

Implementation:
Pollution fines have remained unchanged in nominal terms since 1998.

Recommendation 2.5:
Environmental liability issues should be included permanently in privatization laws, requiring an adaptation of the resources of the legal expertise of the DEP.

Implementation:
The authorities are convinced that the environmental liability issues related to privatization are satisfactorily dealt with by existing legislation, the 1991 Law on Privatization. In the case of large asset sales, a resolution

of environmental liability issues is specified in the privatization contract. In other cases, existing legislation enables the buyer of State assets to demand compensation for undisclosed environmental liabilities within one year of the sale.

Recommendation 2.6:
An initiative by a competent authority to promote the development of insurance schemes against environmental risks could possibly contribute to improving the handling of liability issues for environmental damage in an industrial context.

Implementation:
In 1999, the Ministry of Environment drafted an act on environmental insurance, which was not promulgated due to the unwillingness of the legislature to impose new financial obligations on firms. The country signed the Protocol on Civil Liability and Compensation for Damage Caused by the Transboundary Effects of Industrial Accidents on Transboundary Waters.

In 2004 several environmental-damage-related guidelines and pieces of legislation were drawn up and published: Temporary methodology on the environmental damage valuation, as a result of violation of water legislation; Instruction on the environmental damage valuation of soil resources; Instruction on the estimation of damage from pollution of the air by stationary sources; Instruction on estimation of environmental damage caused as a result of non-compliance of natural resources legislation; and Instruction on the air damage payments as a result of using salvage and consumption waste.

Recommendation 2.7
A method should be implemented that prevents real revenues from the water tax from falling due to inflation.

Implementation:
The principal water tax rate remained unchanged at 1.8 lei per ten m³ from 1998 to 2002. The rate was increased to five lei per ten m³ in 2003 and remained fixed in the following years. The consumer price index increased by 165 per cent between 1998 and 2004.

Chapter 3:   International cooperation

Recommendation 3.1:
The Department for Environmental Protection's capacities for project management, including cooperation with international funding partners, need strengthening. Among the necessary remedial measures, staff should receive language training, as well as intensive training in substantive aspects of environmental policy, management and enforcement.

Implementation:
With the purpose of strengthening the potential of European integration and cooperation with international partners, the MENR created the Division of Science, Technical Assistance and European Integration. Under the Ministry of Foreign Affairs, courses were organized on foreign languages and European integration matters, which were attended by ministry employees.

To raise the level of management in Government, special courses were taught with the participation of representatives from other Ministries and Departments. A number of employees get post-graduate education on environment and international relations at the Academy of Public Administration.

Recommendation 3.2:
The role and resources of the National Commission for the Implementation of International Environmental Conventions should be strengthened.

Implementation:
Each international environmental agreement has a working group that includes the MENR and other representatives from Ministries, Departments and NGOs. For example, the Parliament Regulation Nr.504

XIV on 14.07.99 created the National committee for the implementation of the Convention on International Trade in Endangered Species of Wild Fauna and Flora (CITES).However, these WGs neither have legal nor binding powers, nor any clearly identified plans, procedures or mandates for their work. These procedures are referred to as "non-written". The WGs meet no more often than once every two months. This does not provide any systematic approach for assessing the progress on agreements implementation. The Ministry's experts recognize that the enforcement section in conventions implementation is severely lacking and needs to be strengthened.

Recommendation 3.3:
The Basel Convention should be ratified, related national legislation established and specific training for the staff organized. Likewise, the ratification of the Danube Convention and other relevant intergovernmental treaties should be promoted.

Implementation:
Since 1998 the Republic of Moldova has become party to 11 new agreements, including the Basel Convention in 1998 and the Danube Convention in 1999. As of today, it is party to 19 international environmental conventions, four protocols and a signatory to five more. Each international environmental agreement has its National focal point.

Recommendation 3.4:
The responsibility for the implementation of the Espoo Convention should be assigned to the institution that assesses environmental impacts.

Implementation:
The SEI within the MENR is the focal point for the implementation of the Espoo Convention. It is also the body responsible for the State Ecological Expertise and the Environmental Impact Assessment.

Recommendation 3.5:
To control transboundary air pollution, additional air monitoring stations should be installed on the borders with Ukraine and northern Romania. "Hydrometeo" should be fully equipped for the analysis of all samples obtained from transboundary air pollution monitoring.

Implementation:
The State Hydrometeorological Service (HMS) restored the air monitoring station for transboundary air pollution in the town of Leova. The station is not able to report fully on daily situations so it is necessary to establish additional observation stations. The number of samples and monitored pollutants has increased. The station also performs the monitoring of some persistent organic pollutants (POPs) and heavy metals in atmospheric precipitations that have a transboundary aspect.

PART II: MANAGEMENT OF POLLUTION AND OF NATURAL RESOURCES

Chapter 4:   Air Management

Recommendation 4.1:
The recent adoption of the Law on Air Protection requires the preparation of implementing regulations that should benefit from contemporary European practices and experience, in particular as regards standards for ambient air quality and deposition levels.

Implementation:
The elaboration of instructions, built on the approach of contemporary European methods and practices (for example determination of emissions under the methodology EMEP/CORINAIR and others, elaborated by the European Ecology Agency) is included partially in a long-term ecological programme – "Programme on environmental security" adopted by a Government Regulation in 2003. The legal acts are still based on previous Soviet Union practices. The air quality standards in force (still more than 1,000) have not been changed and also date from the same period. The principles of a combined approach to establishing

requirements are not used i.e., in addition to existing air quality limit values there are no emission standards set directly by legal acts. Emission limit values in permits are still based on pollutant dispersion calculations.

Recommendation 4.2:
The administrative authority for setting environmental standards relevant for air management should be streamlined in such a way that it clarifies responsibilities and enforces appropriate coordination mechanisms between the sectoral interests involved. The new set of standards should become the basis for strict enforcement in the very near future.

Implementation:
In 2000, the National Ecological Institute has created a committee for the elaboration of standards in the field of air quality protection. Practical results in this field have not yet been obtained.

Recommendation 4.3:
The future development of the energy economy should be steered in such a way that the use of cleaner fuels and of cleaner technologies is promoted through the introduction and application of market-oriented instruments.

Implementation:
The recommendation has been partly implemented. There is a tax differentiation on imported fuels: one per cent of the customs value on leaded petrol and diesel and 0.5 per cent on the value of unleaded petrol. The authorities have addressed the air pollution problem with a number of regulations, including restrictions on imports of old cars and stricter norms for imported fuels that promote the use of unleaded petrol and desulphurized diesel. The decrease of energy demand and the replacement of solid and liquid fuels by natural gas in combustion units also contributed to lower emissions.

However, there are no tax reductions or exemptions on energy saving investments or other economic tools for the promotion of energy efficiency improvements and cleaner production. In addition, pollution taxes and user charges are low and are imposed based on calculations instead of actual emission monitoring. Therefore they do not stimulate the implementation of pollution abatement measures and acquisition of offsets for pollution taxes as stipulated by the 1998 *Law on Payments for Environmental Pollution*.

Recommendation 4.4:
In accordance with the recently adopted Law on Payments for Environmental Pollution, the charges and fines used to combat air pollution should be enforced without delay in the country as a whole.

Implementation:
The enforcement rate of existing pollution charges has improved to about 50 per cent in recent years though the charge rates have remained stable since 1998. The enforcement of fines remains more limited.

Recommendation 4.5:
The existing inventory, monitoring and reporting systems for air pollution should be expanded with regard to the most important air pollutants.

Implementation:
The statistical reporting on air pollution has been enlarged to include the following pollutants: aromatic polycyclic hydrocarbon, heavy metals, and persistent organic pollutants. HMS stations measure a limited number of meteorological and chemical parameters (SO_2, NO_x, dust, CO, B(a)P and Pb) in urban air. Several chemical parameters required by national standards (Cu, Cr, Ni, V and Co) are not measured, and neither are air concentrations of NH_3, VOC (except B(a)P), O_3, PM_{10}, Hg and POPs. Since 2004, measurements have been made of aerosols, some POPs and some heavy metals (Cd, Hg and Pb) in precipitation at one station in Chisinau and at the Leova station.

Reporting on emissions of pollutants in the atmosphere under the Secretary of the Convention on Long-range Transboundary Air Pollution and its authorized bodies was enlarged and improved.

Recommendation 4.6:
The gradual implementation of a comprehensive nationwide monitoring programme should begin with the drawing-up of a programme of required investments and lead to the installation of continuous measuring and sampling devices, especially in urban areas. See also Recommendations 2.3 and 2.4.

Implementation:
The HMS has set some measures to update the system of climate monitoring. For that, six automatic stations for monitoring parameters linked to climate were installed in 2004. This is the first prerequisite for integration with the European Observation System.

Recommendation 4.7:
In the immediate future, air management authorities should focus on the control of: (a) emissions from road vehicles, preferably in accordance with relevant UNECE regulations; and (b) emissions of nitrogen and particulates in human settlements. Moldova should consider acceding to the 1994 Sulphur Protocol to the Convention on Long-range Transboundary Air Pollution.

Implementation:
Annually, the Ministry of Ecology and Natural resources estimates vehicle emissions using the elements of COoRdinated INformation AIR (CORINAIR) methodology. In 2001, the Government approved the *Programme for Reduction of Motor Vehicle Emissions*, which prescribes the method and priority actions for reducing pollution. Several towns are taking stock of air pollution, including of solid particles and nitrogen dioxide.

The Republic of Moldova is not planning to comply with the 1994 Oslo Protocol on Further Reduction of Sulphur Emissions. The country signed the 1999 Gothenburg Protocol to Abate Acidification, Eutrophication and Ground-level Ozone in 2000. In the Protocol's Addendum II the country's obligations on reducing the emissions of sulphur until 2010 are included. The country intends to ratify the Gothenburg Protocol in the near future.

Chapter 5:   Water management

Recommendation 5.1:
The existing water supply programmes should be updated, alternative sources of supply should be included, and the involvement of local authorities should be increased.

Implementation:
The 2001 Complex Scheme on public water supply and water disposal until 2010 contains an alternative water supply for those localities that do not have access to high quality drinking water. The scheme foresees the construction of corresponding new supply systems and water abstraction (at present the layout has been examined and has to be approved by the Government).

The 2002 *Programme of Water Supply and Sanitation for Municipalities until 2006* contains a complete list of water supply systems that must be modernized and enlarged for a better supply of high quality drinking water. According to the Programme projects are to be financed from the State Budget, World Bank, Denmark and the NEF.

The Department for Construction and Planning Area coordinates the issues related to water supply policy development.

Recommendation 5.2:
The assessment of the costs of water abstraction and supply, wastewater collection, treatment and discharge should be seen as a priority for Moldova's water resource management. It is essential for revising the national water tariff policy. The assessment should include all economic costs related to the operation of all relevant technical installations, their maintenance and their replacement.

Implementation:
In 2000 the Danish Environmental Protection Agency performed a cost assessment for water abstraction and supply in the framework of a technical co-operation project. In the following years, further cost calculations were done by the Association Moldova "Apa Canal" (AMAC) and the National Agency for Energy Regulation (ANRE). Water tariffs continue to be heavily influenced by social considerations.

Recommendation 5.3:
As a precondition for the implementation of effective cooperation between all administrations involved, water management should be represented at ministerial level as part of overall environmental management. Separating policy authority from actual exploitation activities is advisable. River basin administrative units should be created for each basin. Cooperation should be extended to NGOs in the context of EIAs. See also Recommendation 1.3.

Implementation:
The State authority on water management is the MENR, which coordinates its own activity with the Republican Concern for Water Administration "Apele Moldovei". River basin administration bodies have not been created yet. But the Parliament Regulation Nr 325-XV of 18.07.03 foresees the delimitation of river basins and the creation of their management bodies. Joint arrangements with NGOs have been organized with the aim of raising the population's sense of duty and civil liability for the protection of water resources, as well as encouraging the cleaning of waterside protection zones from any source of pollution.

Recommendation 5.4:
The necessary streamlining of the monitoring system between the different partners should, among other results, lead to more reliable and more complete monitoring data.

Implementation:
The HMS facilitated the procedure of data control with the approval of the MENR. Data control is systematically made based on the approved monitoring scheme. Monthly information about the state of the environment is disseminated to all interested organizations.

Recommendation 5.5:
The enforcement of bilateral water treaties with neighbouring countries should lead to common monitoring systems, specifications for the use of common water resources during droughts, as well as for detailed limit values for the water parameters to be aimed at by the partners in the treaties.

Implementation:
Under bilateral and trilateral agreements with Romania and Ukraine, a working group is going to be established. All aspects of environmental protection will be taken into account, particularly under the agreements with Romania. The HMS is implementing a joint sampling programme with the IASI Environmental Protection Agency of Romania on the Prut River. Agreements on Use of Fish Reserves were prepared and approved by the Government of the Republic of Moldova and the Romanian Government.

The Danube Convention proposes to draw up a joint plan for Prut River management. An information exchange is being carried out on monitoring and sewage purification technologies. The agreement with Ukraine sets water levels in the case of spring floods and emergency situations.

The OSCE project, in which Ukraine and the Republic of Moldova participate, foresees recommendations for the improvement of environmental conditions of the Dniester River, including establishing joint monitoring and water distribution systems.

Recommendation 5.6:
The supply of safe drinking water to the rural population should be ensured with the help of a legal and administrative (including budgetary) framework that enables local authorities to control and enforce effectively all relevant water quality standards and the implementation of related water policies. See also recommendation 1.5 and recommendations 11.3, 11.4 and 11.5.

Implementation:
Public health and environmental protection authorities are engaged in monitoring the quality of water sources in rural localities. The SEI made an inventory of 2259 artificial water objects in March 2002, 4520 wells that were finished in April 2003 and 310 wastewater disposal facilities in June 2004.

For the implementation of the 2004 Presidential Decree on Clean Water Week "Water-source of life", National and local Action Plans were drawn up. As a result of a nation-wide inventory of wells (draw-wells) and springs, 69744 wells and 1343 springs were equipped with modern amenities. A National contest was held with the theme "The best equipped with modern amenities water source in localities".

Recommendation 5.7:
The water management authorities should avoid all unnecessary delays in the introduction of appropriate metering systems as a prerequisite for the recovery of water costs. See also recommendation 9.5.

Implementation:
A gradual installation of metering systems started in 1998. The majority of residential buildings and more than 30 per cent of apartments are equipped with water consumption meters. However, there are large measurement discrepancies (around 15 per cent of the water supplied to households is not accounted for) due to unreliable equipment and meter tampering by a non-negligible proportion of households.

Chapter 6:   Nature conservation, forest and biodiversity management

Recommendation 6.1:
The envisaged comprehensive national biodiversity strategy should be finalized as a matter of priority. It should be supplemented with an action plan including specific projects, coordinated with all other relevant sectoral strategies, notably those governing the development of sustainable agriculture.

Implementation:
The Parliament approved the *National Strategy and Action Plan on Conservation of Biodiversity* in 2001. The State Agency for Land Relation and Cadastre receives suggestions annually for amendments to the Land cadastre concerning the inclusion of new areas protected by the State, although the area of protected territories have not increased since 1998 (1.96%).

Recommendation 6.2:
Competing claims on land should be coordinated in the context of territorial planning at all levels of government (national, regional and local). The coordination should involve public participation. It may result in the identification of areas to be excluded from the privatization process in accordance with the national biodiversity strategy.

Implementation:
The principles of this recommendation were not sufficiently applied during the privatization. Privatization took place before the adoption of key documents such as the 1998 *Law on the Fund of State Protected Natural Areas* and the 2001 *National Strategy and Actions Plan on Conservation of Biodiversity.* Some claims on land-for-land or water protection were not taken into consideration during the privatization. As an example, due to lack of coordination between the different authorities, there were difficulties in establishing the Moldovan National Ecological Network. It is positive that municipalities can to some extent influence land use and land distribution.

Recommendation 6.3:
A long-term programme should be developed to define (explain and justify) what natural habitats and ecosystems will need future protection, under what regimes and in what specific geographic zones. The planning at an early stage of a future ecological network would facilitate the setting of priorities. Environmental bilateral agreements with neighbouring countries (Romania and Ukraine) should include the protection of transboundary aquatic habitats, and their ecosystems and species; the continuity of transboundary ecological corridors/networks; and agreement on objectives and harmonized programmes for the management of protected transboundary zones.

Implementation:
Based on the 2001 *National Strategy and Action Plan on Biodiversity Conservation* and the 2001 *Strategy for Sustainable Development of the Forestry Fund*, the *General Action Plan on Introduction of the Strategy for Sustainable Development of Forestry Fund* and the *State Programme on Forest Fund Areas Regeneration and Forestation for 2003-2020* were approved by the government in 2003.

Also the *Concept for the Development of a National Ecological Network*, the drafting of a *Law on the National Ecological Network* (ready for adoption) and the mapping of the National Ecological Network were elaborated. The country is implementing the Kiev Resolution on Biodiversity, adopted during the fifth Kiev Ministerial Conference "Environment for Europe".

Recommendation 6.4:
The Law on the Protection of Riparian Zones (1995) should be enforced, starting in priority regions, i.e. where vegetation cover is poor and water ecosystems and resources are threatened. Actions should involve the national as well as the local level and could include:

- *Informing of local and regional levels of their tasks,*
- *Requesting municipalities to identify problems on their territory, priorities and resources needed,*
- *Requesting municipalities to issue and enforce the necessary municipal decrees, and*
- *Ensuring that the necessary resources (from national and local sources) are made available at the local level to fulfil these tasks.*

Implementation:
The recommendation has not been implemented. Even though the Government adopted the 2001 Decision "Arrangements on Establishing of Coastal River and Water Reservoirs Protection Zones", its implementation is very slow due to lack of finances and a low commitment from other involved authorities. Furthermore, these zones are not clearly demarcated. The realization of this decision has also been hampered by the privatization of water protection zones in some localities. Nevertheless, the legislation has restricted agricultural activity in water protection zones and prohibited the use of pesticides and the settlement of livestock farms, oil product deposits and others in these zones.

Recommendation 6.5:
A separation of policy authority and actual exploitation of forest is advisable.

Implementation:
The recommendation has not been implemented.

Recommendation 6.6:
A national strategic forest action plan should be developed as a basis for the management of the forest resources as a whole. It should take relevant aspects of the Pan-European Ecological Network and the Pan-European Strategy on Biodiversity and Landscape Protection into account. The action plan should address the question of forest management regimes and should be fully coordinated between the national government (i.e. Moldsilva) and local authorities. A programme for the extension of forest area should be included in the strategic forest action plan.

Implementation:
The 2001 *Strategy for Long-term Development of the National Forestry Fund*, the 2003 *General Action Plan on Introduction of the Strategy for Sustainable Development of Forestry Fund* and the 2003 *State Programme on Forest Fund Areas Regeneration and Forestation for 2003-2020* include an extension of the forest area and conservation of biodiversity, but do not include details such as the establishment of an National Ecological Network. The National Ecological Network of Moldova is still at a conceptual stage.

Recommendation 6.7:
All laws prohibiting the cutting of trees, catching of fish or hunting should be properly enforced.

Implementation:

The *Law on Environmental Protection* prohibits the felling of trees and bushes without permission from appropriate official bodies. The SEI as well as Moldsilva has established a subdivision to fight illegal felling and poaching. Hunting and fishing in natural reservoirs are allowed with a special permit from the MENR. The existent laws and regulations are sufficient but the level of their observance is low, even where sanctions were increased and hardened to encourage adherence. It is necessary to increase the involvement of legal bodies on all levels and of local authorities. Cases of illegal hunting and fishing in scientific reserves such as "The lower Prut" and "Padurea Domneasca" (the Princely Forest) were registered.

Chapter 7:   Waste management and cleaner production

Recommendation 7.1:
The necessary translation of broadly formulated general policy objectives into concrete action plans should start from NEAP. The totality of action plans should be comprehensive to the extent that it constitutes a waste management strategy. It should result in enforceable actions and improved legal instruments, which should explicitly replace all existing action plans in the respective areas of concern.

Implementation:

The 1997 *Law on Municipal and Industrial Waste* requires the Government to develop a National Waste Management Programme. The 2000 *National Programme on Management of Industrial and Domestic Wastes up to 2010* sets priorities and establishes main actions for industrial waste management. The main targets of the Programme are: waste disposal and utilization; reduction of waste accumulated; reduction of hazardous waste and its toxicity before its withdrawal from technological processes; and implementation of separate waste collection principles. The legislative framework in relation to waste was also amended.

The 2003 Regulation on the Control of Transboundary Transport of waste products and their utilization includes the principles of the Basel Convention, as well as parts of the European Directive on Waste. The *Law on Environmental Protection* obliges Local Governments to develop local Environmental Protection Plans that when developed include plans for local waste management. In addition to the existing National Programme no waste management plans have been developed yet on regional (*rayon*) level.

Recommendation 7.2:
A plan is required for the provision of resources for the acquisition of waste treatment technologies, training of staff at all levels of waste management, and the development of an adequate information system. All three aspects are expensive. The plan should therefore take into account the fact that successful waste management will increasingly become an instrument for the achievement of export growth.

Implementation:

The *2000 National Programme on Management of Industrial and Domestic Wastes up to 2010* is based on the principles of waste minimization and the inclusion of waste in economic turnover (processing and utilization). It details the implementation of measures and actions and the authorities responsible for their execution. Its main goals are:

- To use and neutralize existing waste, and reduce waste accumulation;
- To reduce the volume and toxicity of waste until it is eliminated from the technological process;
- To strictly avoid the use of toxic raw material; and
- To develop clean industrial technologies, based on the rational utilization and reduction of raw material and energy until the complete cessation of industrial waste generation is achieved.

No financial plan was developed to define the resources necessary for the implementation of the related actions, including the acquisition of waste treatment technologies and the development of adequate information systems.

Recommendation 7.3:
Moldova should ratify the European Agreement concerning the International Carriage of Dangerous Goods by Roads (ADR). An implementation programme, including an analysis of costs and training for the staff involved in its implementation, should be established. See also Recommendation 3.2.

Implementation:

The country has ratified the *Agreement on the International Carriage of Dangerous Goods by Roads* by Parliament Decision in 1998. But no cost analysis for implementation was performed. Nevertheless the certification procedures and related capacities were developed and training programmes for drivers carrying dangerous goods were carried out. Five training centres were created. To date, 383 drivers for the carriage of dangerous goods have been trained.

Recommendation 7.4:
Technological change for the purposes of cleaner production should be promoted through the creation of a centre for cleaner production, including the preparation of the national programme for the phase-out of ODS. The centre should be jointly supported by the Government and the representative industrial organizations. It should be responsible for the promotion of the ISO 14000 series among Moldovan enterprises.

Implementation:

In 1999 the Centre for Prevention of Industrial Pollution as a non-governmental non-commercial organization was established. Norway and the NEF finance its activities. The Centre started a 4-year Programme "Cleaner Production and Energy Efficiency in Moldova". Four combined training and project development programmes on Cleaner Production and Energy Efficiency in Moldovan industry have been completed in four cities: Balti, Chisinau, Comrat and Tiraspol. A Revolving Fund for Cleaner Production and Energy Efficiency projects was established and managed by the Centre. A training programme on Environmental Management Systems (EMS) and the promotion of ISO 14000 series among enterprises have been completed.

Recommendation 7.5:
The relevant fiscal instruments, particularly profit taxes and import duties, should be used to encourage cleaner production by removing any disincentive to the installation of cleaner technologies, and by introducing appropriate depreciation schemes.

Implementation:

The improvement of the legal basis and the introduction of measures stimulating waste recycling and usage of secondary materials were foreseen in the *National Programme for the Use of Industrial and Domestic Wastes*. This Programme stipulates the introduction of profit tax exemptions for secondary materials collection and supply, and tax exemptions and soft loans for persons using waste as raw materials. However these measures were not implemented.

Recommendation 7.6:
The development of an action plan to reduce the volume of municipal waste for final disposal, destruction (with energy recovery where applicable) or reuse should be started without delay. The first step should be the drawing-up of a study on the installation of treatment facilities, including their costs, the possibility and costs of separate collection and pretreatment of different types of municipal waste, the need and possible success of public education programmes for waste separation in cooperation with NGOs, and the possible scope of markets for recycled materials.

Implementation:

The recommendation has not been implemented. Management of Municipal Solid Waste (MSW) is a big problem in Moldova. Currently about 1,750 MSW landfills are located throughout the territory. The non-observance of waste disposal and accounting rules leads to soil and river contamination. There is neither study on the installation of waste treatment facilities nor is there the development or implementation of an action plan to reduce the volume of MSW by separate collection and destruction, with energy recovering where applicable. The *National Programme on Management of Industrial and Domestic Wastes up to 2010* includes an action plan with concrete measures for MSW; however the cost of these measures was not assessed. There is no separate MSW collection or pre-treatment in Moldova.

Recommendation 7.7:
An inventory should be established of industrial wastes of high potential hazard, which are either stored on industrial premises or were (or continue to be) dumped on landfill sites, including information on the site where they might have been discharged, whether legally or illegally. The inventory should be the basis for urgent clean-up or decommissioning, as the case may be.

Implementation:
On the basis of the 1997 *Law on Utilization of Industrial and Domestic Waste,* the Department of Statistics and Sociology evaluates the production, utilization and neutralizing of industrial wastes, including toxic wastes. In 1997 the Statistical Waste Classifier (CS001-96) was introduced and includes all types of waste. In 2003 local authorities together with the SEI made an inventory of dangerous wastes and technologies processed in the country. Also the 2004 National Implementation Plan for Persistent Organic Pollutants (POPs) establishes priority actions such as establishing an inventory of industrial waste of high potential hazard that is stored on industrial premises or dumped on landfill sites. Due to limited financial means, the processing and neutralization of these wastes are not possible at this stage.

PART III: ECONOMIC AND SECTORAL INTEGRATION

Chapter 8:   Environmental concerns in agriculture

Recommendation 8.1:
A policy programme aiming at sustainable agriculture should be developed as a matter of top priority. The programme should deal with soil conservation as one main focus. It should be implemented simultaneously with agrarian reform, with measures that focus initially on research, training and the creation of extension and technical advisory services. It is also important to remove obstacles to the full and rapid implementation of land privatization.

Implementation:
The recommendation has been partly implemented, but not as a consolidated programme. Arable land has been fully privatised and achievements have been made with regard to the development of extension services. Several land protection programmes have been developed. The 2000 *National Concept on Organic Farming, Production and Marketing of Organic and Genetically Unmodified Products* is being implemented.

Recommendation 8.2:
Programmes to control the introduction of foreign species should be developed.

Implementation:
The Government had approved the Procedure on permitting import and export of birds and plants, including birds and plants covered by the CITES Convention. It is still questionable as to whether the procedure is being properly enforced.

Recommendation 8.3:
A comprehensive system for territorial planning should be introduced at all levels of government (local, regional, national). It should be based on: (a) the need to respect environmental objectives in land-use decisions, and (b) the requirement to provide the necessary infrastructure and communal services for all types of land use. See also recommendation 6.2.

Implementation:
The 1996 *Law on Urbanization and Areas Planning Principles* stipulates that environmental requirements have to be taken into account in the elaboration of territorial planning at all levels. The Government has approved the *State Programme on Town Construction and Planning Activities.*

Recommendation 8.4:
Soil conservation as an aim in itself should be the subject of special legislation. It should concentrate on vulnerable soils and protect the endemic xerophyte forest chernozem. Soil conserving measures should be

envisaged for all agricultural practices (crop patterns, land use, vegetation cover, machinery used, production techniques, etc.). Economic instruments should be developed and used to make soil conservation economically viable for all types of farm management.

Implementation:
The recommendation has not been implemented. A draft law on soil protection and a draft regulation on the management of pasture have been developed, but none of them has reached Parliament. The Government approved in 2003 the *Programme on New Land Use and Improvement of Soil Fertility for 2003-2008.*

Recommendation 8.5:
Farm management practices should systematically be aligned with soil conservation targets, primarily by changing crop patterns and production techniques, and by promoting organic farming methods.

Implementation:
The recommendation has been partly implemented in that organic farming is being promoted with some success in the framework of the *Improving Agricultural Productive Process through an Environmental Sustainable Approach*, as well as during the period when Tacis gave education support in 2002. Nothing has been achieved with regard to crop patterns and production techniques.

Recommendation 8.6:
A programme for the reduction of water pollution from agricultural sources should be developed and implemented. It should introduce water protection objectives into the designation of agricultural lands (e.g. river banks), the suitability of water for use in irrigation, and the handling and application of agro-chemicals. The programme should also provide effective mechanisms for the dissemination of information on the use of pesticides to all farmers.

Implementation:
The recommendation has been partly implemented. Efforts to decrease run-off from animal production are being made within the 2004 project "Agricultural Pollution Control Project". Extension services provide information on the use of pesticides to farmers. Water protection zones have been introduced, but their establishment is slow.

Recommendation 8.7:
The agricultural and environmental information systems should be rapidly adapted to the transition conditions, so that a comprehensive agricultural information system becomes available for decision-making. The funds required in this context could perhaps be mobilized partly through international cooperation projects.

Implementation:
The 2000 *Law on Access to Information* regulates principles, conditions, methods and procedures for access to official information. A Centre for Environmental Information has been established to give public access to environmental information (see implementation of recommendation 1.8). Agricultural information will be added in the future.

Chapter 9:   Environmental concerns in energy

Recommendation 9.1:
The policy for the de-monopolization of electricity generation, and the electricity and gas acts should be implemented as a matter of priority.

Implementation:
The market-oriented legal framework on laws on energy, electricity and gas was passed in 1998. In 1997 the country vertically integrated the electricity monopoly "Moldenergo", which was unbundled into five distribution companies, four generation companies, and a separate transmission and dispatch company, Moldelectrica. The country's district heating networks were transferred from the State to the municipal governments. Three of the five electricity distribution companies were sold in February 2000 to Union

Fenosa, a Spanish international investor and electricity operator. The remaining generation and distribution companies were all announced for full privatization at a later stage.

Recommendation 9.2:
The envisaged national agency for energy regulation should be created so that it can deal with the full range of tasks entrusted to it. It should have sufficient resources to ensure programme delivery.

Implementation:
The National Agency for Energy Regulation (ANRE) was established in December 1997 as an independent authority to support the introduction of market mechanisms in the energy sector, while protecting the interests of consumers and investors. It issues licenses, regulates electricity and natural gas prices, and establishes energy pricing principles and calculation methodology. The tariff setting for heat supply was transferred from ANRE to municipalities in 1999. Prices of centralized heating and hot water supply are set by the suppliers in coordination with agencies of local governments based on a methodology prepared by ANRE. ANRE is setting tariffs for steam and hot water supplied by the State-owned Combined and Heat Power (CHP) plants. ANRE has started to regulate tariffs for technical water.

Recommendation 9.3:
The timely introduction of integrated energy resource planning should be seen as a matter of urgency, calling for the rapid development of appropriate demand-side management techniques and cost-benefit analyses, as well as the training of staff at all levels.

Implementation:
Although the heating sector has been transferred from the State to municipal governments, there are no evident examples of demand-side management techniques or other integrated resource management schemes being implemented on behalf of municipalities.

Recommendation 9.4:
A programme for energy efficiency and the increased use of renewable forms of energy should be developed and implemented.

Implementation:
The *Law on Energy Conservation* was adopted in 2000. The implementation of the 2003 *Energy Conservation Programme* faces many difficulties because of the evident lack of economic incentives to introduce energy saving measures in industries. The *National Programme for Use of Renewal Source of Energy until 2010* is under adoption by the Government. Also, in the frame of the Secretariat of Energy Charter a detailed review of policies and programmes on energy efficiency is carried out. Under the UNDP/GEF project "Climate Change: Enabling Activity", two studies were conducted:

- Technology Needs and Development Priorities - a national report on the technology needs for the reduction of GHG emissions; and
- Renewable Energy Feasibility Study, assessing the technological, economic and environmental needs regarding the implementation of Renewable Energy Sources in the country.

Recommendation 9.5:
Initiatives are required to facilitate the creation of national production facilities for energy metering equipment. Administrative procedures and related practical routines for the installation of the required production capacity that could interest joint ventures (particularly between SMEs) should be reviewed to make them as attractive as possible (simplicity of regulations; realistic taxation of profits).

Implementation:
The country is elaborating the National Calculation System for Natural Gas and Electric Power Consumption for the promotion of national production facilities for energy metering equipment.

Recommendation 9.6:
A complete and detailed inventory of environmental effects of the production and use of energy should be developed, and lead to an action plan to mitigate the negative effects, including the installation of

desulphurization and denitrification equipment at energy plants. The setting of priorities should make use of a general method, in which damages are assessed.

Implementation:
The inventory has not been completed. However some progressive steps in this area can be noticed. The Energy Institute at the Academy of Sciences is involved in the preparation of a scientific programme on the evaluation of the impact of energy generating sources on human health, crops, etc. The results of this study will further be applied for drafting an action plan to mitigate negative effects and will assist in setting more realistic pollution taxes for pollutants emissions. The National Institute for Economy and Information in cooperation with the Energy Institute is involved in reviewing real pollution costs and identifying accurate future levels of fees and fines.

Recommendation 9.7:
The tool kit of economic instruments for the environmental management of the production and use of fuels should be revised and applied, as appropriate. Particular attention needs to be paid to the introduction of instruments that are capable of producing the envisaged results, including possibly tax reductions and/or exemptions for investments that are instrumental in energy savings.

Implementation:
To stimulate economic agents to use ecological fuel, differential payment for utilization of oil depending on its sulphur content was introduced in 2003. Otherwise, there are no tax reductions or exemptions on energy saving investments or other economic incentives for energy efficiency improvements.

Chapter 10:   Environmental concerns in transport

Recommendation 10.1:
A working group on sustainable transport development should be established. It should consist of experts, be headed by the Ministry of Transport and involve all relevant public institutions (DEP, Ministry of Finance, Department of Standards, Department of Energy, and others). The group should set relevant objectives for sustainable transport, time schedules for legislative and investment activities, and measures to encourage public participation.

Implementation:
Under the Ministry of Transport and Communication a working group on sustainable transport development was created. This group consisted of experts from eight Ministries and Departments, representatives of the Association of New Road Motor-Vehicle Importers, and Motorists and Road – a workers Union. The State Environment Inspectorate was never invited. At the time of this review, it is difficult to have a real picture of the group's current work.

Recommendation 10.2:
A master plan for the training of (a) the members of the sustainable transport group, and (b) environmental managers of transport activities, should be developed and implemented.

Implementation:
The Ministry of Transport and Communication organizes courses for managerial authorities and other categories, where its department staff gives lectures on standardization, environmental protection, sustainable development of transport and introduction of technological innovation.

Recommendation 10.3:
The selection of road vehicle standards for imported cars should be reconsidered and possibly adapted to advanced EU legislation.

Implementation:
At present, the above-mentioned standards are not adapted to European Union legislation.

Recommendation 10.4:
Fuel standards that are aligned on European practices should be introduced in accordance with a clear programme. The use of unleaded petrol for all cars should be promoted in all possible manners.

Implementation:
The Department of Standardisation and Metrology (DSM), starting with the specification of new motor fuel norms in 2002 and continuing with their amendment in 2004, gradually brought fuel standards closer to EU practices. The latest standards, effective as of January 2005, specify content limits of benzene, lead and sulphur in motor fuels. The use of unleaded petrol became increasingly dominant, accounting for some 99 per cent of domestic consumption by 2003.

Recommendation 10.5:
The full range of economic instruments should be developed to meet environmental objectives. Preferential import duties and other taxation should be levied on road vehicles incorporating advanced technology to reduce air emissions.

Implementation:
Emission trading has not yet been developed. Eco-taxes on imported fuel were introduced in 1998, the relevant excise tax rate on leaded petrol and diesel being twice as high as that on unleaded petrol. Since 2003, import duties on cars are differentiated according to the engine size and age of the vehicle. However, imports of used cars from the CIS region predominate and there are no reduced duties for the models incorporating advanced emission controls. Trucks and tractors continue to be exempt from excise taxes.

Recommendation 10.6:
A new system of vehicle emission control under the exclusive authority of the Ministry of Transport should be implemented and enforced.

Implementation:
In 2001 the Government approved the *Programme on Reduction of Air Pollution by Motor Vehicles*. It foresees the testing of all vehicles. The MENR and the Ministry of Internal Affairs approved a joint order to guide a State action twice a year on "Clean air", and every year "The town without my vehicle" action. At present 12 vehicle-testing stations are open. It is expected that 12 more will be opened by 2006.

Recommendation 10.7:
A comprehensive policy encouraging the use of public transport and rail goods traffic should be developed and implemented. It should be well coordinated with urban development and other forms of spatial planning. The policy should include provisions enabling the licensing institution to control the implementation of environmentally sustainable provisions for transport.

Implementation:
The recommendation has not been implemented. Issues are still pending since the first EPR review, especially on ecological transport safety. In practice, rail and air transport is not under ecological control. Road transport is partially controlled. Transport authorities have no staff responsible for environmental matters and lack mobile stations to police toxic substance emissions into the air. The quota of transport discharges account for 85-90 per cent of total emissions. To enforce environmental requirements in transport, the country has to enforce compliance with related normative acts.

Recommendation 10.8:
The economic restructuring of municipal public transport companies, as well as the modernization of their vehicle fleets, have become top priorities. To avoid major disruptions in public transport systems, provisions for improved market access by competitors of the public companies have to be complemented by the implementation of adequate financial safety provisions for the public companies.

Implementation:

The prices for State-owned and private public transportation are equal (30% of public transportation belongs to the State; the other 70% is private). A renewal of the car fleet is being carried out both in the public and the private sector. An open competitive market exists between companies.

Recommendation 10.9:
The possible future role of inland waterway transport should be explored.

Implementation:

The country intends to effectuate transportation by inland waterway. There are some harbours, but there is not a full coastal transport infrastructure (berths, storage and port facilities, and cranes). The issue requires further examination.

Recommendation 10.10:
The air emission inventory should be revised for reliability and completeness, making use, to the extent possible, of CORINAIR practices. The implications of this task are such that the producers of environment, transport and energy data should cooperate in it.

Implementation:

The air emissions inventory is still under revision and is yet to be completed. For air emissions the elements of CORINAIR methodology were included in the calculations. Data exchange is also performed with the energy and transport sectors.

Chapter 11:   Environmental pollution and human health

Recommendation 11.1:
The drafting of the national environment and health action plan should be finished, taking into account the work already completed under the National Environmental Action Plan. Both plans should be implemented in close coordination.

Implementation:

The 2001 *National Environment and Health Action Plan* (NEHAP) is supplementing the 1995 National Environment Action Plan (NEAP).

A Presidential Decree proclaimed 2004 as the Year for Health. A specific *Programme of Measures* then was approved. The same year, the MENR in collaboration with the Ministry of Health conducted a conference "Children's Health and Environment" for the fifth Conference of Health Ministers and prepared a joint report "Children's Health and Environment". The 2004 *Economic Growth and Poverty Reduction Strategy Paper* envisages targets in health protection and environment.

Recommendation 11.2:
National capacities should be developed for applied health research, into the quality of the environment and the effects of pollution.

Implementation:

Among the targets specified in the National Environment and Health Action Plan, harmonization and improvement of the collection of environmental data were achieved. Data are used for the development and assessment of the national health policy, as well as for scientific targets. This will have in influence on public health.

Recommendation 11.3:
The enforcement of the options of existing programmes for the supply of safe drinking water should be the main management concern once they are selected. It is necessary to reduce the population's exposure to fluoride in drinking water so as to eliminate fluorosis, observed in large parts of the population living in high-risk areas.

Implementation:
The Government's priority issue is the extension of the population proportion that receives high quality water. These priorities are determined in basic strategy documents, such as the *Economic Growth and Poverty Reduction Strategy Paper* and the Programme *"Economy Revival- Country Revival"*. The 1999 *Law on Drinking Water* regulates water supply, inspection and responsibility for drinking water supply.
The 2002 *Concept on the organization and functioning of social and health monitoring* was approved with a view to preventing the unhealthy influence of risk factors on people's health. Alternative water supplies, such as deep underground waters and water from the Prut and Dniester rivers, are utilized to reduce the risk of using water containing excessive fluorine.

Recommendation 11.4:
Improving the microbiological quality of drinking water should be recognized as a top priority. Nitrate pollution is another priority concern.

Implementation:
See Implementation of recommendation 11.3. A regular control on drinking water was also implemented according to available funding and is functioning. Wells and springs were inventoried and as a result arrangements were made for the amelioration of water source conditions. The 2005 National Programme *"Moldovan Village"* foresees the extension of public access to high quality drinking water.

Recommendation 11.5:
Surface and ground waters should be better protected from contamination by communal sewage and run-off from agricultural land.

Implementation:
Regular samples of surface water have been taken. In 2001, with a view to preventing surface and subsoil water pollution, a Government Decision *"Arrangements for Establishment of Protection of River and Reservoir Frontiers"* was approved. Economic activity, use of pesticides, livestock farms layout, oil-products terminal stores and others are prohibited in protected water zones. Some reconstruction and regular maintenance has been carried out in these zones since 2001. Nevertheless, the process is rather slow.

Recommendation 11.6:
The air quality monitoring system should be reviewed and modified to better assess the health risks and better control pollution.

Implementation:
Since 2004, the HMS has enlarged the scope of its air quality monitoring by starting measurements of aerosols, some POPs and some heavy metals in precipitation at one station in Chisinau and at the Leova station.

Recommendation 11.7:
A system for controlling the quality of food consumed by the population should be improved and should include the control of food produced by suppliers without special licences.

Implementation:
In 2003, to improve the system of management for quality of products and goods and to establish a legal framework for consumer rights, the Government approved the *Law on Consumer Protection*, which makes clear the responsible authorities and their function to protect consumers. Two laboratories are responsible for food analysis. One is under the Department of Standardization and Metrology and the other within the National Scientific Centre of preventive medicine of the Ministry of Health. Regular checks are done; for example, an every day control is done in Chisinau market.

Annex II

SELECTED ECONOMIC AND ENVIRONMENTAL DATA

Selected economic data

	1998	1999	2000	2001	2002	2003	2004
TOTAL AREA (1,000 km²)	33.8	33.8	33.8	33.8	33.8	33.8	33.8
POPULATION							
Total population, (1,000 inh.)	3,655	3,649	3,644	3,635	3,627	3,618	3,607
% change (1998=100)	100.0	99.8	99.7	99.4	99.2	99.0	98.7
Population density, (inh./km²)	120.4	120.3	120.1	119.8	119.5	119.2	118.9
GROSS DOMESTIC PRODUCT							
GDP, (current prices million lei)	9,122	12,322	16,020	19,052	22,556	27,619	31,992
GDP, (million US$)	1,700	1,117	1,288	1,481	1,662	1,958	2,594
% change (1998=100)	100	65.7	75.8	87.1	97.8	115.2	152.6
per capita, (US$ 1,000/cap.)	0.5	0.3	0.4	0.4	0.5	0.5	0.7
INDUSTRY							
Value added in industry (% of GDP)	16.7	..	..	..	..	17.8	..
Industrial production % change (1998=100)	100	88.4	95.2	108.3	119.7	136.0	..
AGRICULTURE							
Value added in agriculture (% of GDP)	25.8	24.9	25.4	22.4	21.0	19.2	18.2
ENERGY SUPPLY							
Total supply, (Mtoe)	2.8	2.2	1.8	1.7	1.8	..	..
% change (1998=100)	100	78.6	64.4	60.9	64.8	..	..
Energy intensity, (Toe/US$ 1,000)	1.6	1.9	1.4	1.1	1.1	..	..
% change (1998=100)	100	119.6	85.1	69.9	66.3	..	..
Structure of energy supply, (%)							
Solid fuels	6.4	3.8	3.7	5.2	5.5	..	..
Oil	22.3	18.7	23.4	26.9	27.2	..	..
Gas	55.4	58.8	50.0	58.5	54.7	..	..
Nuclear	..	..	..	..	..	..	..
Electricity	15.8	18.7	22.9	9.3	12.6	..	..
ROAD TRANSPORT							
Road traffic volumes							
billion vehicle-km	..	0.6	0.6	0.6	0.7	0.8	..
% change (1999=100) [1]	..	100	101.8	103.3	127.3	141.1	..
per capita (1,000 veh.-km/cap.)	..	..	..	..	..	..	..
Road vehicle stock,							
10,000 vehicles	29.5	30.0	30.0	31.9	33.3	33.0	..
% change (1998=100)	100	101.8	101.5	108.1	112.8	112.0	..
per capita (veh./100 inh.)	8.1	8.2	8.2	8.8	9.2	9.1	..

Sources: UNECE and National Statistics, 2005

Notes :

.. = not available.   - = nil or negligible.

[1] No data for 1998 therefore 1999 used as a baseyear

Selected environmental data

	1998	1999	2000	2001	2002	2003	2004
LAND							
Total area (1,000 km^2)	33.8	33.8	33.8	33.8	33.8	33.8	33.8
Major protected areas (% of total area)	2.0	2.0	2.0	2.0	2.0	2.0	2.0
Mineral fertilizer use (ton/km^2 arable land) *	..	..	0.5	0.9	1.1	3.7	3.4
Nitrogenous fertilizer use (ton/km^2 arable land)	..	..	..	..	..	..	..
FOREST							
Forest area (% of land area)	9.5	9.6	9.7	9.7	9.7	9.8	9.9
Use of forest resources (harvest/growth)	..	..	..	..	..	..	..
Tropical wood imports (US$/capita)	..	..	..	..	..	..	..
THREATENED SPECIES							
Mammals (% of species known) **	..	..	..	..	..	..	14.0
Birds (% of species known) **	..	..	..	..	..	..	39.0
Fish (% of species known) **	..	..	..	..	..	..	12.0
WATER							
Water withdrawal (million m^3/year)	1,262.9	999.5	918.4	874.0	865.6	864.0	852.5
Fish catches (% of world catches)	..	..	..	..	..	..	..
Public waste water treatment (% of population served)	..	..	..	..	..	..	..
AIR							
Emissions of sulphur dioxides (kg/capita)	6.8	2.7	3.0	2.8	3.7	3.9	..
" (kg/US$ 1,000 GDP)	14.3	8.4	8.4	6.8	8.1	7.3	..
Emissions of nitrogen oxides (kg/capita)	6.4	4.6	4.7	4.8	5.7	6.3	..
" (kg/US$ 1,000 GDP)	13.9	14.4	13.2	11.9	12.5	11.6	..
Emissions of carbon dioxide (ton/capita)	1.9	2.0	2.2	2.4	2.5	2.7	2.8
" (ton/US$ 1,000 GDP)	4.8	7.8	7.3	6.8	6.4	5.8	4.6
WASTE GENERATED							
Industrial waste (kg/US$ 1,000 GDP)	..	..	..	..	..	..	..
Municipal waste (kg/cap.)	..	..	..	..	..	..	..
Nuclear waste (ton/Mtoe of TPES)	..	..	..	..	..	..	..
NOISE							
Population exposed to leq > 65 dB (A) (million inh.)	..	..	..	..	..	..	..

Source: UNECE and National Statistics, 2005.

.. = not available.   - = nil or negligible.

Notes:

* In 1998 57.7 % of the land was in agricultural use. This percentage was used in calculations for the years 2000 to 2004.

** Figure from The Red Book of the Republic of Moldova. 2nd Edition, 2000.

Annex III

SELECTED REGIONAL AND GLOBAL ENVIRONMENTAL AGREEMENTS

Selected bilateral and multilateral agreements

	Worldwide agreements		Republic of Moldova	
Year	**As of October 2005**		**Status**	**Year**
1951	(ROME) International Plant Protection Convention		Ad	2001
1961	(PARIS) International Convention for the Protection of New Varieties of Plants			
1971	(RAMSAR) Convention on Wetlands of International Importance especially as Waterfowl Habitat		Ra	1999
	1982 (PARIS) Amendment			
	1987 (REGINA) Amendments			
1971	(GENEVA) Convention on Protection against Hazards from Benzene (ILO 136)			
1972	(PARIS) Convention Concerning the Protection of the World Cultural and Natural Heritage		Ra	2002
1972	(LONDON, MOSCOW, WASHINGTON) Convention on the Prohibition of the Development, Production and Stockpiling of Bacteriological (Biological) and Toxin Weapons, and their Destruction			
1972	(GENEVA) International Convention for Safe Containers			
1973	(WASHINGTON) Convention on International Trade in Endangered Species of Wild Fauna and Flora		Ac	2001
	1983 (GABORONE) Amendment			
	1987 (BONN) Amendment			2001
1977	(GENEVA) Convention on Protection of Workers against Occupational Hazards from Air Pollution, Noise and Vibration (ILO 148)			
1979	(BONN) Convention on the Conservation of Migratory Species of Wild Animals			2001
	1991 (LONDON) Agreement Conservation of Bats in Europe			2001
	1992 (NEW YORK) Agreement on the Conservation of Small Cetaceans of the Baltic and North Seas (ASCOBANS)			
	1995 (THE HAGUE) African/Eurasian Migratory Waterbird Agreement (AEWA)			2001
	1996 (MONACO) Agreement on the Conservation of Cetaceans of the Black Sea, Mediterranean Sea and Contiguous Atlantic Area (ACCOBAMS)			
1985	(VIENNA) Convention for the Protection of the Ozone Layer		Ac	1996
	1987 (MONTREAL) Protocol on Substances that Deplete the Ozone Layer		Ac	1996
	1990 (LONDON) Amendment to Protocol		Ac	2001
	1992 (COPENHAGEN) Amendment to Protocol		Ac	2001
	1997 (MONTREAL) Amendment to Protocol		Ac	2005
	1999 (BEIJING) Amendment to Protocol			
1986	Convention Concerning Safety in the Use of Asbestos			
1986	(VIENNA) Convention on Early Notification of a Nuclear Accident			
1986	(VIENNA) Convention on Assistance in the Case of a Nuclear Accident or Radiological Emergency			
1989	(BASEL) Convention on the Control of Transboundary Movements of Hazardous Wastes and their Disposal		Ac	1998
	1995 Ban Amendment			
	1999 (BASEL) Protocol on Liability and Compensation			
1992	(RIO) Convention on Biological Diversity		Ra	1995
	2000 (CARTAGENA) Protocol on Biosafety		Ra	2003
1992	(NEW YORK) Framework Convention on Climate Change		Ra	1995
	1997 (KYOTO) Protocol		Ac	2003
1993	(PARIS) Convention on the Prohibition of the Development, Production, Stockpiling and Use of Chemical Weapons and on Their Destruction			
1994	(PARIS) Convention to Combat Desertification		Ac	1999
1998	(ROTTERDAM) Convention on the Prior Informed Consent Procedure for Certain Hazardous Chemicals and Pesticides in International Trade			
2001	(STOCKHOLM) Convention on Persistent Organic Pollutants		Ra	2004

Ac = Accession; Ad = Adherence; De = denounced; Si = Signed; Su = Succession; Ra = Ratified.

Regional and subregional agreements		Republic of Moldova	
Year	As of October 2005	Status	Year
1950	(PARIS) International Convention for the Protection of Birds		
1957	(GENEVA) European Agreement - International Carriage of Dangerous Goods by Road (ADR)		
	European Agreement Concerning the International Carriage of Dangerous Goods by Road (ADR) Annex A Provisions Concerning Dangerous Substances and Articles Annex B Provisions Concerning Transport Equipment and Transport Operations		
1958	(GENEVA) Agreement - Adoption of Uniform Conditions of Approval and Reciprocal Recognition of Approval for Motor Vehicle Equipment and Parts.		
1958	Convention Concerning Fishing in the Water of the Danube		
1968	(PARIS) European Convention - Protection of Animals during International Transport		
	1979 (STRASBOURG) Additional Protocol		
1969	(LONDON) European Convention - Protection of the Archeological Heritage		
1976	(STRASBOURG) European Convention for the Protection of Animals Kept for Farming Purposes		
1979	(BERN) Convention on the Conservation of European Wildlife and Natural Habitats	Ra	1993
1979	(GENEVA) Convention on Long-range Transboundary Air Pollution	Ac	1995
	1984 (GENEVA) Protocol - Financing of Co-operative Programme (EMEP)		
	1985 (HELSINKI) Protocol - Reduction of Sulphur Emissions by 30%		
	1988 (SOFIA) Protocol - Control of Emissions of Nitrogen Oxides		
	1991 (GENEVA) Protocol - Volatile Organic Compounds		
	1994 (OSLO) Protocol - Further Reduction of Sulphur Emissions		
	1998 (AARHUS) Protocol on Heavy Metals	Ra	2002
	1998 (AARHUS) Protocol on Persistent Organic Pollutants	Ra	2002
	1999 (GOTHENBURG) Protocol to Abate Acidification, Eutrophication and Ground-level Ozone	Si	2000
1991	(ESPOO) Convention on Environmental Impact Assessment in a Transboundary Context	Ac	1994
	2003 (KIEV) Protocol on Strategic Environmental Assessment	Si	2003
1992	(HELSINKI) Convention on the Protection and Use of Transboundary Waters and International Lakes	Ra	1994
	1999 (LONDON) Protocol on Water and Health	Ra	2005
	2003 (KIEV) Protocol on Civil Liability and Compensation for Damage Caused by the Transboundary Effects of Industrial Accidents on Transboundary Waters	Si	2003
1992	(HELSINKI) Convention on the Transboundary Effects of Industrial Accidents	Ra	1994
1993	(OSLO and LUGANO) Convention - Civil Liability for Damage from Activities Dangerous for the Environment		
1994	(SOFIA) Convention on Cooperation for the Protection and Sustainable Use of the Danube River	Ra	1999
1994	(LISBON) Energy Charter Treaty		
	1994 (LISBON) Protocol on Energy Efficiency and Related Aspects		
1998	(AARHUS) Convention on Access to Information, Public Participation in Decision-making and Access to Justice in Environmental Matters	Ra	1999
	2003 (KIEV) Protocol on Pollutant Release and Transfer Register	Si	2003
2000	(FLORENCE) Convention on European Landscape	Ra	2002

Ac = Accession; Ad = Adherence; De = denounced; Si = Signed; Su = Succession; Ra = Ratified.

Annex IV

LIST OF ENVIRONMENT-RELATED
LEGISLATION IN REPUBLIC OF MOLDOVA

Abbreviations

GD   Government Decision
PD   Parliament Decision
PR   Parliament Resolution
PD   President Decree

Legislation

1979
- Forestry Code, (revised in 1996)

1991
- Land Code, № 828-XII of 25 December (revised in 1995)

1992
- Law on Enterprises and Entrepreneurship, № 845–XII of 03 January

1993
- Law on Environmental Protection, № 1515–XII of 16 June
- Law on Sanitary and Epidemiological Protection of the Population, № 1513-XII of 16 June
- Subsoil Code, № 1511-XII of 152 June
- Law on Cultural and Natural Monument Protection, № 1530–XII of 22 June
- Water Code, № 1532-XII of 22 June

1994
- Law on Civil Protection, № 271-XIII of 9 November

1995
- Law on Health Protection, № 411-XIII of 28 March
- Law on Fauna, № 439-XIII of 27 April
- Law on Protection Zones for Water Rivers and Basins, № 440-XIII of 27 April
- Law on Standardization, № 590-XII of 22 September
- Law on State Service, № 647-VII of 17 November

1996
- Law on Secondary Material Resources, № 787-XIII of 26 March
- Law on Principles of Urbanism and Territorial Planning, № 835-XIII of 17 May
- Law on Ecological Expertise and Environmental Impact Assessment, № 851-XIII of 29 May
- Forest Code, № 887-XIII of 21 June
- GD on Improvement of Forests and Forest Vegetation Management, № 595 of 29 October

1997

- Law on Hazardous Substances and Products Management, № 1236 XII of 03 July
- Law on Industrial and Domestic Wastes, № 1347 of 09 October
- Law on Atmospheric Air Protection, № 1422-XIII of 17 December

1998

- Law on Hydrometeorological Activity, № 1536-XIII of 25 February
- Law on the Fund of Natural Areas protected by the State, № 1538-XIII of 25 February
- Law on Payments on Environmental Pollution, № 1540-XIII of 25 February
- GD on approval of Regulation on Environmental Impact Assessment of privatized enterprises, № 394 of 8 April
- Government Decision on approval of Regulation on Environmental Audit of Enterprises, № 395 of 8 April
- Law on Energy, № 137_XIV of 17 September
- Regulation on Environmental Funds, № 988 of 21 September
- Regulations on the System of Integrated Environmental Monitoring. Ministry of Environment № 20 of 10 November

1999

- Law on Drinking Water, № 272-XIV of 10 February
- Law on issuing licenses for certain types of activities, № 332-XIV of 26 March, (has been replaced by the Law on Licensing Certain Types of Activities, № 451-XV of 30 July 2001)
- Law on Foundations, № 581-XIV of 30 July
- Law on Green Areas in Urban and Rural Settlements, № 591-XIV of 23 September
- Law on international agreements, № 595-XIV of 24 September
- Law on Plant Protection, № 612-XIV of 1 October
- Law on Certification, № 652-XIV of 28 October

2000

- Regulation on Public Participation on Elaboration and Adoption of the Environmental Decision, № 72 of 26 January
- Law on Industrial Safety of Dangerous Industrial Objects, № 803-XIV of 11 February
- Law on Access to Information, № 982-XIV of 11 May
- Law on Amelioration of Degraded Territories through Afforestation № 1041-XIV of 14 May

2001

- Law on the Licensing of Certain Types of Activities, № 451-XV of 30 July
- Law on Biosafety, №755 of 21 December
- Law on Geodesy and Cartography, № 778-XV of 27 December

2002

- Law on Approval of Regulation on Commercial Regime and Control of Use of Halogenated Hydrocarbons that Deplete Ozone Layer, № 852-XV of 14 February
- Decree on the Adoption of the Water Supply and Sewage Programme of the Localities until 2006, № 519 of April 23
- Civil Code, № 1107-XV of 6 June
- Decree on the Adoption of the Concept of the Organization and Functioning of Social and Health Monitoring and of the Regulation on Social and Health Monitoring, N 717 of 7 June
- Law on Philanthropy and Sponsorship, № 1420-XV of 31 October

2003

- Law on Consumers Rights Protection, № 105-XV of 13 March
- Law on Local Public Administration, № 123-XV of 18 March
- Decree of the Government on the Adoption of the National Programme on Insurance of Environmental Safety, N 447 of 17 April
- GD on National Commission for Biosafety, № 603 of 20 February
- GD on the Approval of the Regulation on Control of Transboundary Transport of Wastes and Their Disposal, № 637 of 27 May
- GD on Regulation on Creation, Registration, Addition, Storage (Custody), Export and Import of Collections of Plants and Animals from Wild Flora and fauna, № 1107 of 11 September

2004

- Regulation on Informing the Public and its Participation in Decision-making on Genetically Modified Organisms, MENR's Order, № 19 of 10 February

2005

- Law on Fertilizers and Products for Phytosanitary Use, № 119-XV of 9 June
- Law on Ecological Agricultural Food Production, № 115-XVI of 9 June
- GD on the Ministry of Ecology and Natural Resources, № 573 of 13 June

Concepts, Plans, Programmes, and Strategies

1995

- National environmental action plan (NEAP)
- Concept of environmental protection, (has been replaced by the Concept on Environmental Policy, № 605 – XV of 2 November 2001)
- Concept of external policy, № 368-XIII from 8 February

1997

- Concept of the development of cynegetics administration, PD № 1442-XIII of 24 December

1999

- National Programme for gradual phase-out of ozone depleting substances, № 1064 of 11 November

2000

- National Action Programme for Combating Desertification, GD № 367 of 13 April
- National Programme on the Management of Industrial and Domestic Wastes, GD № 606 of 28 June
- Programme of Water Supply and Sanitation for Municipalities until 2006
- National Concept on Ecological Agriculture, Production and Marketing of Ecological and Genetically Unmodified Food Products, GD № 863 of 21 August
- Energy Strategy of the Republic of Moldova until year 2010, GD № 360 of 11 April

2001

- National Action Plan to Combat Desertification
- Programme for the Reduction of Air Pollution Level from Vehicles, GD № 1047 of 04 October
- National Environment and Health Action Plan (NEHAP), GD № 487 of 19 June
- Programme of Government Activity for 2001-2005 "Economy Revival-Country Revival"
- Complex Programme for Protection of Soils against Erosion, 2003-2012
- Concept on Sustainable Development of Municipalities and Settlements, № 1491 of 28 December
- Concept of Environmental Policy, № 605-XV, 02 November
- Biodiversity Conservation National Strategy and Action Plan, PD № 112-XV of 27 April
- Strategy of the Sustainable Development of the Forest Fund, PD № 350-XV 0f 12 June
- National Strategy of Social and Economic Development for the medium term until , GD № 1415 of 19 December

2003

- National Programme on Energy Conservation for the Years 2003-2010, GD № 1078 of 05 September
- National Human Rights Action Plan for 2004-2008, PR № 415-XV of 24 October
- National Programme on Utilization of New Land and Improvement of Soil Fertility for 2003-2010, № 728 of 16 June
- National Programme on Insurance of Ecological Safety, GD № 447 of 17 April
- Programme for Energy Efficiency Improvement in Industry for 2004-2005
- Concept on Creation and Development of the National Network of International Transportation, GD № 365 of 28 March
- Investment Strategy, GD № 234 0f 27 February
- Concept of National Policy in Water Resources for 2003-2010, PD № 325-XV of 18 July
- National Strategy for Sustainable Development of Forestry Fund and State Program on Forest Fund Areas Regeneration and Forestation for 2003-2020
- Strategy on Sustainable Development of Tourism for 2003-2005

2004

- National Implementation Plan for the Stockholm Convention on Persistent Organic Pollutants, GD № 1155 of 22 October
- Economical Growth and Poverty Reduction Strategy Paper, Law № 398-XV of 2 December
- Concept of Transboundary Cooperation for 2004-2006, № 1069 of 20 September
- National Strategy on Reduction and Elimination of Persistent Organic Pollutants, GD № 1155 of 20 October

2005

- Presidential programme "Moldovan Village", GD № 242 of 01 March 2005
- Programme of Activities for 2004-2009, "Modernization of the country - Wealth People"
- Implementation of the Refrigerant Management Plan : technical assistance program

SOURCES

Personal authors:

1. Fiodorov, A. Nature Conservation in Moldova. (From: Moldovan Nature on My Mind. 2003).
2. Gheorghiu, V. IPP. European Strategy of Moldova.
3. Herd, R. A comment, UNECE Economic Survey of Europe, 2003 No. 2, pp. 68-70. (www.unece.org/ead/pub/surv_032.htm).
4. Newbury, D.M. 'Sectoral dimensions of sustainable development: energy and transport.' UNECE Economic Survey of Europe, 2003 No. 2, pp. 73-93. (www.unece.org/ead/pub/surv_032.htm).
5. Ridker, R. G. and A. Lipschitz. The Seeds of Democracy Program in the West NIS: An Evaluation. December 1999.
6. Seghal, M. Republic of Moldova. Agricultural Pollution Control Project. (GEF Investment Fund for Nutrient Reduction in the Black Sea/Danube Basin). 2001.

Material from Moldova:

7. Constitution of Moldova. Adopted on July, 29, 1994; Published in Monitorul Oficial al R. Moldova, N1, July 18, 1994.
8. Department for Statistic and Sociology. Statistical Yearbook of the Republic of Moldova 2004. Chisinau 2004.
9. Department of Environmental Protection. Provisional Instructions on the Application of the Standards Governing Payments for pollution. Chisinau, 1991.
10. Department of Statistical and Sociological Surveys of the Republic of Moldova. The shadow economy parameters in Moldova's national accounts. Chisinau 2000.
11. Development of the environmental legislative framework in the Republic of Moldova Legislation.
12. Fiscal Code of the Republic of Moldova.
13. Government decision on approval Millennium development goals in the Republic of Moldova till 2015, No. 288 on 15 Mar. 2005.
14. Government decision on approval of National programme to combat desertification, No. 367 on 13 Apr. 2000.
15. Government decision on approval of National strategy on limiting of emissions and neutralisation of POPs and National plan on implementation of Stockholm convention provisions, No. 1155 on 20 Oct. 2004.
16. Government decision on approval on Concept of transboundary cooperation for the years 2004-2006, No. 1069 on 29 Sep. 2004.
17. Government decision on creation of the National commission on implementation and realisation of UNCCCF provisions as well as mechanisms and provisions of Kyoto protocol, No. 1574 on 26 Dec. 2003.
18. Government decision on National technical assistance programme for 2005-2006, No. 302 on 21 Mar. 2005.
19. Government of the Republic of Moldova. Economic Growth and Poverty Reduction Strategy Paper (2004-2006). Chisinau, May 2004.
20. Government of the Republic of Moldova. Economic Growth and Poverty Reduction Strategy Paper (2004-2006). Chisinau, May 2004. Annexes.
21. Land Code.828-XII of Dec. 25, 1991 including all amendments as of July 22, 1999.
22. Law of Associations. No. 837-XIII on 17 May 1996.
23. Law of the Republic of Moldova on Instituting Center for Combating Economic Crimes and Corruption. No. 1104-XV of 06.06.2002. "Monitorul Oficial" of the Republic of Moldova Nos. 91-94/668 of 27.06.2002.
24. Law on acceding to Rotterdam convention. No. 2129-III on 7 Dec. 2004.
25. Law on access to information. No. 982-XIV on 11 may 2000.
26. Law on adherence of the Republic of Moldova to the CITES. No. 1246-XIV on 28 Sept. 2000.
27. Law on foreign Investment. No. 988-XII on 1. Apr. 1992.
28. Law on free economic zones. No. 440-XV on 27.July 2001.
29. Law on international agreements of the Republic of Moldova. No. 595-XIV on 24 Aug. 1999.
30. Law on Payments for Environmental Pollution No. 1540 on 25.02.1998.
31. Law on Privatization Program 1997-1998. (Extended up to December 31, 2002).
32. Law on ratification of Stockholm convention on POPs. No. 40-XV on 05 Mar. 2004.
33. Law on state budget for 2005. No. 373-XV on 11 Nov. 2004. Published in Monitorul Oficial No. 224-225 (1578-1579) on 5 Dec. 2004.
34. Law on the Protection of Plant Varieties. No. 915 / 1996. Adopted June 1996 and amended June 2000.
35. Ministry of Ecology and Natural Resources and National Institute of Ecology. Republic of Moldova. State of

the Environment Report 2003. Chisinau, 2004.

36. Ministry of Ecology and Natural Resources of the Republic of Moldova. 2004.

37. Ministry of Ecology and Natural Resources: State Hydrometeorological Service 60 years. 2005.

38. Ministry of Ecology, Constructions and Territorial Development of the Republic of Moldova. National Institute of Ecology. Republic of Moldova – State of the Environment Report 2002. Chisinau 2003.

39. Ministry of environment and natural resources, United Nations environment programme, and Global environment facility. National Biosafety framework. 2004.

40. Ministry of Environment. Construction and Territorial Development. National Declaration on cleaner production. 2003.

41. National Preparation of the Republic of Moldova to the Earth Summit "Rio + 10" in Johannesburg, 2002. General Overview, September 2001.

42. Order of the MENR on creation of the Interministerial commission for the implementation of the Danube Convention and preparation for taking over the Republic of Moldova Presidency in the ICPDR for the year 2006.

43. Parliament decision on: Coordination of interministerial activity on European integration policy No. 197 on 2 Mar. 2004.

44. Parliament decision on: Draft Law on ratification of MoU between Government of Republic of Moldova and Government of Kingdom of Denmark on cooperation for implementation of CDM established in the Kyoto Protocol to the UNFCC, No. 75-XV on 11 Mar. 2004.

45. Parliament decision on: Draft of Law on acceding Convention on Conservation of Migratory Species of Wild Fauna (Bonn, 1979), Agreement on Conservation of bats in Europe and Agreement on Conservation of African – Euro-Asian Migratory Water Birds, No. 1243 on 28 Sept. 2000.

46. Parliament decision on: Ratification of MoU "Danish assistance to Moldova, 1998". No. 202-XIV on 25 Nov. 1998.

47. Parliament decision on: Regulation regarding mechanism of conclusion of international agreements, No. 120 on 12 Feb. 2001.

48. Republic of Moldova. Concept of the Environmental Policy of the Republic of Moldova. Adopted by the Parliament of the Republic of Moldova, Decision N 605-XV from 02.11.2001, published officially at 15 January 2002.

49. Republic of Moldova. Country Profile Implementation of Agenda 21: Review of Progress Made Since the United Nations Conference on Environment and Development, 1992.

50. Republic of Moldova. Economic Growth and Poverty Reduction Strategy Paper (2004-2006). Chisinau, May 2004.

51. Republic of Moldova. Interim Poverty Reduction Strategy Paper. November 15, 2000.

52. Republic of Moldova. Ministry of Environment and Territorial Development. First National Communication of the Republic of Moldova under the United Nations Framework Convention on Climate Change. 2000.

53. Republic of Moldova. Ministry of Finance. Medium Term Expenditure Framework (2005-2007). Chisinau, 2004.

54. Republic of Moldova. Moldova. Interim Poverty Reduction Strategy Paper. April 21, 2002.

55. Republic of Moldova. National concept of policy in the field of water resources up to 2010. 2002.

56. Republic of Moldova. National Human Development Report 2003. Good Governance & Human Development.

57. Republic of Moldova. National Institute of Ecology. State of the Environment Report 2002. Chisinau, 2003.

58. Republic of Moldova. National Institute of Ecology. State of the Environment Report 2003. Chisinau, 2004.

59. Republic of Moldova. National plan for environmental hygiene, 2001.

60. Republic of Moldova. National Program for Production and Domestic Wastes Use, 2000.

61. Republic of Moldova. National strategy for the implementation of Stockholm convention on persistent organic pollutants. Chisinau, 2004.

62. Republic of Moldova. Second National Report on the Implementation of the Convention on Biological Diversity. 2001.

63. Republic of Moldova. Strategy of industrial development until 2006. Chisinau, 2004.

64. Republic of Moldova. The Economic Growth and Poverty reduction strategy for 2004-2006. 2004.

65. Republic of Moldova. The National programme for environmental safety, 2003.

66. Republic of Moldova. The National Programme of Water Supply and Sewage for human settlements up to 2006. 2002.

Regional and international institutions:

67. 479 microproiecte implementate (479 Micro-projects Implemented). Alternative rurale, Special Edition, 2004, p. 2-3.

68. ADB and Republic of Moldova. National Implementation Plan for Persistent Organic Pollutants (POPS).

Chisinau, 2004. 1st Discussion Draft. Thursday, October 21, 2004.

69. Association Moldova Ape-Canal (AMAC). Reform of the Municipal Water Supply and Wastewater Treatment in the Republic of Moldova. Chisinau, 2004. (in Russian)

70. Center for International Studies. International Studies Journal. Romania's Relations with the Republic of Moldova. Andreescu, G. Stan, V. and Weber, R. 1994.

71. Center for Strategic Studies and Reforms. Moldova in Transition. Economic Survey No. 11, 2003. Chisinau, April 2003.

72. Chemonics International Inc. and Environment International Ltd. Biodiversity Assessment for Moldova. Task Order under the Biodiversity and Sustainable Forestry IQC (BIOFOR). Submitted to: USAID/Kiev. August 2001.

73. CISR. "Republic of Moldova: Strategy for Development". Annex B. Strategy for Sustainable Development of Agricultural and Food Security. 1998.

74. Commission of the European Communities. European Neighbourhood Policy. Country Report. Moldova. Commission Staff Working Paper. SEC(2004) 567. Brussels, 12.5.2004.

75. Convention on Biological Diversity. Thematic Report on Alien Species. 2002.

76. Convention on Biological Diversity. Thematic Reports on Forest Ecosystems. 2002.

77. Danish Environmental Protection Agency. Assistance to Moldova in the Implementation of the Aarhus Convention, Second Phase. Report on Environmental Monitoring System. November 2002.

78. Danish Environmental Protection Agency. Assistance to Moldova in the Implementation of the Aarhus Convention – Second Phase. FINAL REPORT. Draft version. February 2003.

79. Danish Environmental Protection Agency. Municipal Water and Wastewater Sector in Moldova: Environmental Financing Strategy. Copenhagen, 2001.
(www.mst.dk/inter/pdf/Municipal%20water%20and%20wastewater%20sector%20in%20Moldova%20environ m_uk.pdf).

80. DEPA Danish Environmental Protection Agency /DANCEE. Municipal Water and Wastewater

81. Sector in Moldova. Environmental Financing Strategy. Submitted to the Government of the Republic of Moldova. 2001.

82. DEPA/DANCEE. Moldova - Background Analyses for the Environmental Financing Strategy. 2000.

83. EAP Task Force. Sixth Annual Meeting of the EECCA Regulatory Environmental Programme Implementation Network (REPIN). REPIN (2004) 12. 26-28 September 2004, Yerevan, Armenia

84. EAP Task Force. Sixth Annual Meeting of the EECCA Regulatory Environmental Programme Implementation Network. 26-28 September 2004 (Yerevan, Armenia). Progress in Implementing the Work Programme of the Regulatory Environmental Programme Implementation Network (REPIN) in Eastern Europe, Caucasus and Central Asia (EECCA). January 2004 – September 2004. REPIN (2004) 2/Eng. September 2004.

85. Earth Trends. Moldova Country Profile. 2003.

86. EBRD. Strategy for Moldova. As approved by the Board of Directors on 1 July 2003.

87. EBRD. Transition report 2004. London, 2004.

88. Economist Intelligence Unit - Country Profile Moldova 2004 Main Report.

89. Energy Charter Secretariat. In-depth Review of Energy Efficiency Policies and Programmes of the Republic of Moldova. Brussels, 2004.
(www.encharter.org/upload/9/116845981066322053334024863033307814092209436 2f2540v1.pdf).

90. Energy Charter Secretariat. Moldova. Investment climate and market structure in the energy sector. data

91. Environmental Approximation in the pilot sector (IPPC and energy sector) in Moldova, Ukraine and Georgia was financed by EC, 2002.

92. Environmental information, Education and Public Awareness, NIS. Sixth Interim report. 25 June 2004, European Commission 02-114. Communications from the MENR on environmental information, public participation and education. 2005.

93. EU-Moldova Action Plan, UE-MD 1101/05, DG E VI.

94. Gosudarstvennyi doklad, sostoyanie prirodnoi sredy I prirodookhrannaya deyatelnost v SSSR v 1989. Gosudarstvenny komitet SSSR po okhrane prirody, Moscoe.

95. IFAD. International Fund for Agricultural Development. Executive board – Eightieth Session

96. Rome, 17-18 December 2003. Report and Recommendation of the President to the Executive Board on a Proposed Loan to the Republic of Moldova for the Agricultural Revitalization Project.

97. IFAD. International Fund for Agricultural Development. Executive board – Sixty-Eight Session, Rome, 8-9 December 1999. Report and Recommendation of the President to the Executive Board on a Proposed Loan to the Republic of Moldova for the Rural Finance and Small Enterprise Development Project.

98. Implementation report. Republic of Moldova. Second Meeting of the Parties to the Convention on Access to Information, Public Participation in Decision-making and Access to Justice in Environmental Matters. UNECE. Geneva. 2005. ECE/MP.PP/2005/18/Add.19.

99. International Crisis Group Europe. Moldova: No Quick Fix. Europe Report N°14712. Chisinau/Brussels, August 2003.

100. International Crisis Group Europe. Moldova: Regional Tensions over Transdniestria. Europe Report N° 157.

Chisinau/Brussels, June 2004.

101. International Energy Agency. Energy Statistics of Non-OECD Countries1999-2000. 2002 Edition.

102. International Energy Agency. Energy Statistics of Non-OECD Countries 2001-2002. 2004 Edition.

103. Moldova Country Report. October 2003. Country Information and Policy Unit.

104. OECD and DEPA. МОЛДОВА. Стратегия финансирования инфраструктуры городского водоснабжения и канализации. Стамбул, 28 января 2004 г.

105. OECD and EAP Task Force. Utility Performance Indicators and Benchmarking in the EECCA. Meeting Summary December 9-10 2004. Chisinau, Moldova.

106. OECD EAP Task Force Secretariat and DEPA. Final Report: Performance Review of the National Environmental Fund of Moldova and the Chisinau Municipal Environmental Fund. Paris, June 2002.

107. OECD EAP Task Force Secretariat and the Danish Environmental Protection Agency. Performance Review of the National Environmental Fund of Moldova and the Chisinau Municipal Environmental Fund. Paris, 2002.

108. OECD EAP Task Force Secretariat. Environmental Pollution and Product Charges in Armenia: Assessment of Reform Progress and Directions for further Improvement. Paris, 2005.

109. OECD EAP Task Force Secretariat. The Use of Economic Instruments for Pollution Control and Natural Resource Management in EECCA. Paris, 2003.

110. OECD. Centre for Co-Operation with Non-Members. Reviews of National Policies for Education. South Eastern Europe. FYROM, Moldova, Montenegro, Romania, Serbia Volume 2. 2003.

111. OECD. EAP Task Force Secretariat and DANCEE. Final Report. Performance Review of the National Environmental Fund of Moldova and the Chisinau Municipal Environmental Fund. Paris, 20 June 2003.

112. OECD. EAP Task Force Secretariat and DANCEE. Final Report. Performance Review of the National Environmental Fund of Moldova and the Chisinau Municipal Environmental Fund. Paris, 20 June 2003. (in Russian)

113. OECD. EAP Task Force. Survey on Enforcement and Compliance with Environmental Laws and Regulations in the New Independent States. Country Report: Moldova. 2002.

114. OECD. Economic Surveys: Poland. Paris, 2001.

115. OECD. Environmental Performance Reviews: Slovak Republic. Paris, 2002.

116. OECD. Good Practices Expenditures. 2001. (in Russian)

117. OECD. Policy Brief. Financing Strategies for Environmentally Related Infrastructure. May 2003.

118. OECD. Policy Brief: Feasible Financing Strategies for Environmentally Related Infrastructure. Paris, 2003.

119. OECD. The St. Petersburg Guidelines on Environmental Funds in the Transition to a Market Economy. Paris, 1995. (www.oecd.org/dataoecd/28/57/2397072.pdf).

120. OECD. The Use of Economic Instruments for Pollution Control and Natural Resource Management in EECCA. Fourteenth EAP Task Force Meeting. 10-11 February, Tbilisi, Georgia.

121. OECD. Thematic Review of National Policies for Education – Moldova. Stability Pact for South Eastern Europe. Table 1 - Task Force on Education. 7 June 2002.

122. OECD/DANCEE. Financing Strategy. (in Russian)

123. PEEREA. Energy Charter. In-depth review of energy efficiency policies and programmes. 2004.

124. Preparatory EU Approximation Work of the Republic of Moldova in Integrated Pollution Prevention Control and Waste Management, 2001.

125. Prototype Carbon Fund. Moldova Soil Conservation Project. Environmentally and Socially Sustainable Development Europe and Central Asia Region. Environmental Analysis and Environmental Management Plan. April 25, 2003. (draft)

126. Raportul a fost pregatit de catre beture-cerec si centrul de date in domeniul apelor. Chisinau. 2005

127. REC Moldova. Preparatory EU Approximation Work of the Republic of Moldova in Integrated Pollution Prevention and Control and Waste Management. Final Report. 2001.

128. Regional Environment Centre – Moldova. Annual Report. Reports of 1998/9, 2000, 2001, 2002, and 2003.

129. Regional Environmental Centre – Moldova. Privatization in the Republic of Tajikistan. Web site of the State Property Committee of the Republic of Tajikistan.

130. Report on the Rio+10 National Assessment Workshop. Moldova, Chisinau June 20, 2001.

131. Tacis. European Commission. Project: SCRE/111232/C/SV/WW Support to the Implementation of Environmental Policies and NEAPs in the NIS Proposed Work Programme: Moldova. March 2002.

132. Tacis. European Commission. Project: SCRE/111232/C/SV/WW Support for the Implementation of Environmental Policies and NEAPs in the NIS Country Inception Report: Moldova. January 2002.

133. Tacis. European Commission. Project: SCRE/111232/C/SV/WW Support for the Implementation of Environmental Policies and NEAPs in the NIS Task 10d: Moldova. A Framework for Water Quality Standards in Rivers and Point-Source Discharges. January 2003. Draft Report.

134. Transparency International Moldova. Corruption and Tax Evasion: Economic Dimensions. Chisinau, 2003.

135. UNECE. Country Profiles on the Housing Sector. Republic of Moldova. New York and Geneva, 2002.

136. UNECE. Environmental Performance Reviews. EPR of Moldova: Report on Follow-up. Geneva, March 2000.

137. UNECE. Environmental Performance Reviews. Republic of Moldova. New York and Geneva, 1998.

138. UNEP. CBD Implementation assessment. National Assessment of Implementation of the Convention on Biological Diversity. The Republic of Moldova. August 2000.
139. United Nations Development assistance framework, the UN in Moldova, 2001.
140. US Department of State. Background note: Moldova. http://www.state.gov/r/pa/ei/bgn/5357.htm
141. USAID. Moldova. Strategic Plan for 2001 – 2005. January 2001.
142. What is the Stability Pact?
143. Working Group for the Preparation of the first Meeting of the Parties to the Aarhus Convention. Summary of activity on Aarhus Convention in the Republic of Moldova. 28-30 November, Geneva.
144. World Bank. 'Transport Sector Overview,' (http://lnweb18.worldbank.org/ECA/Transport.nsf/Countries/Moldova?Opendocument), 2004.
145. World Bank. Environmental Compliance and Enforcement Capacity Building in Moldova. Component 2: Upgrading Compliance Monitoring Capabilities of the State Ecological Inspectorate. Final Report. 2002.
146. World Bank. Environmental Compliance and Enforcement Capacity Building in Moldova. Component 3: Development of the Environmental Quality Management Information System. Assessment Report. 2003.
147. World Bank. Moldova country assistance evaluation, Report No. 28981, on 22 Oct 2004.
148. World Bank. Report No. 28556-MD. International Development Association. Country Assistance Strategy for the Republic of Moldova. November 12, 2004.
149. World Bank. The Millennium Development Goals in Europe and Central Asia.

Internet Addresses:

Ministries and government institutions:

150. Statistica Moldovei — http://www.statistica.md/index.php?lang=en
151. The Parliament of the Republic Moldova — http://www.parliament.md/en.html
152. National Bank of Moldova — http://www.bnm.org/english/index_en.html
153. Republica Moldova — http://www.moldova.md/

Other internet sites:

154. CIA factbook — http://www.cia.gov/cia/publications/factbook/geos/md.html
155. Commission of the European Communities. European Neighbourhood Policy. Country Report. Moldova. — http://europa.eu.int/comm/world/enp/pdf/country/Moldova_11_May_EN.pdf
156. Commission of the European Communities. European Neighbourhood Policy (main webpage) — http://europa.eu.int/comm/world/enp/document_en.htm
157. Commission of the European Communities. European Neighbourhood Policy Action Plan — http://europa.eu.int/comm/world/enp/pdf/action_plans/Proposed_Action_Plan_EU-Moldova.pdf
158. Conventions — http://www.unece.org/env/environment-conventions.html
159. EEA European Environmental Agency — http://countries.eea.eu.int/SERIS/SoEReports/view_on_coverage?country=md
160. Electionworld — http://www.electionworld.org/moldova.htm
161. Environment for Europe. Fifth Ministerial Conference. Kiev 2003. — http://www.unece.org/env/proceedings/html/Item7a.speeches.docum.html#7adoc
162. EU external relations — http://europa.eu.int/comm/external_relations/moldova/intro/index.htm
163. FAO Country Profile Moldova — http://www.fao.org/countryprofiles/index.asp?iso3=MDA&lang=en
164. Governments on the web — http://www.gksoft.com/govt/en/md.html
165. Grida State of the Environment — http://www.grida.no/enrin/soe.cfm?country=MD
166. Human Rights Watch — http://hrw.org/doc/?t=europe&c=moldov
167. IMF and Moldova — http://www.imf.org/external/country/MDA/index.htm
168. Infoplease — http://www.infoplease.com/ce6/world/A0833615.html
169. Integrated data on external assistance to Moldova at — http://www.ncu.moldova.md/
170. REC Moldova — http://www.rec.md/index_en.html
171. Republic of Moldova: Legal documentation — http://www.docs.md

172.	State of the Environment Report	http://www.grida.no/enrin/htmls/moldova/soe/
173.	Technical Assistance with Implementation of the IPPC Directive in the Power Generation Sector of Moldova	http://www.unece.org/env/epr/experts/moldova/Year%202%20IPPC%20in%20Moldova.htm
174.	Timer Country Statistics	http://timer.kub.nl/country.statistics/countrystats_moldova.html
175.	UN DESA Division for Sustainable Development	http://www.un.org/esa/sustdev/natlinfo/nsds/nsds.htm
176.	UN DESA Division for Sustainable Development: National information	http://www.un.org/esa/agenda21/natlinfo/countr/moldova/
177.	UNDP Human Development Report 2004	http://hdr.undp.org/reports/global/2004/
178.	UNECE Trends	http://www.unece.org/stats/trends/mda.pdf
179.	UNECE Working Group for Environmental Monitoring and Assessment	http://unece.unog.ch/enhs/wgema/
180.	UNEP Country Profile	http://www.unep.net/profile/index.cfm
181.	USAID	http://www.usaid.gov/pubs/cbj2003/ee/md/
182.	World Bank	http://web.worldbank.org/WBSITE/EXTERNAL/COUNTRIES/ECAEXT/MOLDOVAEXTN/0,,menuPK:302256~pagePK:141159~piPK:141110~theSitePK:302251,00.html
183.	World Bank Country Brief Moldova	http://www.worldbank.org.md/WBSITE/EXTERNAL/COUNTRIES/ECAEXT/MOLDOVAEXTN/0,,menuPK:302260~pagePK:141132~piPK:141107~theSitePK:302251,00.html
184.	World Bank. Moldova: Projects and Programs.	http://www.worldbank.org.md/